CAMPSITE SYMBOLS

Facilities

 A 4WD is required to reach the campsite.

 Towed camper trailers can access the campsite.

 There is an undercover camp kitchen area with some equipment.

 A camping fee applies; you may need to pay it in advance or at the campsite.

 Caravans can access the campsite.

 Cold showers are available at the campsite.

 The park, forest or conservation area charges a daily fee, which may be per person or per vehicle.

 The toilets are wheelchair-accessible; showers at this campsite are not necessarily suitable for disabled visitors.

 Some pets are allowed, usually small dogs, and they will need to be on a leash when outside. Always request permission before bringing your pet.

 Drinking water is available. It may need to be boiled/ treated before drinking; bore water may taste unpalatable, despite being safe to drink, due to high mineral content.

 Vehicles of any kind (2WD or 4WD) can only reach the campsite in dry weather.

 There is a facility to dump caravan toilet waste.

 No campfires are allowed.

 A gas or electric BBQ is at the campsite. It may be coin-operated.

 Hot showers are available at the campsite. A fee may be charged for access to the shower block, or coins required to turn on the hot water.

 Information about the area is available at, or near, the campsite.

 The camping area or caravan park has a kiosk where basic food supplies or prepared food can be bought.

 No pets are allowed.

 There are no rubbish disposal facilities. Bring rubbish bags with you, and take rubbish away when you leave.

 The camping area is not accessible to vehicles. All gear must be carried in; distances are usually indicated in the entry.

 There is a sheltered picnic table at the campsite.

 There is a picnic area with tables at, or near, the campsite.

... sually

... t be a
... ut one
... ation

 This is one of our favourite campsites.

 There is a toilet at the campsite. It may be a pit or composting toilet.

 The campsite is suitable for a vehicle with a pop-up tent, or for a tent to be erected beside a vehicle.

 When fire bans are not in place, fires can be lit at this campsite, generally in designated fireplaces or BBQs.

Activities

 A boat ramp is within easy access of the campsite.

 Canoeing or paddling is possible. BYO canoe/kayak, unless otherwise mentioned in entry.

 Crocodiles live in waters near the campsite. Observe warnings.

 Cycle trails are nearby, suitable for either normal bikes or mountain bikes.

 Salt- or fresh-water fishing is allowed.

 Hiking trails are nearby (these are more strenuous than walking trails). Recommended for fit adults.

 A horseriding trail is nearby, or horses may be brought by float to the campsite; facilities are available.

 The campsite is in a scenic area, or a scenic lookout is close by.

 There is a walk near the campsite with information or signage about the flora and fauna in the area.

 There is no swimming at, or near, the campsite.

 The sea or reservoir near the campsite is suitable for sailing small boats. It does not mean there is a boat ramp.

 There is a scenic drive within a reasonable distance of the campsite.

 Swimming is allowed at, or near, the campsite.

 A generally flat or gently sloping walking trail is nearby.

 Facilities for waterskiing are available at, or near, the campsite.

CAMPING
AROUND QUEENSLAND

CONTENTS

BEFORE YOU GO

WHY CAMP?

It's the end of another sensational day in the outdoors. The sun slips towards the horizon, and birds and wallabies come out to feed in the twilight. A campfire is lit, and close friends and family gather around its glow to sink a sundowner, cook a meal and share the adventures of the day – waves that were caught, fish that got away, discoveries that were made.

The darkness deepens and the stars – much brighter away from the city lights – twinkle and shine over possums, gliders, owls, frogs and other creatures that begin to explore the night.

Around the campfire, senses are heightened so the meal tastes better, the jokes seem funnier and the ties that bind are strengthened.

Camping refreshes the mind, revives the soul and reminds us of what is special. Through it, we gain new experiences, visit parts of the world we otherwise wouldn't see, and relearn the importance of the simple things in life.

The guide you hold in your hands is packed with great ideas of where to take your next camping holiday or weekend away in Queensland. There's information on all the best campsites for enjoying the wonders of the Great Barrier Reef, exploring the remote four-wheel-drive tracks of the Far North or escaping to the magnificent rainforests of the Hinterland. So start planning that next unforgettable excursion in the great outdoors.

WHERE TO GO?

Planning a trip is often the hardest part of camping. There are so many questions! Do you keep going to the same places that you know and love, or do you venture somewhere new? Will you go to a well-placed campground that has hot showers, flushing toilets and firewood supplied, or slip off the beaten track to an isolated, more rugged spot? Should you stay near the coast with its beaches, lush forests and nearby facilities, or venture inland, where sites are usually quieter, and the landscape so spacious and vastly different? Do you need to camp in school holidays or public holidays when many campsites are overflowing, or can you slip away mid-week or at other non-peak times?

It's also worth considering what sort of a camping experience you want. Driving to a campsite is the most common way to get there, but have you considered hiking with a backpack? For a first hiking trip, it's best to start with an overnight walk over not too great a distance (no more than about 10 kilometres each way). Many campers love this form of isolated camping so much, they disappear for weeks at a time.

But if hiking isn't your thing, what about a canoe or kayak camping trip, a boat trip to an island or mountain-biking? All of these activities can deliver you to some exceptional out-of-the-ordinary camping experiences.

Whatever your method of transport, if your planned route takes you through or on to Aboriginal land, make sure you start applying for permits with the relevant Land Council well in advance, as it can take some time to have permits approved.

WHAT TO TAKE

It is almost impossible to define what any single individual will need on a camping trip – the amount and type of gear varies greatly with the style, length and location of the trip. A tough, three-day hike in a remote area will require a vastly different list of essentials compared to a week spent with children in a well-established caravan park in summer.

Even when camping in the same conditions, people will choose to bring varying amounts and type of gear. Some campers (or 'glampers') bring along so much tonnage that you wonder why they left home at all: fairy lights, gas fridges, bikes, wine glasses, pillows and TVs. Others at the same campground may have decided to 'get back to basics' and bring little more than a 'hoochie', or mosquito net, and a billy.

Outdoor/camping shops will nearly always try to sell you more gear than you actually need. It isn't necessary to own the latest 'must-have' gizmo to have a satisfactory, fun and safe camping trip. The best advice is to start simply, with a few basic necessities, and to then add any extra items as you gain experience and discover what would be helpful or desirable for your style of camping.

Whatever style of camping trip you are undertaking, you will need to consider three key areas: bedding and shelter, food and cooking, and safety.

Bedding and shelter

Most people immediately think of a tent when contemplating camping, but in many situations a tent is unnecessary. If you are camping in dry conditions, a swag can be one of the nicest ways to spend the night. They're comfy and sleeping directly under the stars is blissful. Swags usually contain a warm layer or two (such as a sleeping-bag), a pillow, a rollable mattress and a canvas outer layer that keeps off the dew. Some even have a small flap that can be erected to keep off the rain.

In a hot conditions, you are often better with a mosquito net that lets through any whisper of breeze, rather than sweltering under potentially stifling plastic or canvas. If you don't have a suitable mosquito net, you can often use a modern tent's 'inner tent' without a fly.

If you *are* going to buy a tent, think of the main purposes for which you will be using it. If backpacking, you will need the lightest tent you can buy that is suitable for the conditions in which you will be travelling (for example, heavy rain, high wind). If you will be setting up in a campground for a week or more with a family, a large walk-in tent with multiple rooms will be more suitable.

Many long-term car campers swear that camping becomes much more pleasurable with a large tarpaulin. A large tarp placed over the tent and extending out beyond it to provide an extra 'living space' gives you extra protection in rain, and also provides vital shade for the tent – and you – on summer holidays.

Although they are one of the most common camping items, sleeping bags may not necessarily be the most appropriate bedding for your camping trip. They can be very hot, and if you are car camping with a trailer, it may be a better idea to bring sheets, a pillow and a comfy mattress, or even a camp bed.

Also remember that you will need to choose the most appropriate sleeping bag for your trip. For example, a lightweight summer sleeping bag will not be adequate if you are camping in winter.

Many air mattresses are very thin (particularly the self-inflating kind) but can still be surprisingly comfortable. If you are camping in very cold conditions, it is advisable to put a second layer – such as a foam mat or groundsheet – between the air mattress and the ground.

Food and cooking

Once again, the style of trip will greatly influence the cooking gear you bring – a backpacking trip will use a small gas-powered or methylated spirits cooker, but most car campers will have a larger, gas-powered cooker. Of course, cooking over a campfire, or using the coals for the camp oven, is often a great alternative, but it's a good idea to bring along an alternative cooking source, in case of fire bans, lack of firewood or incessant rain. As you will see in this guide, many campgrounds now also have gas barbecues on site.

When compiling your camp list, it is also worth thinking about the peripheral items relating to preparing food and hygiene: a cotton bag to hang your plates and cutlery can be helpful, alcoholic gel is a great tool for cleaning hands and, if you're staying at a campground with sinks, a plug can be helpful for washing up.

For great recipes, and more ideas on what to bring along for your campsite kitchen, pick up a copy of Explore Australia's *Camping Chef* by Heidi Marfurt.

Safety

No medical kit is useful if you don't know how to use its contents, or if it is left at home. Stock your medical kit with more medications than you think you will need (for example, antihistamines, pain killers) as well as bandages and saline solution. It is very worthwhile for at least someone in your group to do a first-aid course, particularly if you will be travelling in remote areas.

SAMPLE CAMPING LIST

The following list is intended as a helpful guide. You will need to modify it for your own trip.

Bedding/shelter

- Tent, poles and pegs
- Tent repair kit
- Hammer/mallet
- Spring-loaded pegs
- Guy ropes
- Large tarpaulin
- Mozzie net
- Ground sheet
- Sleeping bag
- Inner sheet
- Swag/airbed/camp bed/mattress
- Airbed repair kit
- Pump
- Pillow

Food/cooking

- Stove and fuel
- Stove stand
- Gas bottle

- Gas attachments
- Barbecue plate or baking paper to place on the dirty hotplate
- Esky/car fridge/gas fridge
- Drink bottles
- Water supply if none available
- Plates/cups/bowls/mugs/cutlery
- Cooking utensils (e.g. a sharp knife)
- Barbecue tools
- Matches
- Water carrier
- Billies or pots and pans
- Camp oven
- Billy lifter or oven mitt
- Can opener
- Dishcloth
- Scourers/scrubbers
- Cutting board
- Washing-up bowl
- Detergent
- Garbage bags
- Tables/chairs
- Fire starters
- Firewood
- Folding saw
- Tomahawk

Safety

- First-aid kit
- Sunscreen
- Water purifying tablets or device
- Toilet paper
- Maps and compass
- Thermals
- Heat blanket
- Mirror and/or whistle for signalling

Extras

- Lights (e.g. solar or gas lantern, torches)
- Swimwear
- Rain gear
- Towels
- Hats
- Toiletries
- Fishing gear
- Shovel or trowel
- Brush and pan
- Doormat
- Camera
- Binoculars
- Water toys
- Ball games
- Card games
- Books
- Clothesline/pegs
- Mozzie coils
- Insect repellent
- Universal sink plug
- Hot-water shower bag
- Toilet system

SELECTING THE TENT SITE

Many campers make poor choices when selecting where to set up camp. However, if you are arriving at a busy or pre-booked campground, your decision about where to camp will probably be limited.

Choosing a flat piece of ground is ideal, but if it is likely to rain make sure the ground isn't the lowest land around. Shade provided by trees is great in summer, but beware of river red gums and other lethal eucalypts that can unexpectedly drop huge branches.

Choosing a campsite with a great view can also be ideal, but beware of how exposed the site is if the weather should turn nasty.

Before placing your tent or swag, always check for sharp rocks, sticks or insect nests that could make your night uncomfortable.

FIRES

Firewood that is gathered from bushland is not 'waste wood' waiting to be burned. Much of it provides habitat to a host of animals – in particular animals such as lizards, numbats, snakes and echidnas – and as it decays it also puts nutrients back into the soil. So, in many national parks, collecting firewood is illegal.

If collecting firewood is legal, be conscious of not using too much – restrict your fire to a size that's appropriate for your group.

Many national parks, particularly in bushfire-prone areas, do not allow fires at all. If you have chosen to camp in these areas, respect the park manager's wishes.

There are many other camping spots where fires are welcome, and you will find those sites listed in this guide.

Fires should be lit in existing fireplaces where possible. If this isn't possible, dig a small pit or use rocks to contain the fire. Make sure your fire is lit in an appropriate place with no overhanging branches. Fires should be completely extinguished before you leave a site, preferably with water, as covering a fire with sand can make the sand ferociously hot for many hours, potentially causing serious burns to the next visitors to the campsite.

If you are likely to be lighting a fire with damp wood and kindling, it may help to use a fire starter or two.

CAMPING WITH KIDS

Taking children into the great outdoors provides them with positive experiences they will remember for life: seeing wildlife up close, enjoying the freedom of the outdoors and toasting marshmallows by the campfire. Many of today's keen adult campers were taken on many a camping trip when they were younger.

Initially, it's advisable to take young children on easy camping trips, where there are good amenities and help is nearby if necessary. However, as they gain experience and confidence, they will enjoy more varied and remote camping trips.

Generally, if the weather is good, children who become comfortable in the outdoors can quickly create their own fun, so there is no need to go overboard with prepared activities. In fact, it's often a great chance to get them away from video games and the television. However, it can be helpful to include card games, board games and books, particularly if you experience a stretch of bad weather.

Make sure all first-time little campers have their own torch to ward off night-time fear, and be extra vigilant with all safety hazards: in particular, fire, water and getting lost.

FIRST AID

There is no substitute for proper first-aid training, and the following advice is not definitive or comprehensive. Treatment regimes can change with new information and regular campers are advised to update their first-aid training with suitable courses.

There are many great courses, including some specifically designed for camping and remote situations. A good starting point is large, respected organisations such as St John Ambulance (www.stjohn.org.au), the Australian Red Cross (www.redcross.org.au) and Australian First Aid (www.australianfirstaid.com.au).

Burns

Cold, clean, running water is the best first-aid treatment for burns. Ideally, place the person or limb under a cold, running shower for at least ten minutes. Place a sterile non-stick dressing over the wound, and seek medical assistance if the burn is severe.

Insect bites and stings

Ticks, sandflies and mosquitoes may all cause itchy bites. An antihistamine may be helpful in severe cases. Ticks can be almost microscopic, so check carefully and remove them with tweezers or a tick remover. Ice can be used to help dull the pain of bee and wasp stings, or the bites of other invertebrates such as ants, scorpions and centipedes.

Spider bites

The general rule of thumb with spiders is that if they are up high, in a web, they are almost certainly not dangerous. Spiders that live in burrows on the ground are most likely to be dangerous. With most dangerous spider bites, do not wash the wound, but apply a firm compression bandage, a splint if possible to immobilise the limb, and seek emergency help immediately. Try to identify the spider.

The exception is red-back spiders: do not bandage the bite, but apply ice and use pain-killers while seeking urgent medical attention.

Bluebottles

Bluebottle stings can certainly take the enjoyment out of a summer ocean dip. The latest treatment is to first place the affected area in warm to hot water, to nullify the sting, then in cold water to help ease the pain, which should fade with time.

Other stings and bites

Although rare, other stings and bites may be caused by animals such as snakes and blue-ringed octopuses. Most animals, such as snakes, will flee from humans if given the chance. Generally, if there is a bite or sting with venom involved, the first-aid treatment is a compression bandage, keeping the patient or limb still, and seeking urgent medical attention. If the bite does not involve venom (such as a dog bite), keep the wound clean and stem the bleeding with bandages.

Sprains and breaks

The basic first-aid treatment for ankle and other sprains is remembered by the acronym RICE – Rest, Ice, Compression bandage (to immobilise and support it) and Elevation (placing it higher than the level of the heart when the patient is lying down).

If bones in a limb or elsewhere have been broken, the patient may well have other serious difficulties, so check breathing, circulation and stem any serious bleeding. Immobilise the limb with padding and a splint if necessary, and seek help.

CPR

Again, all regular campers should receive proper training on this resuscitation technique that can save lives. The current recommended CPR technique is two breaths, and then 30 chest compressions, repeated until the patient recovers.

RESPONSIBLE CAMPING

Many people who profess to love camping and the outdoors show little respect for the places they visit, and for other campers. Commonsense and courtesy should cover most issues, but all campers should think of the following.

Leave no trace

As a general rule, a campsite should look better when you leave than when you arrived. That means all rubbish needs to be removed, including fruit peel and lolly wrappers. Simply piling rubbish on top of, or beside, an already overflowing rubbish bin is ridiculous and leads to foraging by dogs, birds and other animals. If there is no suitable place to leave rubbish, take it with you. If you carried it in, you can carry it out.

And remember, just because you are camping doesn't mean you can ignore the principles of recycling. If possible, separate your recyclables and dispose of them accordingly.

For more information on the principles of 'leave no trace' camping, see www.lnt.org.au.

Toileting

If there are toilets in a campsite, use them. If not, dig a hole at least 20 centimetres deep, a long way from water sources (at least 100 metres) and other campers. As wild dogs and some other animals will dig up used toilet paper, leaving it to blow around unpleasantly, you should burn the used paper either in the hole, or place it in a small paper bag and burn it on the campfire. This will not be possible if a fire ban is in place. Used tampons, sanitary pads and disposable nappies should be carried out.

Camping with pets

You will see in this guide that many campsites do allow pets, such as dogs on leashes, but that doesn't mean that every other camper will instantly fall in love with your animal. Keep pets under control, away from other campers, and clean up their faeces.

Noise and light pollution

Generators, loud music and wild parties can ruin the quiet ambiance that many seek when they camp. Only use generators in the places and times they are allowed, and be sensitive to the wishes of others.

CAMPING IN SENSITIVE AREAS

Some beautiful but vulnerable natural areas need extra protection – for example, the no-fire zones in many national parks – and so there are special rules and tips about camping in those areas.

In some areas, rather than burying toilet waste, you are encouraged or required to carry all human waste out. The easiest way is to bring along a chemical toilet, which you can buy at outdoor and camping stores.

In such sensitive areas, also consider the other chemicals you may be inadvertently leaving behind. Choose toothpaste with little or no fluoride (often children's toothpastes are

best), and use biodegradable detergents and soaps or, preferably, none at all. (A combination of sand or grit and hot water can usually clean most things.) Never do the washing up directly in a water source, and make sure any fats and grease are poured out a long way from the water, preferably into a small hole.

If swimming in pristine waterholes or creeks, avoid the use of sunscreen as it can pollute the water. Swim in clothes if necessary to protect yourself from the sun.

BE PREPARED TO CHANGE PLANS

No matter how much planning you have done, some things can still go wrong. A camping trip may be plagued by sickness or injury, incessantly bad weather, or crowded or unpleasant campsites. Although most keen campers are prepared to put up with a little discomfort, being flexible can save a camping trip from complete disaster, and leave you keen and willing to camp again.

HOW TO USE THIS BOOK

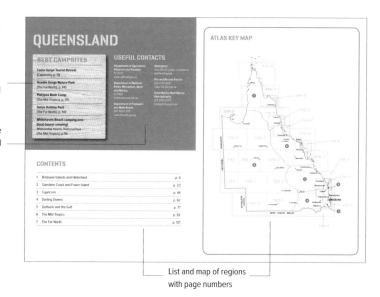

List of the best campsites in the state with region names and page numbers

Useful contacts include information on national parks, fire services, roads authorities and emergency contacts

List and map of regions with page numbers

Region name

Regional introduction highlights the area's parks, activities and natural attractions

National parks, state forests and reserves are listed in alphabetical order within each region; campsites in these areas are also listed alphabetically

Introduction provides information on national parks, state forests and reserves

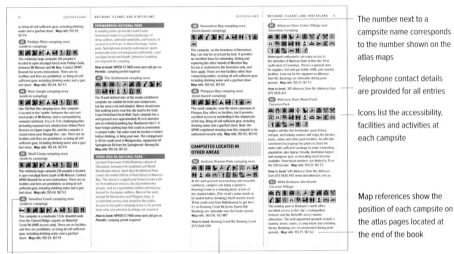

The number next to a campsite name corresponds to the number shown on the atlas maps

Telephone contact details are provided for all entries

Icons list the accessibility, facilities and activities at each campsite

Map references show the position of each campsite on the atlas pages located at the end of the book

Campsite entries provide information on individual campsites

Campsites outside national parks, state forests and reserves are listed alphabetically in a section following those entries

Index

There is an extensive index starting on page 200. It includes place names and campsites and lists both text and map references. For easy reference, campsite names include the national park, state forest or reserve in which they are located.

Campsite location and number enables easy cross-referencing to campsite entry

QUEENSLAND

BEST CAMPSITES

Cania Gorge Tourist Retreat
(Capricorn), p. 58

Granite Gorge Nature Park
(The Far North), p. 145

Platypus Bush Camp
(The Mid-Tropics), p. 119

Seisia Holiday Park
(The Far North), p. 149

**Whitehaven Beach camping area
(boat-based camping)**
Whitsunday Islands National Park
(The Mid-Tropics), p. 116

USEFUL CONTACTS

**Department of Agriculture,
Fisheries and Forestry**
13 2523
www.daff.qld.gov.au

**Department of National
Parks, Recreation, Sport
and Racing**
13 7468
www.nprsr.qld.gov.au

**Department of Transport
and Main Roads**
(07) 3834 2011
www.tmr.qld.gov.au

Emergency
Dial 000 for police, ambulance
and fire brigade

Fire and Rescue Service
(07) 3247 8100
www.fire.qld.gov.au

**Great Barrier Reef Marine
Park Authority**
(07) 4750 0700
www.gbrmpa.gov.au

CONTENTS

ATLAS KEY MAP

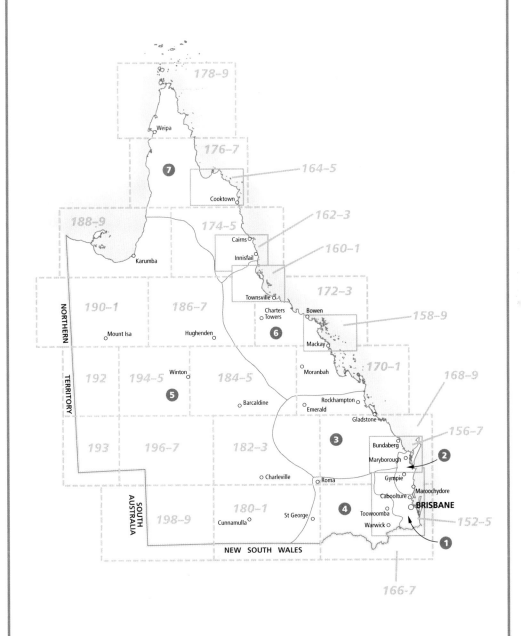

Elabana Falls, Lamington
National Park (p. 9)

BRISBANE ISLANDS AND HINTERLAND

Don't bother packing that extra jacket or scarf – you're heading to the state of never-ending summers, sensational surf beaches and an average 300 days of sunshine per year. South-east Qld's wonderfully mild and temperate climate, gorgeous tropical islands and stunning inland protected forests give it the edge as one of the best camping regions in the country.

Moreton Bay's magnificent islands – North Stradbroke, Bribie and Moreton – are easily accessed from Brisbane and offer postcard-perfect foreshore campgrounds. Camp on a surf beach on North Stradbroke, at a secluded site on Bribie accessible only by boat or by a beautiful lagoon on Moreton.

Half an hour's drive inland from the Gold Coast lie the spectacular rainforests, waterfalls, mountains and hiking trails of Springbrook and Lamington national parks. The tranquil national park hinterland campgrounds are a world away from the theme parks and tourist traps on the coast – you can camp near the dramatic cliffs of Binna Burra in Lamington or chill out at the secluded Settlement camping area in Springbrook. Whatever you choose, it's sure to be peaceful and relaxing.

The lakeside campgrounds in south-east Qld are perfect for thrill-seeking jetskiers, waterskiers, boaties and keen anglers. North of Brisbane, Lake Somerset and Lake Wivenhoe are fantastic watersports playgrounds, and further north you can spend your days fishing, sailing or canoeing on Lake Boondooma. Maroon Dam, Bjelke-Peterson Dam and Atkinson Dam also have popular lakeside campgrounds.

Other national parks in the region offer everything from scenic drives and picnicking spots to challenging bushwalks on rugged terrain for experienced hikers. Check out Benarkin State Forest, Bunya Mountains, D'Aguilar or Mt Barney.

CAMPSITES LOCATED IN PARKS AND RESERVES

BENARKIN STATE FOREST

Known for its towering hoop pines and eucalypt forests, Benarkin is a stunning subtropical rainforest near the regional town of Blackbutt. The forest is popular with wilderness bushwalkers seeking amazing views on the National Bicentennial Trail. Vehicle access to the forest is from Benarkin Forest Dr (be wary of logging trucks). Advance bookings are required for camping.

How to book: NPRSR 13 7468 www.nprsr.qld.gov.au
Permits: camping permit required

1 Clancys camping area

Beside Emu Creek (a tributary of the Brisbane River) and adjacent to the Bicentennial National Trail, this campground has sizeable, open grassy areas suitable for large groups. The site is accessible by conventional vehicles via a gravel road, around 11 km south of D'Aguilar Hwy. Note: there is no mobile phone coverage. Bring your own firewood and drinking water – or treat or boil the tap water at this campsite. **Map refs: 152 D4, 167 F1**

2 Emu Creek camping area

Great for families, with enough space for up to 200 campers, you need to bring firewood and drinking water to this camping area (or treat or boil the water available before drinking). The gravel road can be steep, narrow and winding at times, but is accessible for caravans, motorhomes and even buses. The camping area is around 13 km south of the D'Aguilar Hwy. **Map refs: 152 C5, 167 F2**

BRIBIE ISLAND NATIONAL PARK

Linked to the mainland by bridge via the Caboolture–Bribie Island Rd, beautiful Bribie is a popular weekend getaway for Brisbane residents and a relaxed holiday spot for tourists seeking sun, sand and a chilled-out vibe. There's no shortage of activities on the island: 2 golf courses, scenic cruises, heritage walks and lawn bowls are on offer. The array of wildlife includes dolphins, dugongs and turtles. Bribie is east of Caboolture in the north of Moreton Bay. Advance bookings are required for camping here.

How to book: NPRSR 13 7468 www.nprsr.qld.gov.au
Permits: permits are required for both camping and 4WD access

3 Gallagher Point camping area

One of Bribie's smallest campsites, with just 6 numbered sites, this camping area is typically popular with backpackers who can easily access the grounds, just 3 km north of White Patch Ranger Headquarters. There is boat access via Pumicestone Passage and 4WD access via White Patch Espl. There is no toilet block. Bring your own drinking water and firewood. **Map refs:** 153 G4, 167 G2

4 Lime Pocket camping area
(boat-based camping)

This tiny campsite (6 numbered sites) is Bribie's most secluded and tranquil, but also one of its most basic. Access is only by boat from Pumicestone Passage, and campers must bring their own drinking water and firewood. Lime Pocket is north of Mission Point and Poverty Creek on western Bribie. There is no toilet block. Fishing is permitted near the campsite but not in nearby Tipcony Bight. **Map refs:** 153 G4, 167 G1

5 Mission Point camping area
(boat-based camping)

Accessible only by boat from Pumicestone Passage, there are 12 numbered sites at Mission Point, along with toilets, picnic tables and fireplaces; bring your own drinking water and firewood. Mission Point is north of Poverty Creek on western Bribie. **Map refs:** 153 G4, 167 G2

6 Ocean Beach camping area

Bribie's biggest camping area, the 64 sites are set behind sand dunes and reached via defined tracks. Access is 4WD only from the Eighth Ave carpark off North St, Woorim, but you'll need to check tide times before departing. Visitors are required not to take their 4WD vehicles on the dunes or to create new tracks. Note: toilet facilities are provided at the camping area accessed by track P. Bring your own drinking water and a gas/fuel stove. **Map refs:** 153 G4, 167 G1

7 Poverty Creek camping area

Poverty Creek campsite is a popular family area, with 12 numbered sites and a group camping area suitable for camper trailers. Bring your own drinking water and firewood. Access is via White Patch Espl (navigable by 4WD only), or by boat from Pumicestone Passage. **Map refs:** 153 G4, 167 G2

BUNYA MOUNTAINS NATIONAL PARK

The Bunya Mountains, peaking at 1135 m, rise abruptly from the surrounding Darling Downs and South Burnett Valley. The most westerly rainforest park in southern Qld, it protects more than 30 rare and threatened species of flora and fauna. Here you will find the largest remaining area of bunya pines in the world, along with cool subtropical rainforests, dry rainforests, and grasslands known as 'balds', containing rare grass species. There are 35 km of walking tracks, ranging from a 500 m stroll to a 10 km hike. The winding roads in the area are not recommended for large camper trailers or caravans. Advance bookings are required for camping.

How to book: NPRSR 13 7468 www.nprsr.qld.gov.au
Permits: camping permit required

8 Burtons Well camping area (walk-in camping)

Camp among the ancient grass trees with beautiful forest surrounds at this large tent-only site, 8.5 km north-west of the QPWS information centre. The carpark is a short walk from the open camping area which caters for up to 50 campers. Fires are permitted, but the park prefers gas/fuel stoves. A donkey boiler is available to heat water for showers. The tap water here must be treated before drinking, or bring your own. You'll find Burtons Well 4 km north of Westcott camping area on Bunya Mountains Rd. **Map refs:** 152 B4, 167 E1

9 Dandabah camping area

Dandabah has large, open grassy areas conveniently close to a small general store, restaurant and public phone. There are sites for up to 70 campers and it can be reached by conventional vehicle. The site is on Bunya Ave, signposted off Bunya Mountains Rd. Tap water must be treated before drinking, or bring your own. Note: there is an information centre close to Dandabah, at the southern entrance to the park. **Map refs:** 152 B4, 167 E1

10 Westcott camping area (walk-in camping)

Suitable for tents only, there is no vehicular access to this partly shaded campground for up to 30 people, but parking is just 20 m away. There are fireplaces but use the firewood sparingly. Tap water must be treated before drinking, or bring your own. The site is 4 km north of Dandabah on Bunya Mountains Rd. **Map refs:** 152 B4, 167 E1

D'AGUILAR NATIONAL PARK

D'Aguilar National Park consists of 2 distinct areas: the southern section (formerly Brisbane Forest Park) and the northern (formerly Mt Mee State Forest). The southern section features open eucalypt woodlands, lush subtropical rainforests and more than 800 plant species – all just a short drive from the Brisbane city centre. The southern section's Walkabout Creek complex has an information centre, cafe and details about the amazing wildlife in the park, which includes endangered giant barred frogs and yellow-bellied gliders. Other features to enjoy include scenic lookouts, picnic and BBQ areas, bushwalking tracks, horseriding and cycling trails. The northern section extends all the way to Woodford, and boasts lookouts and excellent walking tracks. For those less active, there's a popular half-day mountain drive covering The Gantry, Rocky Hole and the relaxing picnic spot at Broadwater. The Falls lookout over D'Aguilar is another must-see in the northern section. Advance bookings are required for all camping in the park.

How to book: NPRSR 13 7468 www.nprsr.qld.gov.au
Permits: camping permit required

11 Archer camping area

Camp in open woodland near a creek at this lovely grassy site just 1 km from the Rasmussen Rd entry to the northern section of the park. It can be accessed by car from Rasmussen Rd, but if you are entering via Mt Mee and The Gantry you'll need a 4WD. There are 9 designated sites and enough space to accommodate large groups. Fire rings are provided but you must bring your own firewood, as collecting wood in the forest is prohibited. Tank water must be treated before drinking, or bring your own. **Map refs:** 153 E4, 167 G2

12 Dundas Road camping area (walk-in camping)

This 15-person bush camp is a 1.6 km walk from Mt Nebo Rd. There are no facilities aside from tank water, which must be boiled or treated before drinking, or bring your own; also bring a gas/fuel stove. It is within striking distance of the Westridge outlook. **Map refs:** 155 F1, 167 G2

13 England Creek camping area (walk-in camping)

This 9-person campsite lies deep within D'Aguilar, next to the picturesque England Creek. No facilities at all are provided and the camp lies at the end of a 10.5 km hike from Mt Glorious Rd. It's for experienced self-sufficient campers only. Bring water and a gas/fuel stove. **Map refs:** 153 F5, 155 F1, 167 G2

14 Light Line Road camping area (walk-in camping)

This tiny campsite (maximum 6 people) provides a small shelter and a water tank (treat or boil water before drinking). It is located 1.7 km from the park boundary at Forestry Rd, Mt Nebo. Bring a gas/fuel stove. **Map refs:** 155 F1, 167 G2

15 Middle Kobble camping area (walk-in camping)

This campsite near the Kobble Creek waterfall is accessed via a 4.7 km uphill track featuring some steep climbs. Bring your own drinking water, as none is provided and Kobble Creek is often dry; also bring a gas/fuel stove. **Map refs:** 153 F5, 155 F1, 167 G2

16 Neurum Creek camping area

A 4WD is recommended for accessing this medium-size campsite off Neurum Creek Rd, about 6 km from the Salin Rd entry (The Gantry) to the northern section of the park and about 13.5 km from the Rasmussen Rd entry (Woodford end). There are 13 numbered sites with raised dirt pads, septic toilets, fireplaces (bring your own firewood) and water to be boiled or treated

Mt Mee Lookout, D'Aguilar National Park (p. 7)

before drinking. Note: mobile phone coverage is unreliable. **Map refs:** 153 E4, 167 G2

17 North Kobble camping area (walk-in camping)

This campsite, north of Middle Kobble, can be accessed only by unmarked trails through steep terrain. Campers must be physically fit, capable of navigating the bush unaided and prepared for emergencies. There are no facilities and Kobble Creek is often dry, so bring your own drinking water and a gas/fuel stove. **Map refs:** 153 F1, 155 F1, 167 G2

18 Northbrook Mountain camping area (walk-in camping)

This small clearing on a high ridge overlooking Kipper Creek hosts only 9 people and provides no facilities whatsoever (bring your own drinking water and a gas/fuel stove). The 4.7 km walk to camp from Lawton Rd is only for experienced hikers. **Map refs:** 153 E5, 155 E1, 167 G2

19 Scrub Road camping area (walk-in camping)

This 9-person bush camp is a 4 km hike within D'Aguilar's southern section from Mt Nebo Rd. Like other campsites in the southern half of D'Aguilar, it is for self-sufficient campers only. There is a small shelter. Boil or treat the tank water before drinking. Bring a gas/fuel stove. **Map refs:** 155 F1, 167 G2

20 South Kobble camping area (walk-in camping)

Like North Kobble, this campsite is very remote and accessible only by unmarked trails through steep terrain. Campers must be physically fit, capable of navigating the bush unaided and prepared for emergencies. There are no facilities and Kobble Creek is often dry, so bring your own drinking water and a gas/fuel stove. **Map refs:** 153 F5, 155 F1, 167 G2

LAMINGTON NATIONAL PARK

The World Heritage–listed Lamington National Park, cresting the McPherson Range, is renowned for its natural beauty, panoramic views, lush rainforests, ancient trees, picturesque waterfalls, prolific birdlife and over 150 km of well-maintained walking trails. It is also famous for 2 exceptional guesthouses (Binna Burra and O'Reillys), where hospitality is combined with informative activities aimed to give all who stay there an appreciation of the precious environment. Bookings are required for all camping in the park.

Who to contact: QPWS Lamington National Park Green Mountains (07) 5544 0634 for access information about bush camping areas ***How to book:*** Binna Burra Mountain Lodge (07) 5533 3622, 1300 246 622 for campsite no. **21**; or NPRSR 13 7468 www.nprsr.qld.gov.au for all other campsites ***Permits:*** camping permit required for all camping areas except campsite no. **21**

21 Binna Burra camping area

A south-east Queensland gem, this privately managed mountain-top site has long been a favourite with campers for its stunning panoramic views of the Numinbah Valley. Activities at Binna Burra include guided bushwalks, abseiling, flying fox, a kids' club and superb dining at the Binna Burra Tea House or Clifftop Dining Room. Also on offer are furnished, safari-style tents (2–6 people) with beds, tables and chairs, lighting and your own private verandah with beautiful valley or rainforest views. This campsite is part of the Gold Coast Hinterland Great Walk. The location is Binna Burra Rd, 28 km south of Canungra. Bookings are essential for weekends and peak periods. **Map refs:** 155 G4, 167 G3

22 Bush camping areas (walk-in camping)

For experienced, self-sufficient campers with good navigational skills, there are 10 remote camping sites (Bithongabel, Darlington, Echo Point, Illinbah, Lost World Creek, Lost World Saddle, Point Lookout, Rat-a-tat, Running Creek and Stinson) in

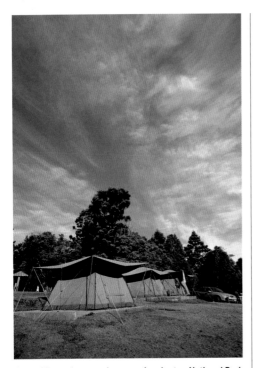

Green Mountains camping area, Lamington National Park

the bush along the walking trails in the national park. These are walk-in only, limited to around 6 people per site and for a single-night stay. Allow 10 business days for processing bookings. Note: these bush-camping sites are closed every year Dec–Jan. For access instructions and locations, contact QPWS Lamington.
Map refs: 155 G4, 167 G4

23 **Green Mountains camping area**

Close to O'Reillys Rainforest Resort, this hillside campground in forest surrounds has designated campsites on terraces on the slope and a separate area designated for those doing the Gold Coast Hinterland Great Walk. It is suitable for walk-in camping, camping beside your car, and campervans, but not for caravans or camper trailers. The nearby day-use area contains BBQs, picnic facilities and wheelchair-accessible toilets. A public phone is available past O'Reillys reception

office. You'll find the campground at the end of the 36 km narrow and winding Lamington National Park Rd (depart from Canungra), just 200 m from the information centre outside O'Reillys. Bookings are essential for weekends and peak periods. Tap water must be boiled or treated before drinking.
Map refs: 155 G4, 167 G3

MORETON ISLAND NATIONAL PARK AND RECREATION AREA

Regarded as the jewel of Moreton Bay's sandy islands, Moreton Island is a haven for off-road adventurers (it's 4WD only) looking for a wilderness experience within easy reach of Brisbane. Here, only a 2 hr barge trip from the mainland, are long sandy beaches, clear freshwater lagoons, wildflower heaths and some of the highest sand dunes in the world. Anglers should check the Moreton Bay Marine Park map before casting off, as fishing is prohibited in some areas of the coast. Advance booking is required for camping.

How to book: NPRSR 13 7468 www.nprsr.qld.gov.au
Permits: camping permit required

24 **Ben-Ewa camping area**

A favourite with families and school groups, Ben-Ewa's valley location provides protection from strong winds and offers many a shady tree. The site is on the western side of the island, 1.5 km north of The Wrecks. There are only 12 camping plots available, but it is accessible for camper trailers. Open fires are permitted in existing fire sites, but you must BYO firewood. Treat or boil the water before drinking, or bring your own.
Map refs: 153 H5, 155 H1, 167 H2

25 **Blue Lagoon camping area**

With beautiful walking trails to the nearby lake and close proximity to the surf beach, this camping area is in a gorgeous spot on the eastern side of the island between Middle Rd and Cape Moreton. Trailers and caravans are permitted, but due to the soft sand on the one-way track they are not recommended. Bring your own firewood and treat or boil the water before drinking, or bring that along too. **Map refs: 153 H5, 167 H2**

26 Comboyuro Point camping area

Within walking distance of the Bulwer township on the island's west coast, this site has 49 camping sites marked with totem poles and plenty of shade. Water is available, but it must be treated or boiled before consumption. Open fires are allowed, but you must bring all firewood from the mainland, as Moreton's natural environment is protected. Note: mobile phone coverage is poor in this area. **Map refs: 153 H5, 167 H2**

27 North Point camping area

On the northern tip of the island between Yellow Patch and Cape Moreton, this is a large grassy site close to the surf beach and within walking distance of Honeymoon Bay. The area is not accessible with a caravan or trailer and is reached by 4WD only. There is a maximum of 17 sites available. Bring a gas/fuel stove from the mainland and treat or boil water before drinking. **Map refs: 153 H4, 167 H2**

28 North-east camping area
(bush camping)

Self-sufficient campers can stay in areas marked with totem poles on this stretch of beach on the east coast of Moreton, spanning between Middle Rd and Spitfire Creek (excluding Blue Lagoon camping area). There are no facilities, so bring your own drinking water and firewood (for use in existing fire sites only) and take all rubbish with you. **Map refs: 153 H5, 167 H2**

29 North-west camping area
(bush camping)

Self-sufficient campers can stay in areas marked with totem poles on this stretch of beach on the west coast of Moreton, spanning the area between Ben-Ewa and Comboyuro Point camping areas. There are no facilities, so bring your own drinking water and firewood (for use in existing fire sites only) and take all rubbish with you. **Map refs: 153 H5, 167 H2**

30 South-east camping area
(bush camping)

Self-sufficient campers can stay in areas marked with totem poles on this stretch of beach on the east coast of Moreton, spanning the area between Middle Rd and Rous Battery. There are no facilities in this camping area, so bring your own drinking water and firewood (for use in existing fire sites only) and take all rubbish with you. **Map refs: 153 H5, 155 H1, 167 H2**

31 South-west camping area
(bush camping)

Self-sufficient campers can stay in areas marked with totem poles on this stretch of beach on the west coast of Moreton, spanning the area between Tangalooma Bypass and Toulkerrie. There are no facilities in this camping area, so bring your own drinking water and firewood (for use in existing fire sites only) and take all rubbish with you. **Map refs: 153 H5, 155 H1, 167 H2**

32 The Wrecks camping area
(walk-in camping)

The Wrecks is a walk-in camping area just a short stroll from Tangalooma near the main barge landing point. There are 21 sites available; the surface is sand (not grass) and is surrounded by native shrubs and trees. Vehicles can park on the beach, a short distance from the campground. The water must be boiled or treated before use. **Map refs:** 153 H5, 155 H1, 167 H2

33 Yellow Patch camping area (bush camping)

Self-sufficient campers can stay in areas marked with totem poles on this stretch of beach at the northern end of Moreton, spanning the area between North Point and Heath Island. There are no facilities in this camping area, so bring your own drinking water and firewood (for use in existing fire sites only) and take all rubbish with you. **Map refs:** 153 H4, 167 H2

MOUNT BARNEY NATIONAL PARK

As one of the state's largest areas of pristine vegetation, World Heritage–listed Mt Barney National Park on the Qld–NSW border is a mecca for experienced bushwalkers and climbers. Out of this rugged wilderness rise 7 peaks, of which Mt Barney is the highest. The Yellow Pinch picnic area at the base of Mt Barney provides wheelchair-accessible toilets, BBQs and tables. Bush camping areas have no facilities. Advance bookings are required to camp here.

How to book: QPWS Boonah (07) 5463 5041 for campsite nos **35, 45**; or NPRSR 13 7468 www.nprsr.qld.gov.au for campsite nos **34, 36, 37, 38, 39, 40, 41, 42, 43, 44, 46** *Permits:* camping permit required; pay fees and arrange permit 3–6 weeks in advance

34 Barney Gorge Junction camping area (walk-in camping)

This basic bush camping area, as its name might suggest, is located in tall eucalypt forest at the junction of Mt Barney Creek and Barney Gorge. There are no facilities and fires are prohibited, so bring all self-sufficient gear, including drinking water and a gas/fuel stove. **Map refs:** 155 E4, 167 F3

35 Bush camping areas (walk-in camping)

Experienced hikers looking for additional challenges can camp in 10 designated bush camping zones in the remotest areas of Mt Barney National Park. Hikers are required to obtain permits and discuss their itinerary directly with QPWS Boonah. There are no facilities and fires are prohibited, so bring all self-sufficient gear, including drinking water and a gas/fuel stove. **Map refs:** 155 E4, 167 F3

36 Cleared Ridge camping area (walk-in camping)

This campsite is located at the top of a ridge on a fire trail, and is a 1.5 hr walk from the carpark of the same name on Waterfall Creek Rd (4WD access only). There are no facilities and fires are prohibited, so bring all self-sufficient gear, including drinking water and a gas/fuel stove. **Map refs:** 155 E4, 167 F3

37 Cronan Creek Site 9 camping area (walk-in camping)

This campsite is reached by a 50 min walk from the Yellow Pinch Reserve day-use area on the east side of the national park, and consists of a clearing in the open eucalypt forest near the upper reaches of the Logan River. There are no facilities and fires are prohibited, so bring all self-sufficient gear, including drinking water and a gas/fuel stove. **Map refs:** 155 E4, 167 G4

38 Cronan Creek Site 10 camping area (walk-in camping)

A 10 min walk from Cronan Creek Site 9, this camping area is accessed from the Yellow Pinch Reserve on Upper Logan Rd. There are no facilities and fires are prohibited, so bring all self-sufficient gear, including drinking water and a gas/fuel stove. **Map refs:** 155 E4, 167 G4

39 Hoop Pines camping area (walk-in camping)

This camping area offers room for a relatively large number of campers (30 people), and is accessed via a 1 hr downhill walk from the Cleared Ridge carpark on Waterfall Creek Rd (4WD only). There are no facilities and fires are prohibited, so bring all self-sufficient gear, including drinking water and a gas/fuel stove. **Map refs:** 155 E4, 167 F3

40 Lower Portals camping area (walk-in camping)

This campsite near Mt Barney Creek is accessed via a 3.7 km walk from the carpark of the same name off Upper Logan Rd. There are no facilities and fires are prohibited, so bring all self-sufficient gear, including drinking water and a gas/fuel stove. **Map refs:** 155 E4, 167 F3

41 Mount May Saddle camping area (walk-in camping)

Thrillseekers will revel in the challenge of accessing this campsite in the 'saddle' between the north and south peaks of Mt May (836 m). Access is via a steep climb including rock scrambles off Waterfall Creek Rd. There are no facilities and fires are prohibited, so bring all self-sufficient gear, including drinking water and a gas/fuel stove. **Map refs:** 155 E4, 167 F3

42 Old Hut Site camping area (walk-in camping)

This small campsite is located beside a small patch of remnant rainforest in the 'saddle' between the east and west peaks of Mt Barney. It is a 4–5 hr challenging hike (including exposed rock climbs) from Yellow Pinch Reserve on Upper Logan Rd, and is closed Dec–Jan every year. There are no facilities and fires are prohibited,

Four-wheel driving on Moreton Island, Moreton Island National Park and Recreation Area (p. 10)

so bring all self-sufficient gear, including drinking water and a gas/fuel stove. **Map refs:** 155 E4, 167 F4

43 Paddys Plain camping area (walk-in camping)

This relatively large campsite (30 people) is located in open eucalypt forest near Paddys Gully, between Mt Maroon and Mt May. Contact QPWS Boonah for access instructions. There are no facilities and fires are prohibited, so bring all self-sufficient gear, including drinking water and a gas/fuel stove. **Map refs:** 155 E4, 167 F3

44 Rum Jungle camping area (walk-in camping)

Like Old Hut Site camping area, this campsite is located in the 'saddle' between the east and west peaks of Mt Barney, and is surrounded by remnant rainforest. It is a 4–5 hr challenging hike (including exposed rock climbs) from Yellow Pinch Reserve on Upper Logan Rd, and the campsite is closed every year through Dec–Jan. There are no facilities and fires are prohibited, so bring all self-sufficient gear, including drinking water and a gas/fuel stove. **Map refs:** 155 E4, 167 F4

45 Skull Camp camping area (walk-in camping)

This relatively large campsite (30 people) is located in open eucalypt forest south of Mt Maroon. Contact QPWS Boonah for access instructions. There are no facilities and fires are prohibited, so bring all self-sufficient gear, including drinking water and a gas/fuel stove. **Map refs:** 155 E4, 167 G3

46 Yamahra Creek camping area (walk-in camping)

This campsite is a moderate 1.5 hr downhill walk from the Cleared Ridge carpark on Waterfall Creek Rd (4WD access only). There are no facilities and fires are prohibited, so bring all self-sufficient gear, including drinking water and a gas/fuel stove. **Map refs:** 155 E4, 167 F4

SPRINGBROOK NATIONAL PARK

A winding drive up into the Gold Coast hinterland leads to a pristine landscape of deep valleys, splendid waterfalls and forests of ancient beech trees. A World Heritage–listed park, Springbrook protects subtropical, warm temperate and cool temperate rainforests, open eucalypt forest and heath. Advance bookings are required for camping.

How to book: NPRSR 13 7468 www.nprsr.qld.gov.au
Permits: camping permit required

47 The Settlement camping area

The 11 well-defined sites at this newly established campsite are suitable for tents and campervans, but the area is not well shaded. Hikers should note that walking tracks near this site lead to the Gold Coast Hinterland Great Walk. Each campsite has a well-grassed area approximately 10 m in diameter and an individual parking bay. Numbered sites 1–4 have longer parking bays that could accommodate a camper trailer. Tap water must be treated or boiled before drinking, or bring your own. The campground is 30 km south-west of Mudgeeraba, signposted off Springbrook Rd from the Springbrook–Nerang Rd. **Map refs:** 155 G4, 167 G3

TEERK ROO RA NATIONAL PARK

Located 4 km west of the Brisbane suburb of Cleveland, between the mainland and North Stradbroke Island, Teerk Roo Ra National Park covers the entire 519 ha of Peel Island in Moreton Bay. The island is a significant historical site both for its traditional owners, the Quandamooka people, and as a quarantine station and leprosy lazaret for European settlers. Most of the park, except for Horseshoe and Platypus bays, is a restricted-access area closed to the public. Access to the park's camping areas is via private boat only, and advance bookings are required.

How to book: NPRSR 13 7468 www.nprsr.qld.gov.au
Permits: camping permit required

48 Horseshoe Bay camping area (boat-based camping)

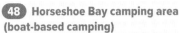

This campsite, on the foreshore of Horseshoe Bay, can only be accessed by boat. It provides an excellent base for swimming, fishing and exploring the other islands of Moreton Bay. Access is restricted to the foreshore only, and fines apply. There are few facilities other than composting toilets, so bring all self-sufficient gear, including drinking water and a gas/fuel stove. **Map refs:** 155 H2, 167 H2

49 Platypus Bay camping area (boat-based camping)

This small campsite, near the stone causeway at Platypus Bay, offers no facilities, but it provides excellent access to snorkelling in the shipwrecks of the bay. Bring all self-sufficient gear, including drinking water and a gas/fuel stove. Note: the QPWS-registered mooring near this campsite is for authorised vessels only. **Map refs:** 155 H2, 167 H2

CAMPSITES LOCATED IN OTHER AREAS

50 Andrew Drynan Park camping area

At this well-grassed area backing onto beautiful rainforest, campers can enjoy a splash in Running Creek or a relaxing picnic at one of the shaded tables. (The creek's water needs to be boiled before drinking.) You'll need to travel 19 km south-east from Rathdowney to get here; it's on Running Creek Rd (Lions Tourist Rd). Bookings are advisable over the Easter period. **Map refs:** 155 F5, 167 G4

How to book: Running Creek Rd, Running Creek (07) 5544 1281

51 Atkinson Dam Cabin Village and Shoreline Camping

Watersports enthusiasts can enjoy access to the shoreline of Atkinson Dam at this site, 8 km south-west of Coominya. There's a general store for supplies, fuel and gas bottle refills, plus laundry facilities. Look out for the signpost on Atkinson Dam Rd. Bookings are advisable during peak periods. **Map refs:** 155 E1, 167 F2

How to book: 381 Atkinson Dam Rd, Atkinson Dam (07) 5426 421

52 Atkinson Dam Waterfront Caravan Park

Anglers will like this freshwater sport fishing hotspot, and holiday-makers will enjoy the kitchen, kiosk, cabins and other park facilities. An officially sanctioned local group has plans to stock the water with sufficient saratoga to make a breeding population, plus bigeye trevally, Australian tarpon and mangrove jack, as breeding stock become available. Powerboat numbers are limited to 15 on the 550 ha lake. **Map refs:** 155 E1, 167 F2

How to book: 545 Atkinson Dam Rd, Atkinson Dam (07) 5426 4151 www.lakeatkinson.com.au

53 BIG4 Brisbane Northside Caravan Village

This holiday park in Brisbane's north offers excellent access to the city's cosmopolitan features and the Redcliffe area's marine attractions. The well-appointed grounds include a laundry, tennis courts, a camp kiosk and a lending library. Bookings are recommended during peak periods. **Map refs:** 155 F1, 167 G2

How to book: Cnr Dorville and Zillmere rds, Aspley (07) 3263 4040, 1800 060 797 http://brisbane-northside-caravan-village.qld.big4.com.au

54 Bigriggen Park camping area

There's plenty of room to sprawl on this 40 ha ground known for its peaceful surroundings and proximity to national parks. Wildlife is aplenty here: tree frogs, possums, wallabies and, if you're lucky, maybe even platypus. The kiosk is open daily for bread, milk, ice, firewood and gas bottle refills (cash only). Bigriggen is 9 km west of Rathdowney, signposted on Bigriggan Rd from Upper Logan Rd. Bookings are required year-round. **Map refs:** 155 F4, 167 G3

How to book: 196 Bigriggan Rd, Rathdowney (07) 5463 6190 www.bigriggen.com.au

55 Boonah Showground camping area

The showground is a top spot for powered sites, only a 3 min walk from Boonah town centre. There's a camp kitchen and laundry facilities, but BYO firewood. The showground provides excellent access to the attractions of the Scenic Rim and Lake Moogerah. Boonah is 50 km west of Beaudesert and 56 km south of Ipswich. **Map refs:** 155 E3, 167 F3

How to book: Melbourne St, Boonah (07) 5463 4080

56 Burgess Park camping area

Much smaller than its sister site at Darlington Park, this flat and grassy 1.2 ha camping area backs onto Christmas Creek, a good spot for swimming and fishing, but the tap water needs to be treated or boiled before drinking. To find it, head for Christmas Creek Rd, 37 km south of Beaudesert; the road is signposted off Mt Lindesay Hwy at Laravale, 14 km south of Beaudesert.

Bookings are recommended for peak periods. **Map refs:** 155 F4, 167 G3

How to book: Christmas Creek Rd, Laravale (07) 5544 8120

57 Burleigh Beach Tourist Park

Set on a prime location directly opposite Burleigh Beach, this tourist park has 73 powered sites and 16 unpowered sites. Facilities include a modern amenities block, laundry, free wireless broadband access and tour desk. Other attractions include the public swimming pool and gym across the street, surf lessons on Burleigh Beach and access to cafes and restaurants at the nearby Burleigh Theatre Arcade. **Map refs:** 155 H4, 167 H3

How to book: 37 Goodwin Tce, Burleigh Heads 1300 672 750 www.goldcoasttouristparks.com.au/park/burleigh-beach

58 Captain Logan Camp

With as much water as 2.5 Sydney Harbours, Wivenhoe Dam is a major water storage reserve for south-east Queensland and a hub for watersports enthusiasts (however boat motors are not to be used on the lake). With 57 unpowered sites, Captain Logan Camp suits both tent and trailer camping. Hot showers are available. You'll find it on Hay Rd, off the Brisbane Valley Hwy, 11 km north of Coominya. The boat ramp is nearby at Lumley Hill. Bookings are recommended for peak periods. **Map refs:** 153 E5, 155 E1, 167 F2

How to book: Logan Inlet Rd, Wivenhoe Hill (07) 5426 4729 www.seqwater.com.au/public/recreation/camping *Permits:* permits needed to fish (under-18s excepted) and to take boats requiring trailers on Lake Wivenhoe

59 Centenary Park camping area

This campground features 8 powered sites, a laundry and an electric BBQ. For stays more than

1 night, the second night is free; maximum stay is 7 nights. Visitors can throw a line in at nearby Lake Dyer or enjoy the walking trails. To get here, follow the signpost on Mulgowie Rd in Thornton, 15 km south of Laidley. Treat or boil tap water before drinking. Advance bookings are required. **Map refs:** 154 D3, 167 F3

How to book: cnr Mulgowie and Thornton School rds, Thornton (07) 5465 3698, 0439 368 561

60 Darlington Park camping area

Sensational for families, this well-shaded campsite has the added bonus of a cricket oval (with artificial turf pitch) and kids' playground on a glorious 12 ha site. The kiosk is handy for basic supplies, including firewood. You'll need to buy drinking water there, bring your own, or treat the water available. Follow the signposted access on Kerry Rd, 25 km south of Beaudesert. Bookings are recommended for peak periods. **Map refs:** 155 F4, 167 G3

How to book: Kerry Rd, Beaudesert (07) 5544 8120

61 First Settlers Park camping area

Available for a single-night stopover, this free site has surprisingly good facilities. There's a powered site suitable for caravans and camper trailers, showers (bring $2 coins for hot water) and a public phone at the general store across the road. It is in Benarkin, signposted off the D'Aguilar Hwy south-east of Nanango. **Map refs:** 152 D4, 167 F1

Who to contact: South Burnett Energy and Information Centre (07) 4171 0100 www.southburnett.qld.gov.au

62 Flanagan Reserve camping area

The natural bush setting makes this one of the most peaceful family-oriented spots in the Scenic Rim. The Logan River offers fantastic bass and

mullet fishing, there's an assortment of wildlife (turtles, lorikeets, kookaburras) and at night you can relax around the warmth of the campfire. To get to this reserve, head south from Rathdowney on the Mt Lindesay Hwy and turn right onto Boonah–Rathdowney Rd. Follow this road for 7 km and then turn left into Upper Logan Rd. Follow this road for 4 km to a T-intersection and turn right into the reserve. Bookings are recommended for peak periods. **Map refs:** 155 E4, 167 G3

How to book: Flanagan Reserve Rd, Barney View (07) 5544 3128, 0408 759 928 www.flanaganreserve.com.au

Gold Coast Hinterland Great Walk

This 54 km hiking trail traverses 2 World Heritage–listed national parks, over the top of a dormant volcano and behind a waterfall. It is best approached from west to east, starting at Green Mountains camping area and finishing at the Settlement. Note: Binna Burra is a privately operated campsite, and bookings for it must be made separately from those made through NPRSR. Walkers are required to purchase a topographic map of the Great Walk before embarking.

Please note that campsites are listed in alphabetical order, not track order. Refer to the map on p. 155 for further information.

How to book: Binna Burra Mountain Lodge (07) 5533 3622, 1300 246 622 for campsite no. **21**; NPRSR 13 7468 for campsite nos **23**, **47**, **63** *Permits:* permits required for all campsites except campsite no. **21**

21 Binna Burra camping area
See p. 9.

23 Green Mountains camping area
See p. 10.

47 The Settlement camping area
See p. 14.

63 Woonoongoora camping area (walk-in camping)

This campsite, on Gold Coast Council land, offers no facilities besides composting toilets. Bring your own drinking water and a gas/fuel stove, as open fires are prohibited. It is 23.6 km from Binna

Burra camping area and 9 km from the Settlement camping area. **Map refs:** 155 G4, 167 G3

64 Lake Boondooma Caravan and Recreation Park

An angler's paradise, the lake camping area features powered sites, hot showers, a dump point and laundry facilities. Other facilities include a kiosk, playground, tennis court and boats for hire. The site is 20 km north-west of Proston, via Boondooma Dam Rd. Bookings are recommended for powered sites. **Map refs:** 152 A1, 156 B5, 169 E4

How to book: 40 Bushcamp Rd, Lake Boondooma (07) 4168 9694 www.lakeboondooma.com.au

65 Lake Dyer Camping and Caravan Ground

The caretakers at Lake Dyer recently renovated the toilet block, installed new gas BBQs and a washing machine, and built a new playground. There are 16 powered sites at the campground. Visitors can enjoy the scenery at nearby Cunninghams Crest or Schultz lookouts, take a drive along the popular Antiques Trail or discover the historic Spring Bluff Railway Station. The lakeside site is 1.5 km west of Laidley. Note: pets must be approved by management in advance. Advance bookings are required. **Map refs:** 154 D2, 167 F2

How to book: Gatton–Laidley Rd, Laidley (07) 5465 3698, 0439 368 561

66 Lake Somerset Holiday Park

Set on a 45 ha property, this holiday park has excellent facilities for campers, caravans and camper trailers, and the option of a log or waterfront cabin for those seeking a little extra comfort. The area is known for its wineries, craft shops and watersports, and there are weekend markets at Esk, Kilcoy and Woodford. The park is on Kirkleagh Rd, 10 km south of Kilcoy off Esk–Kilcoy Rd. Note: bring your laptop as there is free wireless internet available. Bookings are recommended during peak periods. **Map refs:** 153 E4, 167 F2

How to book: Kirkleagh Rd, Hazeldean (07) 5497 1093, 1800 689 679 www.lakesomerset.com.au

67 Lumley Hill camping area

Just a short distance from Captain Logan Camp, Lumley Hill has powered sites. The campground is on Logan Inlet Rd, off Hay Rd, signposted off the Brisbane Valley Hwy. Lake Wivenhoe is a major water storage reserve where popular pastimes include canoeing, sailing and fishing (do not operate boat motors on Lake Wivenhoe). Bookings are required for powered sites. **Map refs:** 153 E5, 155 E1, 167 F2

How to book: Logan Inlet Rd, Wivenhoe Hill (07) 5426 4729 www.seqwater.com.au/public/recreation/camping *Permits:* permits required to fish (under-18s excepted) and to take boats requiring trailers on Lake Wivenhoe

68 Maidenwell camping area

This free stopover (maximum 24 hr) has a BBQ, toilets and picnic tables on Coomba Falls Rd in Maidenwell, 25 km south-west of Nanango. Have a hot shower in the town hall (pick up the key from the general store), and bring your own firewood and drinking water (tap water must be treated or boiled before drinking). **Map refs:** 152 B4, 167 E1

Who to contact: South Burnett Energy and Information Centre (07) 4171 0100 www.southburnett.qld.gov.au

69 Main Beach Tourist Park

This large, busy tourist park – across the road from Main Beach and 2 min drive from Surfers Paradise – has 100 powered sites and an additional 24 ensuite powered sites. Facilities include a swimming pool, BBQ areas, kids' playground and free wireless broadband internet. Also available are laundry facilities, a tour desk, surfboard hire and gas refills. **Map refs:** 155 H3, 167 H3

How to book: 3600 Main Beach Pde, Main Beach 1300 672 720 www.goldcoasttouristparks.com.au/park/main-beach

North Stradbroke Island

Called Minjerribah by the Indigenous Quandamooka people, and affectionately known as 'Straddie' among locals, the laid-back vibe and subtropical beauty of Stradbroke Island will have you blissfully relaxed from the moment you arrive. Spot dolphins and manta rays on the North Gorge Headlands Walk, take a scuba-diving adventure, hike through bushland to magnificent freshwater lakes, enjoy a 4WD tour on the beach, go fishing, or simply sit back at the Point Lookout pub and enjoy the glorious sunsets. Several areas of North Stradbroke Island are now part of Naree Budjong Djara National Park and Minjerribah Recreation Area, jointly administered by the Quandamooka and NPRSR. All campsites must be booked and paid for in advance of travel.

Who to contact: for Minjerribah Recreation Area contact NPRSR 13 7468 www.nprsr.qld.gov.au
How to book: Straddie Holiday Parks (07) 3409 9602, 1300 551 253 www.straddieholidayparks.com.au *Permits:* an annual permit is required to drive 4WDs on Flinders and Main beaches

70 Adder Rock camping area

Sheltered in the bushland behind a cove, Adder Rock is a shady campground with 26 powered sites and plenty of room for tents. There's a

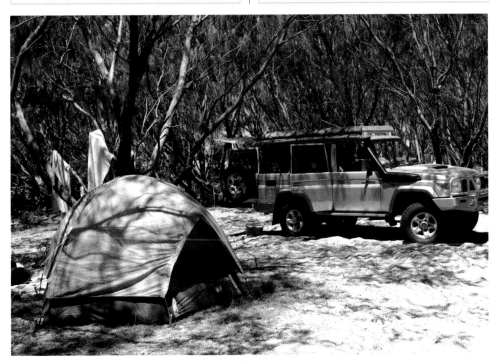

Camping at Flinders Beach, North Stradbroke Island (p. 20)

general store and public phone within 100 m, and you have the option of hiring a 2-bedroom cabin on site. The campground is on East Coast Rd at Point Lookout, around 20 km north-east of Dunwich. **Map refs:** 155 H1, 167 H2

71 Amity Point camping area

A lovely, quiet spot for swimming and dropping in a line, Amity is ideal for camping with the family. It is suitable for conventional vehicles and has 23 powered sites; there's also cabin accommodation at the campground. It is on Claytons Rd at Amity, 18 km north of Dunwich. **Map refs:** 155 H1, 167 H2

72 Bradbury's Beach camping area

Popular with boaties and fishing enthusiasts, this small campsite is just 1 km from the ferry terminal. Go past the information centre and turn left into Ballow Rd, follow it around to the right where it becomes Bingle Rd, then turn left into Flinders Ave (just before the cemetery). The park is 200 m on the right. **Map refs:** 155 H2, 167 H2

73 Cylinder Beach camping area

Straddie's most popular campground is metres from Cylinder's patrolled surf beach and close to Point Lookout's shops and pub. There are 60 unpowered sites, 8 powered sites and plenty of shade. From the ferry at Dunwich, take East Coast Rd about 19 km to Point Lookout, and follow the signs to Cylinder Beach. The park is on the left-hand side at the bottom of the hill. Note: there are electric BBQs in the adjacent public park. **Map refs:** 155 H1, 167 H2

74 Flinders Beach camping area

Accessible by 4WD only, the camping areas are behind the sand dunes and designated with blue tent signs. The only facilities on Flinders Beach are 4 composting toilets, so bring all of your self-sufficient camping equipment and supplies, including firewood and drinking water. From the ferry, follow the signs to Flinders Beach or drive out to Point Lookout and enter the beach at the Adder Rock Beach access (the first street on your left at Point Lookout, opposite the bus stop/ Tramican St). **Map refs:** 155 H1, 167 H2

75 Main Beach camping area

You'll need a 4WD to access this area and there are no facilities – not even composting toilets. Bring drinking water and a gas/fuel stove. Camping areas commence 7.5 km south of the causeway and tracks are designated by red numbered zone signs. From the ferry, follow Tazi Rd past the turn-offs to Brown Lake and the North Stradbroke Golf Course until you reach Main Beach. Or from East Coast Rd turn right onto George Nothling Dr at Point Lookout; the beach is 2 km further. **Map refs:** 155 H2, 167 H2

76 Thankful Rest camping area

Adjacent to Home Beach at Point Lookout, this secluded campground is only open during peak periods. Nearby you'll find a general store, restaurants, a bowls club, library, community markets and skater's half-pipe. It is on East Coast Rd, 20 km north-east of Dunwich. **Map refs:** 155 H1, 167 H2

77 Pointro camping area

A 1 min walk from the water's edge of Maroon Dam, Pointro is a mown site with plenty of clear spaces and a few gum trees if you prefer shade.

The dam is popular for fishing and watersports. You'll need to bring drinking water (or treat/boil the on-site water) and stock up on supplies at the stores in Boonah or Rathdowney, but firewood can be obtained on site. The campground is on Burnett Creek Rd, 28.5 km south of Boonah. Bookings are advised during peak periods. **Map refs:** 155 E4, 167 F3

How to book: Ministry Education Commission (07) 5463 6209

78 Seven Mile Diggings camping area

You can still dig around in this old fossicking area 11 km south of Nanango, though it's unlikely you'll find any gold. The campgrounds at the end of the sealed section of Old Esk North Rd are drive-in, but if you want to camp further down in the diggings themselves you'll have to carry your equipment in. This site has no facilities and suits self-sufficient campers (bring water and firewood). Camping is free but visitors must obtain a permit from the South Burnett Energy and Information Centre. **Map refs:** 152 C3, 167 F1, 169 F5

Who to contact: South Burnett Energy and Information Centre (07) 4171 0100 www.southburnett.qld.gov.au *Permits:* camping permit required

79 Sharp Park River Bend Bush Camping

Only 30 min from the Gold Coast's theme parks, this no-frills family site is split into 2 areas by the Coomera River. It's 4 km south of Canungra, which in turn is 27 km east of Beaudesert. Ideal for daytrips to Mt Tamborine, Lamington National Park or O'Reillys, you'll find it on Beechmont Rd off the Beaudesert–Nerang Rd. Bookings are recommended during peak periods. **Map refs:** 155 G4, 167 G3

How to book: 3095 Beechmont Rd, Canungra 0409 550 745

80 Somerset Park camping area

Waterskiing enthusiasts and keen anglers enjoy staying at this basic site, 25 km north-east of Esk and 26 km south of Kilcoy. The camping ground is on the western shore of the lake, reached via the Esk–Kilcoy Rd. There is a boat ramp 1.2 km away and a shop on site. Advance bookings are required for peak periods. **Map refs:** 153 E5, 167 F2

How to book: Esk–Kilcoy Rd, Somerset Dam (07) 5426 0176 www.seqwater.com.au/public/recreation/camping *Permits:* permits are required to fish (under-18s excepted)

81 Stinson Park camping area

In 1937 local legend Bernard O'Reilly led the Stinson air crash survivors to safety from this historic site. O'Reilly found the wreckage in dense rainforest and saved the lives of 2 men who had been lost in the mountains for 2 days. Experienced, well-equipped bushwalkers can take the 'stretcher track' to the site of the crash. To get to the campsite, take the Mt Lindesay Hwy at Beaudesert (towards Rathdowney). At Laravale (14 km) turn left into Christmas Creek Rd. Note: tap water needs to be treated or boiled before drinking. **Map refs:** 155 F4, 167 G4

How to book: Christmas Creek Rd, Christmas Creek (07) 5544 8008

82 Swinging Bridge Park camping area

This site has no showers or toilets, but public toilets are available nearby and the Cooyar Hotel is happy for you to use their facilities; they charge a small fee for showers. If you are using one of the powered sites, collect the key to the power box from the pub (a small fee applies). The campground is beside Cooyar Creek on Fergus St (off Munro St). Cooyar is on the New England Hwy, 90 km north of Toowoomba. **Map refs:** 152 C4, 167 E1

Who to contact: Toowoomba Regional Council 13 1872

Tipperary Flat camping area

This spot on the D'Aguilar Hwy in Nanango offers free overnight camping with a few surprising mod cons, including disabled toilets and a dump point for caravans. Grab a key to the town hall from the Nanango information centre (open every day of the year except Christmas Day) for a free hot shower. **Map refs:** 152 C3, 167 F1, 169 F5

Who to contact: South Burnett Energy and Information Centre (07) 4171 0100

84 **Waterfall Creek Reserve camping area**

On the edge of Mt Barney National Park, this very basic campsite with no facilities is suitable for self-sufficient campers and experienced bushwalkers. You'll find it on Waterfall Creek Rd, 35 km south of Boonah and 28 km west of Rathdowney. Access is via Newmans Rd off the Boonah–Rathdowney Rd. Note: during wet weather the reserve can only be accessed by 4WD vehicles. Fires are only permitted in the fire rings provided; bring your own firewood. Advance bookings are required. **Map refs:** 155 E4, 167 F3

How to book: Scenic Rim Regional Council Customer Service (07) 5540 5222 www.scenicrim. qld.gov.au *Permits:* camping permit required

85 **Yallakool Caravan Park on Bjelke-Petersen Dam**

Outdoor movies and friendly tennis competitions might not be typical tourist park activities, but Yallakool offers more bang for your buck. Situated 13 km south-east of Murgon, there are sheltered swimming areas, good fishing at Bjelke-Petersen Dam, kayaks available for hire and wildlife such as koalas, wallabies and kangaroos are often spotted in the grounds. The camp kitchen includes a fridge, hotplates, oven and microwaves. The park is signposted off Barambah Rd, from the Burnett and Bunya hwys. **Map refs:** 152 C2, 169 F5

How to book: Haager Dr, Moffatdale (07) 4168 4834 www.yallakoolpark.com.au

SUNSHINE COAST AND FRASER ISLAND

Stretching from Caloundra to Cooloola north of Brisbane, the Sunshine Coast's pristine coastline and year-round warm weather are a magnet for surfers, holidaying families and anyone seeking the laid-back seaside lifestyle. Venture just a few kilometres inland from the sunny coast to find the region's national parks shaped by forested mountains, rocky outcrops and spectacular waterfalls – the perfect location to relax, unwind and enjoy scenic camping.

North of Noosa, the Cooloola section of Great Sandy National Park features a range of beachfront and riverside campsites offering superb bushwalking, four-wheel driving, fishing, canoeing and boating. Further inland, the Amamoor, Beerburrum and Brooyar state forests have picturesque camping and day-use areas, as well as swimming holes and creeks for taking a leisurely paddle or dropping a line in.

World Heritage–listed Fraser Island, part of Great Sandy National Park, is the world's largest sand island, with 184 000 ha of exceptional beauty. You can go four-wheel driving on the beach, fish for whiting and bream on the famous 75 Mile Beach, or visit the coloured sands of The Pinnacles. Fraser is a must-see for wildlife-watchers; the long sandy beaches and beautiful rainforests provide a valuable habitat for dingoes, wallabies, flying foxes, echidnas and possums. The waters surrounding Fraser Island are home to dolphins and dugongs, and the region off Hervey Bay is one of the world's best known whale-watching spots. There are numerous bush camping sites on the island and well-established campgrounds at Central Station, Dundubara and Waddy Point.

Back on the mainland, state forests and reserves such as Imbil, Jimna, Tuan and Wongi are popular with campers and daytrippers. Imbil has scenic forest tracks for four-wheel driving, several bushwalking circuits and is one of the few protected reserves in Queensland that permits horseriding.

CAMPSITES LOCATED IN PARKS AND RESERVES

AMAMOOR STATE FOREST

Known for its riverine rainforests, hoop and bunya pine plantations and scenic walking tracks, Amamoor State Forest is 180 km north of Brisbane. Popular walks include a short path (with wheelchair access) to a platypus-viewing platform, a 1 km return rainforest walk and, for experienced hikers, the 4.6 km (4 hr) Cedar Grove trail. The forest is the traditional home of the Gubbi Gubbi, Wakka Wakka, Jinibara and Kabi Kabi peoples. The traditional owners maintain strong cultural links and strive to protect the land by sharing their culture. Advance bookings are required for all camping.

How to book: NPRSR 13 7468 www.nprsr.qld.gov.au
Permits: camping permit required

86 **Amamoor Creek camping area**

A rare find for pet owners, this camp is dog friendly. Take care though, as the creek is home to platypus and a variety of frogs. The flat, grassy campsites are suitable for tents and caravans, and surrounded by majestic ironbark and blue gum forest. Toilets and showers are wheelchair-accessible and there is a public phone. The campsite is closed to the public for a week each Aug during the annual Country Music Muster. Bring a gas/fuel stove or your own firewood, as collecting wood in the forest is illegal. Tap water needs to be boiled or treated before drinking.
Map refs: 153 E2, 167 F1, 169 F5

Lake McKenzie, Fraser Island,
Great Sandy National Park (p. 27)

87 Cedar Grove camping area

Cedar Grove camping area in Amamoor State Forest has tent and caravan campsites in open grassy areas beside riverine rainforest of white and red cedars, as well as tall open forest and Amamoor Creek. Bring along a gas/fuel stove or your own firewood, as collecting wood in the forest is illegal. Tap water needs to be boiled or treated before drinking, or bring your own. **Map refs:** 153 E2, 167 F1, 169 F5

BEERBURRUM STATE FOREST

A 1 hr drive north of Brisbane, Coochin Creek camping area in the north-east of Beerburrum State Forest is a renowned spot for fishing and boating. It is close to the site of Campbellville, an 1880s timber town. To get here, take Roys Rd from the Bruce Hwy. Advance bookings are required for camping.

How to book: NPRSR 13 7468 www.nprsr.qld.gov.au
Permits: camping permit required

88 Coochin Creek camping and day-use area

A great find for those who enjoy fishing and boating, this flat and grassy site beside Coochin Creek is on Roys Rd, 3 km upstream from the Pumiceton Passage. Access is 9 km east of Beerwah and 4 km east of the Bruce Hwy. There are 23 numbered campsites, various surfaces (sand, dirt, concrete, grass) and access for all vehicles. Open fires are not permitted except in provided fireplaces; bring firewood. **Map refs:** 153 F4, 167 G1

BROOYAR STATE FOREST

West of Gympie, Brooyar State Forest is known for having some of Qld's best hoop pine plantations and cliff-top lookouts. Visitors can take rainforest walks or kick through the shallows of Glastonbury Creek. Northern access is from Petersen Rd from the Wide Bay Hwy 20 km west of Gympie. From the south, follow the sign from Glastonbury on Gympie–Woolooga Rd. Bookings must be made in advance for all camping.

How to book: NPRSR 13 7468 www.nprsr.qld.gov.au
Permits: camping permit required

89 Glastonbury Creek camping area

This large grassy camping area with a maximum capacity of 120 people is on the south-eastern edge of Brooyar State Forest. There is a day-use area with picnic tables and wood BBQs, and open fires are allowed in the designated fire rings. From the south, the campground is on the right just past the entrance to the forest; from the north it is on the left, 2 km past the entrance. Bring your own firewood, as gathering wood is prohibited. **Map refs:** 153 E1, 169 F4

CONONDALE NATIONAL PARK

The beautiful forests and gorges of Conondale National Park are reached by Booloumba Creek Rd, off Maleny–Kenilworth Rd 6 km south of Kenilworth. The park has waterfalls and lookouts, plus more than 120 bird species. Serious hikers will appreciate the challenge of the Conondale Range Great Walk, a 56 km hiking trail with 3 designated campsites, and its reward of stunning lookouts. Advance bookings are required for camping.

How to book: NPRSR 13 7468 www.nprsr.qld.gov.au
Permits: camping permit required

90 Booloumba Creek no. 1 camping area

This area offers secluded camping in a rainforest setting, ideal for tents but not for caravans or trailers, which are not permitted here. To reach it, go through Maleny and follow the signs to Kenilworth. You'll pass through the small town of Conondale; the turn-off to Booloumba is about 13 km past Conondale. Bring your own firewood and treat or boil the water before drinking. Conventional vehicle access is only possible in dry weather; there is 4WD access at all times. **Map refs:** 153 E3, 167 G1, 169 G5

Much like site no. 1, no. 3 offers secluded tent camping in a rainforest setting. No caravans or camper trailers are permitted. To get here, go through Maleny and follow the signs to Kenilworth; the turn-off to Booloumba is about 13 km past Conondale. Bring your own firewood and treat or boil the water before drinking. Conventional vehicle access is only possible during dry weather; there is 4WD access at all times. **Map refs:** 153 E3, 167 G1, 169 G5

Booloumba Creek's no. 4 campground is suitable for campervans, caravans and trailers. To get here, go through Maleny and follow the signs to Kenilworth; the turn-off to Booloumba is about 13 km past Conondale. Bring your own firewood and use existing fire sites. Treat or boil the water before drinking. Conventional vehicle access is only

possible during dry weather; there is 4WD access at all times. **Map refs:** 153 E3, 167 G1, 169 G5

Conondale Range Great Walk

Please note that campsites are listed in alphabetical order, not track order. Refer to the map on p. 153 for further information.

93 Summer Falls camping area (walk-in camping)

This campsite near the picturesque Summer Falls offers simple facilities for a maximum of 24 campers. Boil or treat the water before drinking and bring a gas/fuel stove, as fires are prohibited. Summer Falls is 12 km from the Booloumba Creek day-use area and 15.2 km from Tallowwood camping area. **Map refs:** 153 E3, 167 F1, 169 F5

94 Tallowwood camping area (walk-in camping)

As the name might suggest, Tallowwood camping area is located in a section of Conondale National

Kauri pines near Central Station camping area, Great Sandy National Park (p. 28)

Park dominated by the tallowwood. The camping area offers simple facilities for a maximum of 24 campers. Boil or treat the water provided before drinking and bring a gas/fuel stove, as fires are prohibited. Tallowwood is 15.2 km from Summer Falls camping area and 17 km from Wongai camping area. **Map refs:** 153 E3, 167 F1, 169 F5

95 Wongai camping area (walk-in camping)

This camping area in the grassy open forest offers simple facilities for a maximum of 24 campers. Boil or treat the water provided before drinking and bring a gas/fuel stove, as fires are prohibited. Wongai is 11 km from the Booloumba Creek day-use area and 17 km from Tallowwood camping area. **Map refs:** 153 E3, 167 F1, 169 F5

GREAT SANDY NATIONAL PARK

Great Sandy National Park encompasses World Heritage–listed Fraser Island, the largest sand island in the world; nearby Woody Island, offering bush camping for self-sufficient visitors; and Cooloola on the mainland. This national park is 4WD only. Bookings are required in advance for all camping sites.

Fraser Island is famous for its giant dunes, some reaching 230 m in height, and its magnificent sand cliffs. Huge sand blows – dunes that continually move and regenerate – are a feature. It is also distinguished by its 40 perched dune lakes, of which Lake Boomanjin, at 200 ha, is the largest in the world. Ringed by white beaches, the water's colour in these freshwater lakes varies, from the sparkling blue of Lake McKenzie to the reddish-brown of Lake Boomanjin, which is stained by tannins from surrounding plants. The Fraser Island Great Walk traverses a 90 km stretch and takes in many of the island's attractions. Note: campfires are prohibited on Fraser Island, except at Dilli Village, Dundubara and Waddy Point. For these sites you need to bring your own firewood; collection of wood locally is prohibited. Many wild dingoes live on Fraser Island; they are dangerous, so read NPRSR's dingo safety information before visiting.

Cooloola offers a scenic experience amid open forests and fringing mangroves, placid waterways and coloured sands. This section of

Great Sandy National Park is on the coast north of Noosa Heads, west of Gympie and south of Rainbow Beach. It contains the Cooloola Great Walk, a 102 km long track that traverses rainforest, dry scrubby regions, waterways and coastal heath. Take time to visit Double Island Point Lighthouse while you're here.

How to book: Fraser Island Learning and Research Centre (07) 4127 9130 for campsite no. 106; (07) 4127 9177 www.cathedralsonfraser.com.au for campsite no. 98; NPRSR 13 7468 www.nprsr.qld.gov.au for all other campsites *Permits:* camping permit required for all NPRSR campsites, and 4WD permits required for all vehicles

96 Burad camping area (bush camping)

Bush camping for self-sufficient campers is available behind the dunes on this stretch of beach south of Corroboree Beach on Fraser Island's east coast. Bring drinking water and a gas/fuel stove (fires are prohibited), and place all rubbish and scraps in containers in your 4WD to avoid attracting dingoes. **Map refs:** 157 H2, 169 H3

97 Carree camping area (bush camping)

This semi-remote camping area at the far north of Fraser Island near Sandy Cape Lighthouse is suitable only for experienced wilderness campers. Bring drinking water and a gas/fuel stove (fires are prohibited), and place all rubbish and scraps in containers in your 4WD to avoid attracting dingoes. **Map refs:** 157 H1, 169 H2

98 Cathedrals on Fraser

This privately managed camping area, part of the Cathedrals on Fraser resort, offers some creature comforts missing from other campgrounds on the island, including fuel sales, a convenience store with bottle shop and laundry facilities. It is a short distance from some of Fraser Island's key attractions, including the multicoloured sand cliff faces of The Pinnacles and the wreck of the SS *Maheno*. **Map refs:** 157 H2, 169 H3

99 Central Station camping area

This fenced family campground in central Fraser Island's rainforest setting has 44 tent sites, 16 camper trailer sites and a group area for 20–40 people. Accessible by 4WD or hiking trails only, it is 13 km east of the Wanggoolba Creek barge landing area and 9 km west of Eurong. Bring coins for the hot showers and use a gas/fuel stove (open fires are prohibited). It is a designated campsite on the Fraser Island Great Walk, and is 6.6 km from Lake McKenzie and 7.5 km from Lake Benaroon. **Map refs:** 157 G3, 169 G3

Cooloola Great Walk

Please note that campsites are listed in alphabetical order, not track order. Refer to the map on p. 153 for further information.

100 Brahminy camping area
(walk-in camping)

This clearing in the coastal heath of Cooloola boasts stunning views of Lake Cootharaba and some modest facilities. It is 17 km from the southern entrance to Cooloola Great Walk and 20 km from Dutgee camping area. Water provided at this campsite must be boiled or treated before drinking. Bring a gas/fuel stove. **Map refs:** 153 G2, 169 G5

101 Dutgee camping area
(walk-in camping)

This sandy campsite next to the Noosa River is named after the local Indigenous word for the boronia flowers that are abundant in the area. Like Brahminy, it has modest facilities, including water (treat or boil before drinking). It is 20 km from Brahminy camping area and 16.5 km from Litoria camping area. Bring a gas/fuel stove. **Map refs:** 153 G1, 169 G5

102 Kauri camping area
(walk-in camping)

The Kauri camping area is so named because it lies at the very southern edge of the kauri pine's range. This camp on a lush forested ridge offers modest facilities, including drinking water (must be treated or boiled before use). Bring a gas/fuel stove. It is 20 km from Litoria camp and 15 km from the northern entrance to Cooloola Great Walk at Carlo Sandblow. **Map refs:** 153 G1, 157 G5, 169 G4

103 Litoria camping area
(walk-in camping)

This campsite, near the shores of the mildly acidic Lake Coolamera, is named after the Cooloola sedgefrog, and you can hear its distinctive call. Boil or treat the water provided here before drinking. Bring a gas/fuel stove. It is 16.5 km from Dutgee camping area and 20 km from Kauri camping area. **Map refs:** 153 G1, 157 G5, 169 G4

104 Coolooloi Creek camping area
(bush camping)

Bush camping for self-sufficient campers is available at this area to the west of the Hook Point barge terminal on Fraser Island, accessible by 4WD or boat. Bring drinking water and a gas/fuel stove (fires are prohibited), and place all rubbish and scraps in sealed containers to avoid attracting dingoes. **Map refs:** 157 G4, 169 G4

105 Cornwells camping area
(bush camping)

Bush camping for self-sufficient campers is available behind the dunes on this stretch of beach at the eastern end of Fraser Island's central lakes scenic drive. Bring drinking water and a gas/fuel stove (fires are prohibited), and place all rubbish and scraps in containers in your 4WD to avoid attracting dingoes. **Map refs:** 157 H3, 169 G3

106 Dilli Village camping area

This privately managed camping area is attached to University of the Sunshine Coast's Fraser Island Research and Learning Centre, and offers reasonable facilities enclosed within a dingo-proof fence. Bring your own firewood for the provided campfire sites, and boil or treat water before drinking. Dilli Village is the southern trailhead for Fraser Island Great Walk, and is 6.3 km from Lake Boomanjin camping area. **Map refs:** 157 G4, 169 G4

107 Diray camping area (bush camping)

Semi-remote bush camping for self-sufficient campers is available behind the dunes on this stretch of beach south of Sandy Cape on Fraser Island's east coast. Bring drinking water and a gas/fuel stove (fires are prohibited), and place all rubbish and scraps in containers in your 4WD to avoid attracting dingoes. **Map refs:** 157 H1, 169 H2

108 Dulara camping area (bush camping)

Bush camping for self-sufficient campers is available behind the dunes on this stretch of beach at the northern end of Hook Point Inland Rd. Generators are prohibited and campers are required to bring a portable toilet (waste disposal facilities are available at Garulim). Bring drinking water and a gas/fuel stove (fires are prohibited), and place all rubbish and scraps in containers in your 4WD to avoid attracting dingoes. **Map refs:** 157 G4, 169 G4

109 Duling camping area (bush camping)

Bush camping for self-sufficient campers is available behind the dunes on this stretch of

beach south of Ngkala Rocks on the northern east coast of Fraser Island. Bring drinking water and a gas/fuel stove (fires are prohibited), and place all rubbish and scraps in containers in your 4WD to avoid attracting dingoes. **Map refs:** 157 H1, 169 H3

110 Dundubara camping area

This popular family campground on Fraser Island has 40 tent sites, 5 camper trailer sites and a separate group camping area for up to 40 people. Accessed by 4WD, it's on the central east coast, about 75 km north of the Hook Point barge landing area and 19 km south of Indian Head. There is a payphone and post box near the campground, plus a waste transfer station 1 km from the site. You'll need to bring coins for the hot showers and to boil or treat the water before drinking. Note: there is a 9pm noise curfew. Bring your own firewood from the mainland. **Map refs:** 157 H2, 169 H3

111 Eli camping area (bush camping)

Bush camping for self-sufficient campers is available behind the dunes on this stretch of beach halfway between Dilli Village and Eli Creek on Fraser Island's east coast. Bring drinking water and a gas/fuel stove (fires are prohibited), and place all rubbish and scraps in containers in your 4WD to avoid attracting dingoes. **Map refs:** 157 H3, 169 G3

112 Eugarie camping area (bush camping)

Bush camping for self-sufficient campers is available behind the dunes on this stretch of beach north of Knifeblade Sandblow on Fraser Island's east coast. Bring drinking water and a gas/fuel stove (fires are prohibited), and place all rubbish and scraps in containers in your 4WD to avoid attracting dingoes. **Map refs:** 157 H3, 169 H3

113   Fig Tree Point camping area

This campground beside Lake Cootharaba in the Cooloola section has basic facilities and a maximum capacity of 25 campers. It can be reached by boat or canoe from the Noosa River, 2 km north of Kinaba, or by a 10 km walk from Elanda Point. Boil or treat water before using, and bring a gas/fuel stove. **Map refs:** 163 F2

Fraser Island Great Walk

Please note that campsites are listed in alphabetical order, not track order. Refer to the map on p. 157 for further information.

99   Central Station camping area

See p. 28.

106   Dilli Village camping area

See p. 29.

114   Lake Benaroon camping area (walk-in camping)

There is a maximum stay of 2 nights and groups should number no more than 8 at this hikers' campsite. Lake Benaroon camping area is 6.3 km from Dilli Village and 7.2 km from Lake Boomanjin camping area. Water from the lake is drinkable but you need to boil or treat it. Bring a gas/fuel stove. **Map refs:** 157 G4, 169 G4

115   Lake Boomanjin camping area (walk-in camping)

See p. 32.

116   Lake Garawongera camping area (walk-in camping)

This site is 13.1 km from Valley of the Giants camping area and about 6.6 km from the Fraser Island Great Walk trailhead at Happy Valley. Treat or boil water before drinking and use gas/fuel stoves only (no open fires are

permitted). A maximum 2-night stay applies. **Map refs:** 157 H3, 169 G3

117   Lake McKenzie camping area (walk-in camping)

This basic clearing with few facilities is 6.6 km from Central Station camping area and 11.9 km from Lake Wabby camping area. The maximum stay is 2 nights and groups should be no bigger than 8. Boil or treat water before drinking, and bring a gas/fuel stove. **Map refs:** 157 G3, 169 G3

118   Lake Wabby camping area (walk-in camping)

This walkers' camp has a maximum 2-night stay and is suitable for groups no larger than 8. Water is available on site (treat or boil first) and there is a toilet. Use only a gas/fuel stove. It is 11.9 km from Lake McKenzie camping area and 16.2 km from Valley of the Giants camping area. **Map refs:** 157 G3, 169 G3

119   Valley of the Giants camping area (walk-in camping)

This walkers' camp, 13.1 km from Lake Garawongera and 16.2 km from Lake Wabby, has a toilet and tap water (treat or boil water before drinking). A 2-night maximum stay applies. Bring a gas/fuel stove as fires are prohibited. **Map refs:** 157 G3, 169 G3

120   Freshwater Campground

Accessible by 4WD only, this campground with 59 sites is 8 km south of Double Island Point off Teewah Beach in Great Sandy's Cooloola section. The camping area is 500 m from the beach in scribbly gum woodland. Travel here via Teewah Beach or Freshwater Rd from the Bymien picnic area, 19 km east of Rainbow Beach Road, 1 km west of the beach. Sites must be pre-booked. Note: bring $1 coins for hot showers. Treat or boil tap water before drinking. Gas BBQs are available at the nearby day-use area. **Map refs:** 153 G1, 157 G5, 169 G4

Gabala camping area (bush camping)

Bush camping for self-sufficient campers is available behind the dunes on this stretch of beach between Poyungan Rocks and Cornwells camping area on Fraser Island's east coast. Bring drinking water and a gas/fuel stove (fires are prohibited), and place all rubbish and scraps in containers in your 4WD to avoid attracting dingoes. **Map refs:** 157 H3, 169 G3

122 Garrys Anchorage camping area

Unfenced campsites and picnic tables in a very quiet, remote location are 19 km south of Ungowa on Fraser Island's south-west coast. Access is by 4WD or boat. Bring drinking water and a gas/fuel stove (fires are prohibited), and place all rubbish and scraps in containers in your 4WD to avoid attracting dingoes. **Map refs:** 157 G4, 169 G4

123 Garulim camping area (bush camping)

Bush camping for self-sufficient campers is available behind the dunes on this stretch of beach halfway between Hook Point and Dilli Village on Hook Point Inland Rd. Generators are prohibited and campers are required to bring a portable toilet (waste disposal facilities available on site). Bring drinking water and a gas/fuel stove (fires are prohibited), and place all rubbish and scraps in containers in your 4WD to avoid attracting dingoes. **Map refs:** 157 G4, 169 G4

124 Govi camping area (bush camping)

Bush camping for self-sufficient campers is available behind the dunes on this stretch of beach north of Dilli Village on Fraser Island's east coast. Bring drinking water and a gas/fuel stove (fires are prohibited), and place all rubbish and scraps in containers in your 4WD to avoid attracting dingoes. **Map refs:** 157 G4, 169 G4

125 Guluri camping area (bush camping)

Bush camping for self-sufficient campers is available behind the dunes on this stretch of beach directly to the north of Happy Valley on Fraser Island's east coast. Bring drinking water and a gas/fuel stove (fires are prohibited), and place all rubbish and scraps in containers in your 4WD to avoid attracting dingoes. **Map refs:** 157 H3, 169 G3

126 Guruman camping area (bush camping)

Bush camping for self-sufficient campers is available behind the dunes on this stretch of beach south of Dundubara camping area on Fraser Island's east coast. Bring drinking water and a gas/fuel stove (fires are prohibited), and place all rubbish and scraps in containers in your 4WD to avoid attracting dingoes. **Map refs:** 157 H2, 169 H3

127 Harrys camping area

This is the only campground in the Cooloola section with vehicle (4WD only) and Upper Noosa River access. It is 10 km east of Cooloola Way on Harrys Hut Rd. Campers should be aware that goannas and brush turkeys often scrounge for food in the area, so do not leave any scraps at the site. Boil or treat drinking water and use a gas/fuel stove. Note: you do not require a 4WD permit to drive along Harrys Hut Rd. **Map refs:** 153 G1, 169 G5

128 Jeffries Beach camping area (boat-based camping)

This bush campground with no facilities is the only camping area on Woody Island. You'll find Jeffries Beach on the south-east side of the island, about 5 min south of the gas shed. Experienced sea kayakers will find the waters of the Great Sandy Strait a delight to paddle in, but beware of the strong currents. You'll need to bring your own water, gas/fuel stove and rubbish bags. Note: mobile phone coverage here is poor. Camping is not permitted on Little Woody Island.
Map refs: 157 G3, 169 G3

115 Lake Boomanjin camping area (walk-in camping)

This fenced campground suitable for tent camping is in open forest between the carpark on Birrabeen Rd and Lake Boomanjin on Fraser Island. It is 6.3 km north of Dilli Village on the Fraser Island Great Walk, or 10 km north-west of Dilli Village on Birrabeen Rd (4WD only). Bring a gas/fuel stove and drinking water.
Map refs: 157 G4, 169 G4

129 Maheno camping area (bush camping)

Bush camping for self-sufficient campers is available behind the dunes on this stretch of beach directly to the north of Eli Creek near the wreck of the *SS Maheno* on Fraser Island's east coast. Bring drinking water and a gas/fuel stove (fires are prohibited), and place all rubbish and scraps in containers in your 4WD to avoid attracting dingoes. Eli Creek is suitable for swimming, but do not swim in the ocean.
Map refs: 157 H3, 169 H3

130 Marloo camping area (bush camping)

Bush camping for self-sufficient campers is available behind the dunes on this stretch of beach between Orchid Beach and Ocean Lake on Fraser Island's east coast. Bring drinking water and a gas/fuel stove (fires are prohibited), and place all rubbish and scraps in containers in your 4WD to avoid attracting dingoes.
Map refs: 157 H2, 169 H3

131 Midyim camping area (bush camping)

Bush camping for self-sufficient campers is available behind the dunes on this stretch of beach between Dulara and Garulim on Hook Point Inland Rd. Generators are prohibited and campers are required to bring a portable toilet (waste disposal facilities are available at Garulim). Bring drinking water and a gas/fuel stove (fires are prohibited), and place all rubbish and scraps in containers in your 4WD to avoid attracting dingoes. **Map refs:** 157 G4, 169 G4

132 Neebs Waterhole camping area (walk-in camping)

Bush camping for self-sufficient hikers is permitted at Neebs Waterhole, 8.1 km (3 hr walk) south of Mullens carpark on Rainbow Beach Rd in the Cooloola section. It is around 12.5 km north of the Wandi Waterhole camping area. Access is walk-in only from the Cooloola Wilderness Trail. Bring in drinking water and a gas/fuel stove (no fires are permitted). **Map refs:** 153 F1, 157 G5, 169 G4

133 Noosa River camping area – no. 1 (boat-based camping)

Take a paddle down the Noosa River in the Cooloola section to this remote campsite, accessible only by small boat or canoe (jetty provided). It caters for a maximum of 8 campers and offers few facilities. Boil or treat the provided water before using. Fires are banned, so bring a gas/fuel stove. **Map refs:** 153 G1, 169 G5

134 Noosa River camping area – no. 2 (boat-based camping)

This campsite, further up the Noosa River in the Cooloola section than camping area no. 1, is similarly low-key and tranquil. It can be accessed by small boat or canoe (canoe landing area provided). It holds a maximum of 8 campers and offers few facilities. Boil or treat the provided water before using. Fires are banned, so bring a gas/fuel stove. **Map refs:** 153 G1, 169 G5

135 Noosa River camping area – no. 3 (boat-based camping)

This campsite, further up the Noosa River in the Cooloola section than camping areas nos 1 and 2, marks the limit of how far motorised vessels can travel up the Noosa. It camps 25 people and has an access jetty, although there are no toilet facilities. Bring your own drinking water – or boil or treat the water here – and a gas/fuel stove. Note: the Cooloola Great Walk passes by this campsite. **Map refs:** 153 G1, 169 G5

136 Noosa River camping area – no. 4 (boat-based camping)

This campsite, just to the north of camping area no. 3 on the Noosa River in the Cooloola section, is the first of a series of isolated bush camps for self-sufficient campers. Accessible only by canoe (no motorised boats), there are no facilities on site and it caters for a maximum of 8 people. Boil or treat water from the river, or preferably bring in your own water. Fires are banned, so also bring a gas/fuel stove. Note: the Cooloola Great Walk passes by this campsite. **Map refs:** 153 G1, 169 G5

137 Noosa River camping area – no. 5 (boat-based camping)

This campsite, a few bends up the Noosa River in the Cooloola section from camping area no. 4, is the last of the riverside camping areas that the Great Walk passes by before turning north-east towards Lake Cooloomera. Like the other campsites, it has no facilities. Boil or treat the river water, or bring your own drinking water, and carry in a gas/fuel stove. **Map refs:** 153 G1, 169 G5

138 Noosa River camping area – no. 8 (boat-based camping)

This campsite is in the semi-remote north of Noosa River in the Cooloola section, 5 km north of camping area no. 5. (The numbered camping areas between are currently closed.) Like the other campsites, it has no facilities. Boil or treat the river water, or bring your own drinking water, and bring a gas/fuel stove. **Map refs:** 153 G1, 169 G4

139 Noosa River camping area – no. 9 (boat-based camping)

This campsite is in the semi-remote north of Noosa River in the Cooloola section, 1 km upstream of camping area no. 8. Like the other campsites, it has no facilities. Boil or treat the river water, or bring your own drinking water, and bring a gas/fuel stove. **Map refs:** 153 G1, 169 G4

140 Noosa River camping area – no. 13 (boat-based camping)

This campsite is in the semi-remote north of Noosa River in the Cooloola section, 2 km upstream of camping area no. 9. Like the other campsites, it has no facilities. Boil or treat the river water, or bring your own water, and carry in a gas/fuel stove. **Map refs:** 153 G1, 169 G4

141 Noosa River camping area – no. 15 (boat-based camping)

If you want to get away from it all, head far up the Noosa River in the Cooloola section to this, the final campsite on the river. Like the other campsites, it has no facilities. Boil or treat the river water, or bring your own water, and bring a gas/fuel stove. **Map refs: 153 G1, 169 G4**

142 Ocean Lake camping area (bush camping)

Bush camping for self-sufficient campers is available behind the dunes between Ocean Lake and the beach on Fraser Island's east coast. Some facilities are available at the nearby Ocean Lake day-use area. Bring drinking water and a gas/fuel stove (fires are prohibited), and place all rubbish and scraps in containers in your 4WD to avoid attracting dingoes. **Map refs: 157 H1, 169 H3**

143 One Tree Rocks camping area (bush camping)

Bush camping for self-sufficient campers is available behind the dunes on this stretch of beach north of Eurong QPWS Information Centre on Fraser Island's east coast. Bring drinking water and a gas/fuel stove (fires are prohibited), and place all rubbish and scraps in containers in your 4WD to avoid attracting dingoes. **Map refs: 157 G3, 169 G3**

144 Poverty Point camping area

This simple campground overlooking Tin Can Bay is 13 km south of Rainbow Beach off Rainbow Beach Rd in the Cooloola section. Follow the 4WD access road a further 6 km to reach the site. Bring your own water and firewoood (for use only in the fire rings provided). There are no facilities on site. **Map refs: 153 G1, 157 G5, 169 G4**

145 Poyungan camping area (bush camping)

Bush camping for self-sufficient campers is available behind the dunes on this stretch of beach north of Poyungan Rocks on Fraser Island's east coast. Bring drinking water and a gas/fuel stove (fires are prohibited), and place all rubbish and scraps in containers in your 4WD to avoid attracting dingoes. **Map refs: 157 H3, 169 G3**

146 Teebing camping area (bush camping)

This very large, remote camping area stretches south from Sandy Cape Lighthouse on Fraser's west coast down to Wathumba camping area. 4WD vehicles are not permitted in this delicate area (boat or walk-in access only), and there are no facilities; bring water and a gas/fuel stove. Note: as this area is remote and difficult to reach in case of emergency, it is suitable only for experienced wilderness campers. Place rubbish and scraps in sealed containers to avoid attracting dingoes. **Map refs: 157 H1, 169 G3**

147 Teewah Beach camping area

You can camp on Teewah Beach in the 15 km zone between Noosa Shire boundary and Little Freshwater Creek in the Cooloola section, but there are no facilities provided. Access is 4WD only, with room for off-road caravans and camper trailers. Beach camping is not permitted from Double Island Point west to Rainbow Beach, north of Little Freshwater Creek, or south of the Noosa Shire boundary. Bring your own water and firewood. Note: use existing tent and fire sites to minimise your impact. **Map refs: 153 G1, 169 G5**

148 Ungowa camping area

Expect plenty of open, shady spots for tents, and defined camper trailer sites, at Ungowa, 12 km south-west of Central Station on the south-west coast of Fraser Island. The facilities are relatively basic but include a sink for washing up. Access is by 4WD or boat. Bring drinking water and a gas/fuel stove, and also insect repellent, as mosquitoes and sandflies are active year-round. **Map refs:** 157 G3, 169 G3

149 Waddy Point camping area

The camping area at Waddy Point on Fraser Island contains a fenced clearing with 30 tent sites and 3 camper trailer sites, a fenced group-camping area for up to 40 people, and unfenced beachfront camping for 90 people. It is on the north-east coast of Fraser Island, about 5 km north of Indian Head, and is accessible only by 4WD. Facilities include flushing toilets, hot showers (coin-operated) and a waste transfer system 500 m from the campground. Use the communal fire rings for campfires – bring your own firewood. Generators are not permitted. **Map refs:** 157 H2, 169 H3

150 Wahba camping area (bush camping)

Bush camping for self-sufficient campers is available behind the dunes on this stretch of beach south of The Pinnacles on Fraser Island's east coast. Bring drinking water and a gas/fuel stove (fires are prohibited), and place all rubbish and scraps in containers in your 4WD to avoid attracting dingoes. **Map refs:** 157 H3, 169 H3

151 Wandi Waterhole camping area (bush camping)

Wandi has clearings for bush camping suitable for self-sufficient hikers, around 12.5 km south of Neebs Waterhole in the Cooloola section. Access is walk-in only from the Cooloola Wilderness Trail. Carry in drinking water and a gas/fuel stove (no fires are permitted). **Map refs:** 153 G1, 169 G4

Teewah Beach camping area, Great Sandy National Park (p. 34)

152 Wathumba camping area

Nearby mangroves ensure mosquitoes and sandflies are ever-present, especially in summer, so come prepared! There are 20 designated sites and plenty of grass at this Fraser Island site, 16 km west of Waddy Point and accessible by 4WD or boat only. Bring drinking water and a gas/fuel stove. **Map refs:** 157 H2, 169 H3

153 Winnam camping area (bush camping)

Bush camping for self-sufficient campers is available behind the dunes on this stretch of beach south of Kirrar Sandblow on Fraser Island's east coast. Bring drinking water and a gas/fuel stove (fires are prohibited), and place all rubbish and scraps in containers in your 4WD to avoid attracting dingoes. **Map refs:** 157 H3, 169 G3

154 Wongai camping area (bush camping)

Bush camping for self-sufficient campers is available behind the dunes on this stretch of beach south of Eurong Beach Resort on Fraser Island's east coast. Bring drinking water and a gas/fuel stove (fires are prohibited), and place all rubbish and scraps in containers in your 4WD to avoid attracting dingoes. **Map refs:** 157 G4, 165 E1, 169 G4, 177 F3

155 Wyuna camping area (bush camping)

Bush camping for self-sufficient campers is available behind the dunes on this stretch of beach south of Burad camping area on Fraser Island's east coast. Bring drinking water and a gas/fuel stove (fires are prohibited), and place all rubbish and scraps in containers in your 4WD to avoid attracting dingoes. **Map refs:** 157 H2, 169 H3

156 Yurru camping area (bush camping)

Bush camping for self-sufficient campers is available behind the dunes on this stretch of beach north of Cathedrals on Fraser resort on Fraser Island's east coast. Bring drinking water and a gas/fuel stove (fires are prohibited), and place all rubbish and scraps in containers in your 4WD to avoid attracting dingoes. **Map refs:** 157 H2, 169 H3

IMBIL STATE FOREST

Adjacent to both Jimna State Forest and Conondale National Park, this state forest provides access to a range of different landscapes – lush rainforests, imposing eucalypts, creeks and waterfalls. It is a popular locale for horseriding, walking through bush, mountain-biking and relaxing with a picnic. Campsites must be booked in advance.

How to book: NPRSR 13 7468 www.nprsr.qld.gov.au
Permits: camping permit required

157 Charlie Moreland camping area

This sizeable campground is suitable for large groups and is accessible by caravans, trailers and campervans. You'll need to bring your own firewood and use existing fire sites. Treat or boil water before drinking. Horses are welcome to stay overnight in the adjoining horse paddock. To get here, go through Maleny and follow the signs to Kenilworth; the turn-off to Charlie Moreland is about 13.5 km past Conondale. **Map refs:** 153 E3, 167 G1, 169 G5

INSKIP PENINSULA RECREATION AREA

Looking onto the southern tip of Fraser Island, north of Rainbow Beach, the peninsula is washed by the Pacific Ocean on its eastern side and by Tin Can Bay and Great Sandy Strait to the west. Fishing and birdwatching are popular pursuits. Inskip's beaches are unpatrolled and sharks are common, so swimming is not recommended. Boaties should familiarise themselves with Great

Sandy Marine Park's zones and regulations before launching. Campsites must be booked in advance. Note: check road conditions for caravan access.

How to book: NPRSR 13 7468 www.nprsr.qld.gov.au
Permits: camping permit required

158 MV Beagle camping area

This small campground is accessible from the road or beach by 4WD only, and is not suitable for caravans, trailers or buses. There are hybrid toilets, and water is available at the service facility on Clarkson Dr in Rainbow Beach. Open fires are permitted in fire sites (bring your own firewood). The sandy campsites are set amid coastal vegetation of casuarina, heath and eucalypt woodland. **Map refs:** 157 G5, 169 G4

159 MV Natone camping area

Accessible from the road or the beach by 4WD only, this campsite is not suitable for caravans, trailers or buses. You can set up camp behind the foredunes and it's only a short walk to the beach. Water is available at the service facility on Clarkson Dr in Rainbow Beach. Bring your own firewood for use in defined fire sites. **Map refs:** 157 G5, 169 G4

160 MV Sarawak camping area

Popular with large groups, this campground off Clarkson Rd is the furthest from the entrance to Inskip Peninsula Recreation Area and can be accessed by road (conventional vehicles, when dry) or beach (4WD). It is accessible for trailers and caravans, but not buses. Water is available at the service facility on Clarkson Dr in Rainbow Beach. Open fires are permitted in fire sites; bring your own firewood. **Map refs:** 157 G5, 169 G4

161 The Oaks camping area

This basic campsite offers only rubbish bins and fire sites; there are no predefined sites, so camping is on a first-come, first-served basis. The campsite is within walking distance of the surf beach, and a boat launch is located close by at Bullock Point. Bring your own firewood, and you can pick up water at the service facility on Clarkson Dr in Rainbow Beach. **Map refs:** 157 G5, 169 G4, 171 F5

162 SS *Dorrigo* camping area

Within walking distance of the surf beach, this is the closest campground to the entrance of Inskip Peninsula Recreation Area. It is accessible by trailers, caravans and buses, but 4WD is recommended, especially in wet weather. Open fires are permitted in fire sites; bring your own firewood. Water is available at the service facility on Clarkson Dr in Rainbow Beach. The boat launch is nearby on Bullock Point. **Map refs:** 157 G5, 169 G4

JIMNA STATE FOREST

At the western edge of Upper Mary Valley, 140 km north of Brisbane and 40 km north of Kilcoy, this state forest has mountains, swimming holes and walking trails to keep visitors occupied. Bookings are required for all camping.

How to book: NPRSR 13 7468 www.nprsr.qld.gov.au
Permits: camping permit required

163 Peach Trees camping and day-use area

This is one for wildlife-watchers; you can spot eastern grey kangaroos, possums and maybe even platypus near here, 45 km north-west of Kilcoy along the Kilcoy–Murgon Rd (access via Peach Trees Rd). Horses can stay overnight in the horse paddock beside Peach Trees; a registered horse trail passes through Jimna State Forest. Grassy sites are beside Yabba Creek, with a cold shower on site and drinking water from a tank (boil or treat it first). Bring your own untreated firewood. **Map refs:** 153 E3, 167 F1, 169 F5

KONDALILLA NATIONAL PARK

Kondalilla National Park, high in the Blackall Ranges, offers a cool retreat for bushwalkers looking to escape Qld's heat. The park is named after Kondalilla Falls, where Skene Creek takes a 90 m plunge into the rainforest valley below. The park protects several important native species, including the pouched frog and the vulnerable *Macadamia ternifolia*. Camping in the park is prohibited except for hikers taking the Sunshine Coast Hinterland Great Walk. Bookings are required in advance for camping.

How to book: NPRSR 13 7468 www.nprsr.qld.gov.au
Permits: camping permit required

164 **Flaxton camping area**
(walk-in camping)

This campsite, set amongst ferns, is on the Sunshine Coast Hinterland Great Walk. It offers simple facilities for up to 48 hikers. Boil or treat the water provided before drinking, and bring a gas/fuel stove, as fires are prohibited. Flaxton camping area is 16.5 km from the walk's trailhead at Baroon Pocket Dam and 13.1 km from Ubajee camping area in Mapleton National Park. **Map refs:** 153 F3, 167 G1, 169 G5

MAPLETON NATIONAL PARK

Just over 100 km north of Brisbane, Mapleton is at the northern end of the Blackall Range in the Sunshine Coast Hinterland. The area has magnificent bushwalks, picnic and day-use

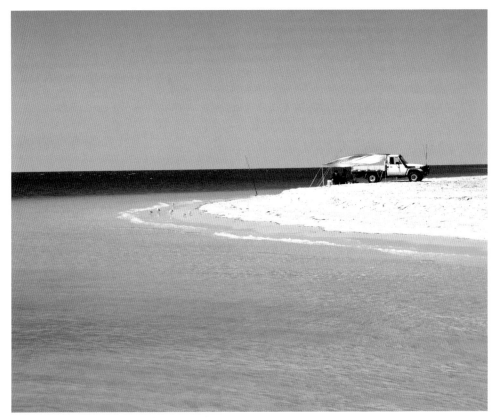

Fishing at Inskip Point, Inskip Peninsula Recreation Area (p. 36)

areas, and abseiling points. Trail-bike riders can make use of 26 km of circuits, provided you have a registered motorcycle. The Sunshine Coast Hinterland Great Walk passes through Mapleton; the campsites at Thilba Thalba and Ubajee are for hikers only. Bookings are required in advance for camping.

How to book: NPRSR 13 7468 www.nprsr.qld.gov.au
Permits: camping permit required

 **Gheerulla camping area**

The Gheerulla creekside camping area is 8 km north-east of Kenilworth, accessed 6 km north-east of Kenilworth along the Eumundi–Kenilworth Rd (4WD only). It is illegal to collect firewood from the forest, so bring your own wood for the BBQs on site, and bring your own drinking water as well. **Map refs:** 153 F3, 167 G1, 169 G5

166 Thilba Thalba camping area (walk-in camping)

This campsite, set high on a ridge above the Gheerulla Valley, is on the Sunshine Coast Hinterland Great Walk. It offers simple facilities for up to 48 hikers. Boil or treat the water provided before drinking, and bring a gas/fuel stove, as fires are prohibited. Thilba Thalba camping area is 16.1 km from the walk's trailhead at Delicia Rd and 13.5 km from Ubajee camping area. **Map refs:** 153 F3, 167 G1, 169 G5

167 Ubajee camping area (walk-in camping)

This campsite, in a blackbutt forest at the edge of the Gheerulla Valley, is on the Sunshine Coast Hinterland Great Walk. It offers simple facilities for up to 48 hikers. Boil or treat the water provided before drinking, and bring a gas/fuel stove, as fires are prohibited. Ubajee camping area is 13.5 km from Thilba Thalba camping area and 13.1 km from Flaxton camping area in Kondalilla National Park. **Map refs:** 153 F3, 167 G1, 169 G5

TUAN STATE FOREST

Around a 20 min drive south-east of Maryborough, the Tuan forest conserves a large range of plant species and is home to diverse wildlife. Visitors can go canoeing along the creeks, enjoy the flower displays in late winter and spring, and stay in one of the campgrounds with water frontage. The entrance to the forest is off Tinnanbar Rd, reached from Maryborough–Cooloola Rd. Bookings are required in advance for campsites.

How to book: NPRSR 13 7468 www.nprsr.qld.gov.au
Permits: camping permit required

168 Hedleys Campground

If you've never accessed a campsite via canoe, here's your chance. Set on a creek, Hedleys also has road access through a private property (fees apply, and the road is suitable for conventional vehicles only in dry weather). It's 3.4 km south of Tinnanbar Rd, signed 11.7 km east of Maryborough–Cooloola Rd on Tinnanbar Rd. Bring drinking water and untreated firewood, or a gas/fuel stove. **Map refs:** 157 G4, 169 G4

169 Log Dump Campground

The Log Dump on Kauri Creek is the only camping area in the region with a toilet; bring drinking water and untreated firewood, or a gas/fuel stove. You'll find it 1 km south-east of Tinnanbar Rd, signposted 7 km east of the Maryborough–Cooloola Road along Tinnanbar Rd. **Map refs:** 157 G4, 169 G4

170 Poona Creek camping area

This very basic clearing for self-sufficient campers can be accessed by entering Tuan State Forest from Cooloola Coast Rd. Campers must bring their own untreated wood for campfires, as gathering wood in the forest is not permitted. Use the fire rings provided and bring in water. Note: this campsite currently operates on a self-registration basis, but will be incorporated with NPRSR's online booking system in future; check NPRSR's webpage for Tuan State Forest before embarking. **Map refs:** 157 G4, 169 G4

WONGI STATE FOREST

Wongi State Forest has several waterholes fringed by paperbarks and surrounded by eucalypt forest. Wongi protects hoop pine rainforest, open eucalypt forest, open woodland with a heath understorey and exotic pine plantations. Visitors can follow a section of the Bicentennial National Trail in the forest. Advance bookings are required for camping.

How to book: NPRSR 13 7468 www.nprsr.qld.gov.au
Permits: camping permit required

 **Wongi camping area**

Chill down with a dip in the beautiful waterholes at Wongi, but note that fishing is not allowed and jumping or diving is not recommended. There is conventional vehicle access and plenty of space for caravans, motorhomes and large groups. Signposted access is along Warrah Rd, 10 km west of the Bruce Hwy. Bring a gas/fuel stove. **Map refs:** 157 E3, 169 F3

CAMPSITES LOCATED IN OTHER AREAS

 **Boreen Point Campground**

This neat and tidy campground, on the shores of Lake Cootharaba, offers an oasis of civilisation next door to the wilds of Cooloola. These well-appointed grounds include a laundry, camp kitchen, hot showers and sporting facilities (basketball, BMX, skateboarding and tennis) to keep the kids amused. The hamlet of Boreen Point is 20 km north-east of Pomona on Louis Bazzo Dr. Fires are only allowed in the designated wood

BBQs. Note: bring your own firewood. Bookings are required. **Map refs:** 153 G2, 169 G5

How to book: The Esplanade, Boreen Point (07) 5485 3244 www.sunshinecoastholidayparks.com.au

 **Borumba Deer Park**

Kids adore this friendly, family-owned park where you can take tours of the grounds and feed the deer. Set on 6 ha of bush along the banks of Yabba Creek, there are powered sites, a kiosk, laundromat, 2 amenities blocks, playgrounds, plus boats and kayaks for hire. Nearby Borumba Dam (3 km west) offers a boat ramp, fishing and waterskiing. To reach the park from Imbil, 12 km away, follow the signs for Borumba Dam and cross Yabba Creek 5 times (9 km); the driveway is 200 m after the fifth crossing. **Map refs:** 153 E3, 167 F1, 169 F5

How to book: 1133 Yabba Creek Rd, Imbil (07) 5484 5196 www.borumbadeerpark.com

 **Coolum Beach Holiday Park**

This popular tourist spot right on the beach at Coolum has room for legions of campers, with 133 powered caravan sites and 101 tent sites. The facilities are very advanced, and include a brand-new camp kitchen with wireless internet access, dump points and hot showers. Coolum beach's excellent surfing, swimming and fishing spots are moments away, and intrepid hikers can tackle Mt Coolum for its stunning views. Note: pets are welcome, but must be approved in advance by the park. Advance bookings are required. **Map refs:** 153 G3, 167 G1, 169 G5

How to book: David Low Way, Coolum Beach (07) 5446 1474 www.sunshinecoastholidayparks.com.au

175 Cotton Tree Holiday Park

This park is the largest operated by the Sunshine Coast Council, with 264 powered sites suitable for caravans and camper trailers, and 139 camping sites. Conveniences include amenities blocks with laundry facilities, dump points and a sheltered camp kitchen. Cotton Tree is conveniently located between the holiday meccas of Maroochydore and Mooloolaba. Bookings are required in advance. **Map refs:** 153 G3, 167 G1, 169 G5

How to book: Cotton Tree Pde, Cotton Tree (07) 5459 9070 www.sunshinecoastholidayparks. com.au

176 Dicky Beach Family Holiday Park

If you're after family-friendly beaches, it doesn't get much better than Dicky Beach, 3 km north of Caloundra. This cosy holiday park offers access not only to the patrolled waters of its namesake but is also within striking distance of a host of others, including Kings, Bullock, Golden, Shelly and Moffat beaches. If the kids haven't exhausted themselves with sand and sun there's an on-site recreation room. Laundry facilities are available. Advance bookings are required. **Map refs:** 153 G4, 167 G1

How to book: Beerburrum St, Dicky Beach (07) 5491 3342 www.sunshinecoastholidayparks.com.au

177 Gympie Caravan Park

This pleasant caravan park offers access to a wide variety of the Sunshine Coast's attractions; it is within easy driving distance of Tin Can Bay, Boreen Point, Pomona and the Cooloola section of Great Sandy National Park. On-site facilities include a laundry, pool and LPG filling station.

Bookings are recommended for peak periods. **Map refs:** 153 E1, 169 G5

How to book: 1 Jane St, Gympie (07) 5483 6800

178 Happy Wanderer Village Caravan Park

This well-appointed and modern caravan park offers all the creature comforts you'd expect from a 4.5 star park, including internet access, pool and spa, games room and laundromat. Its central location in Hervey Bay allows access to the Sunshine Coast's great tourist attractions, including whale-watching and coral-viewing tours. Bookings are recommended. **Map refs:** 157 G3, 169 G3

How to book: 105 Truro St, Torquay (07) 4125 1103 www.happywanderer.com.au

179 Huntsville Caravan Park

Maryborough, 40 km south of Hervey Bay, offers an excellent base to explore the natural attractions of the Sunshine Coast – especially during the whale-watching season, when campsites can be difficult to find in Hervey Bay. This caravan park offers easy access to Maryborough's central shopping district, a saltwater pool and laundry facilities. Bookings are recommended during peak periods. **Map refs:** 157 F4, 169 G4

How to book: 23 Gympie Rd, Maryborough (07) 4121 4075 www.huntsvillecaravanpark.com.au

180 Maroochydore Beach Holiday Park

This moderately sized holiday park (117 sites) is smaller than many of its fellow council-operated parks, but what it lacks in size it makes up for with its absolute waterfront location. Campers looking for a fix of civilisation will be pleased to find wireless internet and a shopping precinct with cafes and restaurants across the road, while swimmers and surfers will revel in Maroochy's iconic golden sands. Advance bookings are required. **Map refs:** 153 G3, 167 G1, 169 G5

How to book: Melrose Pde, Maroochydore (07) 5443 1167 www.sunshinecoastholidayparks.com.au

181 Mooloolaba Beach Holiday Park

This small campsite on Parkyn Pde in Mooloolaba is so popular that it extends to a separate area 1 km up the road at Ocean Beach. Both these locations offer absolute beachfront camping for tents, caravans and camper trailers, as well as modern facilities including laundry and wireless internet. Note: visitors at Ocean Beach need to visit the Parkyn Pde reception area before setting up camp. Bookings are required in advance. **Map refs:** 153 G3, 167 G1, 169 G5

How to book: Parkyn Pde, Mooloolaba (07) 5444 1201 www.sunshinecoastholidayparks.com.au

182 Mudjimba Beach Holiday Park

Mudjimba, across the river to the north of Maroochydore, is home to this quiet haven of a holiday park. Visitors are minutes away from the beach and excellent surfing, but if the surf is too rough you can take a dip in the park's pool. Dogs are permitted on application, so mention your canine friend when booking. There's also a laundry and wireless internet. Bookings are required in advance. **Map refs:** 153 G3, 167 G1, 169 G5

How to book: Cottonwood St, Mudjimba (07) 5448 7157 www.sunshinecoastholidayparks.com.au

183 Noosa North Shore Beach Campground

Entirely surrounded by Great Sandy National Park and the Coral Sea, Noosa North Shore is the most rustic of the council-operated camping areas, but also one of the most charming. Being surrounded by nature doesn't mean giving up modern conveniences: this park features a well-stocked kiosk, hot showers and a laundry. Campfires are prohibited here and there are no gas or electric BBQs, so bring your own portable cooker or rent one from reception. Bookings are required in advance. **Map refs:** 153 G2, 167 G1, 169 G5

How to book: 240 Wilderness Track, Noosa North Shore (07) 5449 8811 www.sunshinecoastholidayparks.com.au

184 Noosa River Holiday Park

This campsite on the banks of Noosa River and Weyba Creek has one of the most enviable positions in Noosa real estate, including stunning views from the camp kitchen and BBQ area. Anglers, boaties and kayakers will find excellent access to Noosa's waterways from this site. A comprehensive kiosk, laundry and wireless internet provide creature comforts. Bookings are required in advance. **Map refs:** 153 G2, 167 G1, 169 G5

How to book: 4 Russell St, Noosaville (07) 5449 7050 www.sunshinecoastholidayparks.com.au

Sunshine Coast Hinterland Great Walk

This 58 km hiking trail traverses Kondalilla, Mapleton and Mapleton Falls national parks. It is best approached from south to north, starting at Baroon Pocket Dam and looping back through Gheerulla Valley to finish at the Delicia Rd entrance. Campsite bookings are required in advance. Note: walkers are required to purchase a topographic map of the Great Walk before embarking.

Please note that campsites are listed in alphabetical order, not track order. Refer to the map on p. 153 for further information.

How to book: NPRSR 13 7468 www.nprsr.qld.gov.au
Permits: camping permit required

164 **Flaxton camping area**
(walk-in camping)
See p. 38.

166 **Thilba Thalba camping area**
(walk-in camping)
See p. 39.

167 **Ubajee camping area**
(walk-in camping)
See p. 39.

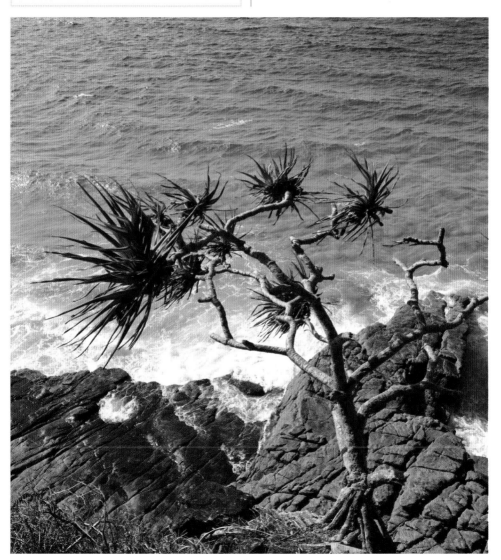

Pandanus growing along the rocky Noosa coastline, near Noosa North Shore Beach Campground (p. 42)

*Stunning cliffs at Blackdown
Tablelands National Park (p. 46)*

CAPRICORN

The diverse charms of the Capricorn region will have you discovering the country charm of coastal centres such as Bundaberg, Gladstone and Rockhampton, exploring the spectacular gorges and waterfalls out west, or setting sail for the southernmost tropical islands of the Great Barrier Reef.

The region is dotted with dozens of wonderfully diverse national parks, state forests, dams and lakes, with some of the best camping locations the state has to offer. Carnarvon National Park is one of the gems. Shaped by dramatic sandstone cliffs, pillars and arches, and featuring rare Aboriginal rock art, the 16 000 ha Carnarvon Gorge is the most popular section of the park for campers. Vehicle-based camping is also permitted at the Mt Moffatt, Ka Ka Mundi and Salvator Rosa sections. For experienced hikers, the 86 km Carnarvon Great Walk leads through the gorge and across the rugged plateaus and valleys of the Consuelo Tableland and Mt Moffatt sections of the national park.

Another unique highlight of the region is Capricornia Cays National Park at the southern end of the Great Barrier Reef, north-east of Gladstone and the town of Seventeen Seventy. Camping is permitted on the coral cays of Masthead Island, North West Island and Lady Musgrave Island. Off the coast of Rosslyn Bay Harbour, camping is allowed on the islands of Keppel Bay Islands National Park – up to 75 people can camp on North Keppel Island at any one time.

Back on the mainland, Lake Murphy Conservation Park, north-west of Taroom, is a great site for birdwatchers. Keen anglers should head for Broadwater Conservation Park, Deep Water National Park or one of the popular water reserves such as Wuruma Dam, Lake Awoonga or Glebe Weir. Only very experienced bushwalkers should attempt to traverse the rugged landscapes and vegetation in Mount Walsh National Park.

CAMPSITES LOCATED IN PARKS AND RESERVES

AUBURN RIVER NATIONAL PARK

Massive granite boulders and steep gorges leading to the Auburn River give this national park a scenic quality like no other. Situated 225 km west of Maryborough, a highlight is the 600 m (15 min) walk to the Gorge Lookout for spectacular views. Bookings are required for all camping.

How to book: NPRSR 13 7468 www.nprsr.qld.gov.au
Permits: camping permit required

185 Auburn River camping area

On the northern bank of the Auburn River, this site has 5 camping clearances close to bushwalking tracks. Don't drink the river water; the tank water available on site must be treated or boiled, and you need to bring milled firewood. To get here from Mundubbera, take Duron Rd for 13 km, then take Hawkwood Rd for 20 km to the signposted park access road. A 4WD is recommended in wet weather. Stay on the road, as soils are treacherous when wet. **Map refs:** 168 D4

BARAKULA STATE FOREST

Expect to see logging trucks on the access roads at Barakula, as this forest is a major supplier of cypress pine. Despite the presence of industry, the forest (about 45 km north of Chinchilla) is known for providing good fishing opportunities after rains, and there's plenty on display for wildlife-watchers. Go west on the Warrego Hwy from Chinchilla, then take Auburn Rd north to Barakula. Advance bookings are required for all camping.

How to book: NPRSR 13 7468 www.nprsr.qld.gov.au
Permits: camping permit required

186 Bush camping areas

Both drive-up and walk-in bush camping for self-sufficient campers is permitted at various locations throughout Barakula. There are no facilities, so bring your own drinking water, a gas/fuel cooker, rubbish bags for taking waste with you and all other necessaries. Camping is prohibited in signposted logging areas. Note: cattle herds are common throughout Barakula; for your safety, do not camp near feeding lots, cattle trails or livestock watering dams. **Map refs:** 168 C5

187 Dogwood Creek camping area

This old sawmill site is now a clearing for campers, but offers no facilities. It is reached from Barakula State Forest Rd off Auburn Rd. Go past the Department of Primary Industries area and look for the forestry camp signs to Dogwood Creek. Bring drinking water and a gas/fuel stove. Open fires are permitted when there are no fire bans, but exercise caution, as there are no formal fire areas. **Map refs:** 168 C5

BLACKDOWN TABLELAND NATIONAL PARK

The traditional home of the Ghungalu people, Blackdown Tableland National Park is in the north-east corner of the central Qld sandstone belt. Its gorges and waterfalls offer spectacular scenery, and rock faces with Ghungalu artwork highlight the wonderful cultural significance of the land. The signed turn-off on the Capricorn Hwy is 11 km west of Dingo or 110 km east of Emerald. Advance bookings are required for all camping.

How to book: NPRSR 13 7468 www.nprsr.qld.gov.au
Permits: camping permit required

188 Munall camping area

Also known as Mimosa Creek, this camping area is 8 km from the park entrance and can be reached with a conventional vehicle. There are 16 numbered sites with a maximum of 6 people per site, ideal for camping beside your car, or for

small camper trailers (no caravans). Bring drinking water and firewood. **Map refs:** 168 A1, 170 C5

BROADWATER CONSERVATION PARK

Broadwater Conservation Park lies between Baffle and Deepwater creeks. Visitors can swim at the beach, but note that it is unpatrolled and marine stingers are present Oct–May. There is 4WD beach access at low tide; check tides and access points before proceeding onto the beach. Anglers need to familiarise themselves with the rules and zones of Great Barrier Reef Marine Park before casting off. Advance bookings are required for all camping.

How to book: NPRSR 13 7468 www.nprsr.qld.gov.au
Permits: camping permit required

189 Mitchell Creek camping area

Fantastic for fishing and wildlife-watching, the campground is accessible by 4WD or boat along Rules Beach; check tides and entry points before proceeding to the beach. There are no facilities so you'll need to bring water, a gas/fuel stove and all self-sufficient camping equipment. **Map refs:** 169 F2

BULBURIN NATIONAL PARK

Formerly a forest reserve and now a national park, Bulburin features vast subtropical rainforests and eucalypt woodlands, home to a variety of wildlife, including the red-eyed tree frog and the rare long-nosed potoroo. Bulburin is 50 km north-east of Monto, with conventional vehicle access from Builyan on the Monto–Gladstone Rd. Advance bookings are required for all camping.

How to book: NPRSR 13 7468 www.nprsr.qld.gov.au
Permits: camping permit required

190 Bush camping areas

Bush camping is permitted anywhere throughout the bunya pines of Bulburin, but the most popular site is a former forestry barracks on Granite Creek Forest Rd. There are no facilities here besides a picnic platform, so campers must be totally self-sufficient. Bring your own drinking water and firewood (open fires are permitted, but no sites are provided). Scenic drives through the forest are recommended; a 4WD loop road passes through the rainforest. **Map refs:** 169 E2

BURRUM COAST NATIONAL PARK

Covering more than 23 000 ha, Burrum Coast National Park boasts a stunning natural environment with mangrove-lined riverbanks, wallum heath wildflowers and tea-tree swamps. Also known for its rare wildlife and quiet beaches, the park is divided into 3 main sections: Woodgate, Kinkuna and Burrum River. Advance bookings are required for all camping.

How to book: NPRSR 13 7468 www.nprsr.qld.gov.au
Permits: camping permit required

191 **Burrum Point camping area**

Whether you prefer swimming at the beach or boating on a river, you're blessed with the choice of both at Burrum Coast National Park. The sandy camping area is just a short walk from the beach at Burrum Point, and Burrum River is also close by. The campground has 13 numbered sites, cold showers and toilets. It is 8 km south of Woodgate; access is signposted on Walkers Point Rd from Woodgate. Note: it is 4WD access only, and roads may be closed during extreme wet weather. **Map refs:** 157 F2, 169 G3

192 **Kinkuna camping area (bush camping)**

Take your pick from 40 sandy sites behind the beach foredunes in the Kinkuna section. There are no facilities but open fires are allowed (except when fire bans apply). Bring drinking water. Note: the Woodgate–Palm Beach Rd through Kinkuna is closed during wet conditions. **Map refs:** 157 E2, 169 F3

CAPRICORNIA CAYS NATIONAL PARK

Part of the Great Barrier Reef World Heritage area, Capricornia Cays is a stunning group of coral cays, islands and reefs off the coast of Gladstone and Seventeen Seventy. The park protects several vegetated coral cays, including Lady Musgrave, North West, Masthead, Wilson, Heron, Erskine and Tryon islands. Commercial operators run daily services to Lady Musgrave Island, and provide charter boats to other islands. Advance bookings are required for all camping.

How to book: NPRSR 13 7468 www.nprsr.qld.gov.au
Permits: camping permit required

193 **Lady Musgrave Island camping area (boat-based camping)**

Lady Musgrave has space for up to 40 campers at any one time from Easter school holidays

Palm Beach, Burrum Coast National Park

until Australia Day in Jan (the campsite is closed between Feb and Mar each year). The campground has composting toilets, an information shelter and emergency radio. Lady Musgrave is the southernmost island in the national park, just south of the Tropic of Capricorn – a great spot for snorkellers. You need to bring drinking water and a gas/fuel stove. **Map refs:** 169 F1, 171 H5

194　Masthead Island camping area (boat-based camping)

Up to 50 people can camp at this site on the north-west corner of the island. Suitable only for self-sufficient campers, there are no facilities and no generators permitted. Masthead Island is known as an important rookery for green turtles and endangered loggerhead turtles; avoid disturbing them. Activities include snorkelling, fishing, birdwatching and reef walking in designated areas. Bring drinking water and a gas/fuel stove. Note: the camping area is closed for regeneration from mid-Oct to Easter each year. **Map refs:** 171 G5

195　North West Island camping area (boat-based camping)

Camping is permitted on the island from Easter until the end of the summer school holidays in Jan each year. The campground has enough space for up to 150 people. Bring drinking water and a gas/fuel stove. There are composting toilets and information displays but no generators are permitted on the island. **Map refs:** 171 G4

CARNARVON NATIONAL PARK

Tucked away in this vast, rambling park in Qld's Central Highlands is the magnificent Carnarvon Gorge. Boasting towering white sandstone cliffs, breathtaking side gorges and some of the finest Aboriginal rock art in Australia, this 160-million-year-old natural wonder is the region's most popular tourist attraction. The Mt Moffat section of the park features grassy woodlands and magnificent sandstone outcrops. Further west, the isolated and unspoiled Ka Ka Mundi and Salvator Rosa sections of the park offer wildlife-watching and bush camping areas. Bookings are required in advance for all sites except Bunbuncundoo Springs and Nogoa River.

How to book: NPRSR 13 7468 www.nprsr.qld.gov.au
Permits: camping permit required *Camping fees:* fees can be paid and permits acquired for campsite nos **197** and **205** at the self-registration stations

Lady Musgrave Island, Capricornia Cays National Park (p. 47)

196 Big Bend camping area
(walk-in camping)

Great for experienced walkers and campers, this site is reached by a 9.7 km walk from the visitor information centre through the gorge; there's no access for vehicles. Once there, you'll find a small campground (the maximum number of campers is 10) in a rainforest setting with a cliff backdrop. A composting toilet and a picnic table are the only facilities, so you'll need to bring all self-sufficient goods and equipment. Note: record your trip details in the registration book at the park's information centre, and log out when you return. Big Bend is a designated campsite on the Carnarvon Great Walk and is 14.8 km from Gadd's camping area. **Map refs:** 183 G3

197 Bunbuncundoo Springs camping area
(bush camping)

This campsite, deep inside Carnarvon's Ka Ka Mundi section, is suitable for self-sufficient campers only; bring water and a gas/fuel stove. There is good wildlife-watching in the area so look out for king parrots and red-necked wallabies. It is 130 km south-west of Springsure. Travel west on the Springsure–Tambo Rd for 50 km, then turn south into Buckland Rd; the campsite is accessible by 4WDs in dry weather only. **Map refs:** 183 F2

198 Bush camping areas
(walk-in camping)

Walk-in bush camping is permitted in all areas of the Mt Moffat section of Carnarvon National Park except restricted-access areas. There are no facilities and fires are prohibited, so bring all self-sufficient gear, including drinking water and a gas/fuel stove. **Map refs:** 183 G3

199 Carnarvon Gorge camping area

Camping is permitted here only during certain Qld school holidays: Easter, winter and spring. There are 35 numbered campsites, plenty of room

for large groups, and good shade under gum trees and cabbage palms. Visitors should note that the site can be reached by conventional vehicle, but the last 20 km of the access road are unsealed and could be impassable in wet weather. The site is 45 km west of the Carnarvon Developmental Rd. **Map refs:** 183 G3

Carnarvon Great Walk

Please note that campsites are listed in alphabetical order, not track order. Refer to the map on p. 183 for further information.

196 Big Bend camping area
(walk-in camping)

See opposite.

200 Cabbage Tree camping area
(walk-in camping)

This open grassy campsite high on the Consuelo Tableland is the last stop on the recommended Carnarvon Great Walk itinerary. It is 13.8 km from Consuelo camping area and 15.3 km from the Carnarvon Gorge information centre. Water is provided from an underground tank, but it must be treated or boiled before drinking. Bring a gas/fuel stove. Note: do not camp within 20 m of the water collection point to avoid damaging the underground tank. **Map refs:** 183 G3

201 Consuelo camping area
(walk-in camping)

High up on the Consuelo tableland – known as 'the roof of Queensland' – this campsite offers no facilities other than water from an underground tank (boil or treat water before drinking). Bring a gas/fuel stove. It is 13.8 km from Cabbage Tree camping area and 17.3 km from West Branch camping area. Note: do not camp within 20 m of the water collection point to avoid damaging the underground tank. **Map refs:** 183 G2

202 Gadd's camping area
(walk-in camping)

This site is situated among the remains of an old cattle station, past the stunning views of

Battleship Spur lookout. There are no facilities other than water from an underground tank, which must be boiled or treated before drinking. Bring a gas/fuel stove. It is 14.8 km from Big Bend camping area and 15.8 km from West Branch camping area. Note: do not camp within 20 m of the water collection point to avoid damaging the underground tank. **Map refs:** 183 G3

203 West Branch camping area

See opposite.

204 Dargonelly Rock Hole camping area

This campground is beside the rock hole at Marlong Creek and can be accessed by conventional vehicles and off-road caravans in dry weather only. Up to 35 people can camp at the site at any one time, and there is a water supply for drinking and cooking only (treat or boil first). Unlike many other national park campgrounds, this one permits generators during the day. You need to bring your own firewood but a gas/fuel stove is preferred. **Map refs:** 183 G3

205 Nogoa River camping area (bush camping)

This bush camping site in the Salvator Rosa section of Carnarvon National Park is for entirely self-sufficient campers. Orange-barked yellow-jacket trees and beautiful wildflower displays are some of the highlights of the area. You can reach the campsite in a conventional vehicle, but need 4WD to explore the park any further. Use a gas/fuel stove for cooking, treat or boil the creek water before drinking, and remove your rubbish. To get to Salvator Rosa from Springsure, head 114 km west along Tambo Rd to the park turn-off. **Map refs:** 183 F2

206 Rotary Shelter Shed camping area

This camping area, about 17 km north-east of the park office, is accessible only by 4WD (suitable

for high-clearance camper trailers). There are no defined sites, but a maximum of 15 people can camp at any one time. Bring all self-sufficient goods and equipment including firewood, and treat or boil the water before drinking. A gas/fuel stove is preferred. **Map refs:** 183 G2

207 Top Moffatt camping area

Accessible only by 4WD and high-clearance camper trailers, this site is at the east branch of the Maranoa River. A maximum of 20 people can use the area at any one time, and it suits self-sufficient campers as the only facilities are a pit toilet and communal fire rings. Bring water and firewood, or a gas/fuel stove. **Map refs:** 183 G3

203 West Branch camping area

This site is near the west branch of the Maranoa River and can be reached by conventional vehicles and off-road caravans in dry weather only. Open fires are permitted only at existing fire rings; check for fire bans. No generators are permitted. The camping area is 9 km north-east of the park office. West Branch is a designated campsite on the Carnarvon Great Walk with a separate area for great walkers; it is 15.8 km from Gadd's camping area and 17.3 km from Consuelo camping area. **Map refs:** 183 G2

CASTLE TOWER NATIONAL PARK

Experienced bush hikers and climbers will relish the challenges in Castle Tower National Park, 35 km south of Gladstone. The dramatic peaks of Mt Castle Tower and Mt Stanley rise out of open eucalypt woodland, and those with the skill and endurance to scale these peaks are rewarded with views over the Boyne Valley and north to Gladstone. Access to the park is on foot only through private property, or via boat across the Awoonga Dam and then on foot through Gladstone Area Water Board land. Permission is required from relevant property owners or GAWB before accessing the park. Advance bookings are required for camping.

How to book: NPRSR 13 7468 www.nprsr.qld.gov.au
Permits: GAWB (07) 4976 3000 www.gawb.qld.
gov.au for camping permit and permission to
access the park; or request permission from
private property owners

208 Bush camping areas
(walk-in camping)

Bush camping is permitted throughout Castle
Tower National Park, wherever hikers can find a
suitable site. No facilities are provided and open
fires are prohibited, so bring all self-sufficient
camping gear, including drinking water and a gas/
fuel stove. **Map refs: 169 E1**

CURTIS ISLAND NATIONAL PARK

This national park is at the north-eastern end
of Curtis Island, off the Qld coast between
Gladstone and Rockhampton. There is a historic
lighthouse at Cape Capricorn, but no other
notable facilities. Fishing, swimming, snorkelling
and wildlife-watching are all popular activities
here, although swimmers and snorkellers should
wear protective clothing during stinger season
(Oct–May). Travel to the island is by private
boat from Gladstone, The Narrows, Port Alma
or Rosslyn Bay. Advance bookings are required
for camping.

How to book: NPRSR 13 7468 www.nprsr.qld.gov.au
Permits: camping permit required

209 Joey Lees camping area
(bush camping)

This secluded campsite north of Turtle Street offers
no facilities, but it comes with a lovely view, beach
access and shady trees – perfect for self-sufficient
campers looking for a quiet getaway. Bring
your own drinking water, a gas/fuel stove (open
fires are prohibited) and all other necessities.
Map refs: 169 E1, 171 F5

210 Turtle Street camping area
(bush camping)

This campsite, the closest to the Southend ferry
terminal, is the most accessible of Curtis Island's
campsites – although it's still very remote and can

only be reached by 4WD. There are no facilities,
so bring your own drinking water, a gas/fuel
stove (open fires are prohibited) and all other
necessities. **Map refs: 169 E1, 171 F5**

211 Yellow Patch camping area
(boat-based camping)

There is bush camping at the north-eastern end
of Curtis Island at Yellow Patch, known for its
bright yellow sand. It is suitable for self-sufficient
campers, with no facilities on site, and can only be
accessed by boat. Bring your own drinking water
and a gas/fuel stove (open fires are prohibited).
Map refs: 171 F5

DAWES RESOURCES RESERVE

Located 109 km south of Gladstone and 58 km
north-east of Monto, this resources reserve
and the surrounding national park preserve the
remains of Glassford, an abandoned mining
town whose fortunes waned as the Glassford
Creek copper lode was diminished. Glassford's
ruins are surrounded by Sydney blue gums and
and blackbutt forests. To access the park, turn
west onto Childs Rd (4WD and dry-weather
access only) off the Gladstone–Monto Rd, 9 km
south of Many Peaks or 16 km north of Kalpowar.

Who to contact: QPWS Gladstone (07) 4971 6505
Permits: camping permit required *Camping
fees:* fees can be paid and permits arranged at
QPWS Gladstone

212 Bush camping areas

Bush camping is permitted throughout Dawes
National Park and Resources Reserve, wherever
campers can find a suitable site. No facilities are
provided and open fires are prohibited, so bring
all self-sufficient camping gear, including drinking
water and a gas/fuel stove. **Map refs: 169 E2**

213 Old Mine camping area
(bush camping)

Those with an interest in history will find this
campsite, near the well-preserved remains of a
copper smelter and mine workings from the early
1900s, a fascinating experience. No facilities

are provided, so bring all self-sufficient camping gear and your own drinking water. Open fires are permitted here; bring your own firewood or a gas/fuel stove. **Map refs:** 169 E2

DEEPWATER NATIONAL PARK

Deepwater National Park, about 100 km north-west of Bundaberg, features diverse vegetation, creeks, beaches and a variety of wildlife. Access to the park is 4WD only, via Wreck Rock Rd from Agnes Water or Tableland Rd from Berajondo. Advance bookings are required for camping.

How to book: NPRSR 13 7468 www.nprsr.qld.gov.au
Permits: camping permit required

214 **Middle Rock camping area (bush camping)**

At the north-eastern side of Deepwater National Park, this sand and woodchip bush camp has undefined sites behind the foredunes and is accessible only by 4WD. There are no facilities provided and you need to take a gas/fuel stove, drinking water and rubbish bags. Also bring along a pair of binoculars and a bird field guide to help identify the diverse birdlife. From Jan–Apr, marine turtle hatchlings emerge, usually at night, from their nests. The beach is unpatrolled and there may be rips and sharks. Beware of marine stingers Oct–May. **Map refs:** 169 F2

Beach in Deepwater National Park

215 **Wreck Rock camping area**

This small campsite behind the frontal dunes at the south-eastern end of Deepwater National Park has 14 sites for a maximum of 6 people each. It provides excellent beachfront camping with sand and woodchip surfaces and is just a skip across the sand dunes to the beach. The park is near the tiny town of Seventeen Seventy where you can join a range of tours and boat trips to Lady Musgrave Island and Fitzroy Reef. Agnes Water and Seventeen Seventy are the closest mainland points to the outer Great Barrier Reef. **Map refs:** 169 F2

EURIMBULA NATIONAL PARK

Protecting tropical forests and coastal mangroves, Eurimbula National Park lies about 110 km north-west of Bundaberg. The park is just 10 km from Seventeen Seventy and 13 km from Agnes Water; both towns are ideal jumping-off points to reach the outer Great Barrier Reef. Access to the park is signposted off Agnes Water–Seventeen Seventy Rd, west of Agnes Water. Take the short but steep walk to Ganoonga Noonga Lookout for beautiful views over Bustard Bay. Bookings are required in advance for camping.

How to book: NPRSR 13 7468 www.nprsr.qld.gov.au
Permits: camping permit required

216 **Bustard Beach camping area**

Set behind the foredunes on the eastern side of the park, this campground with a sand-and-woodchip surface has 17 defined camping sites with a maximum of 6 people per site. You're just a short stroll to the beach, but remember that it's unpatrolled and there may be rips and sharks. Beware of marine stingers Oct–May. The campsite is signposted off the Eurimbula Access Rd, which is signposted off the Agnes Water–Seventeen Seventy Rd, 10 km west of Agnes Water. **Map refs:** 169 E1

217 Bustard Head camping area (boat-based camping)

Self-sufficient campers can boat into this camping area on Bustard Head. There are no facilities and open fires are not permitted, so bring your own water, a gas/fuel stove and all other necessaries. **Map refs:** 169 E1, 171 G5

218 Middle Creek camping area

About 35 km north-west of Agnes Water, this campsite can be accessed by boat or by 4WD (off the Eurimbula Access Rd). Bring your own drinking water, rubbish bags and a gas/fuel stove, as fires are prohibited. **Map refs:** 169 E1

219 Rodds Peninsula camping area (boat-based camping)

A second boat-only campsite in Eurimbula exists on Rodds Peninsula. There are no facilities and open fires are not permitted, so bring your own water, a gas/fuel stove and all other necessaries. **Map refs:** 169 E1, 171 G5

EXPEDITION NATIONAL PARK

Part of the Central Qld Sandstone Belt, Expedition National Park's eucalypt and gum forests are about 130 km west of Taroom. There are 3 main sections: Robinson Gorge, Lonesome and Beilba. Stencil art indicates that Aboriginal people have lived in the area for thousands of years. Signposted access to Robinson Gorge is 18 km north of Taroom from the Leichhardt Hwy; both Lonesome and Beilba sections are accessed via Carnarvon Developmental Rd north of Injune.

Who to contact: NPRSR 13 7468 www.nprsr. qld.gov.au *Permits:* camping permit required *Camping fees:* fees can be paid and permits acquired at the self-registration stations

220 Bush camping areas

Bush camping is permitted throughout the Robinson Gorge section and in certain areas of Beilba and Lonesome sections for self-sufficient and experienced campers. For a unique outback Qld experience, set up camp inside the house at the old cattle station in the Beilba section, or camp by the banks of the Dawson River in the Lonesome section. There are no facilities, so bring your own drinking water and all other necessaries. Open fires are allowed when fire bans do not apply, but a gas/fuel stove is recommended. **Map refs:** 168 A3

221 Starkvale camping area

Self-sufficient campers with 4WD vehicles can access this grassy clearing in the Robinson Gorge section of Expedition, 4 km south-east of Robinson Gorge Lookout (dry-weather access only). There are approximately 8 campsites suitable for walk-in camping, high-clearance camper trailers, or camping beside your car. No generators are permitted. Tank water is provided (it must be treated or boiled before use) but supply is unreliable, so bring your own water. **Map refs:** 168 A3

GOODEDULLA NATIONAL PARK

Located 80 km west of Rockhampton, this national park protects a large number of rare and threatened species, including the black ironbox and the greater glider. This hilly, semi-remote park is perfect for birdwatching. To get there, take the Capricorn Hwy south-west from Rockhampton to Gogango, then follow the signs north to Rookwood Station. Follow further signs to the park from Rookwood along a rough, unsealed and difficult road (4WD only). Advance bookings are required for camping.

How to book: NPRSR 13 7468 www.nprsr.qld.gov.au *Permits:* camping permit required

222 Kings Dam camping area (bush camping)

This bush campsite is 35 km north of Goodedulla's southern entrance. There are no facilities here, so campers must bring their own water, rubbish bags and other necessaries. Open fires are allowed when fire bans do not apply, but a gas/fuel stove is recommended. **Map refs:** 170 D4

223 The Palms camping area (bush camping)

This bush campsite is located in open woodland next to a waterhole on the seasonal Melaleuca Creek, 50 km north of the park entrance. There are no facilities here, so campers must bring their own water, rubbish bags and other necessaries. Open fires are allowed when fire bans do not apply, but a gas/fuel stove is recommended. **Map refs:** 170 D4

224 Wadlow Yards camping area (bush camping)

This bush campsite is located in open woodland next to a waterhole on the seasonal Melaleuca Creek, 6 km north of the park entrance. There are no facilities here, so campers must bring their own water, rubbish bags and other necessaries. Open fires are allowed when fire bans do not apply, but a gas/fuel stove is recommended. **Map refs:** 170 D4

ISLA GORGE NATIONAL PARK

This park of rugged landscapes lies 36 km south-west of Theodore, in central Qld's sandstone belt. It protects not only Isla Gorge, created by erosion from Gorge Creek, but also remnants of dry rainforest, mulga and brigalow scrub, eucalypts and natural grasslands. Access to the park is off the Leichhardt Hwy, 55 km north of Taroom and 35 km south of Theodore.

Who to contact: NPRSR 13 7468 www.nprsr.qld.gov.au *Permits:* camping permit required *Camping fees:* fees can be paid and permits acquired at the self-registration station

225 Isla Gorge camping area

If you're seeking a campsite with a view, you'll love watching the sun set over the orange-coloured cliffs of Isla Gorge at this camping area. There are undefined walking tracks for experienced walkers. Bring your own firewood, and treat or boil the tank water before drinking.

The site is just over 1 km off the Leichhardt Hwy and can be reached by conventional vehicles. Note: the campsite is next to an unfenced cliff face; be cautious when walking and supervise children closely. **Map refs:** 168 C3

KALPOWAR STATE FOREST

More than 150 plant species exist amongst rainforest, eucalypt forest and hoop pine plantations in Kalpowar State Forest, 38 km north-east of Monto. The 20 km Kalpowar Forest Drive is a good way to get around and see the forest. The forest is reached by Fireclay Rd or the Kalpowar–Gin Gin Rd, both off the Monto–Gladstone Rd. Advance bookings are required for camping.

How to book: NPRSR 13 7468 www.nprsr.qld.gov.au *Permits:* camping permit required

226 Kalpowar camping area

This campground beside Crane Creek has plenty of grassy sites for camping beside your car, and also accommodates those with caravans and trailers. To get here from Monto, travel 37 km north-east on the Monto–Gladstone Rd and take the gravel road turn-off. You need to be self-sufficient, preferably with a gas/fuel stove, and bring your own firewood. The water here must be treated or boiled before use. **Map refs:** 169 E2

KEPPEL BAY ISLANDS NATIONAL PARK

This national park covers the region from Curtis Island to Corio Bay off the central Qld coast and includes 15 islands. Travel to the islands is by private boat or water taxi from Rosslyn Bay Harbour, 15 km east of Yeppoon. Access to Barren and Peak islands is restricted. Note: swimmers should take precautions against marine stingers, particularly from Oct–May. Advance bookings are required for camping.

How to book: NPRSR 13 7468 www.nprsr.qld.gov.au *Permits:* camping permit required; campers are required to notify QPWS Rosslyn Bay (07) 4933 6595 immediately before departure from the mainland

227 Conical Island camping area (boat-based camping)

Conical Island has a small camping area with space for 6 campers. There are picnic tables but no other facilities, so you need to be self-sufficient, bringing water and a gas/fuel stove. Coral reefs to the west of the island are within easy snorkelling distance of the beach. **Map refs:** 171 F4

228 Divided Island camping area (boat-based camping)

Self-sufficient campers can pitch a tent at this small campground. The maximum number of people permitted to camp at the site is 6; there are no facilities. The beach on the western side is a recommended spot for picnicking. Bring water and a gas/fuel stove. **Map refs:** 171 F4

229 Humpy Island camping area (boat-based camping)

The national park's most popular camping area, Humpy Island has space for up to 60 self-sufficient campers. The campground is on the island's northern beach; taps throughout the site provide bore water not suitable for drinking, so bring water and a gas/fuel stove. **Map refs:** 171 F4

230 Miall Island camping area (boat-based camping)

This tiny camping site behind the foredunes only has space for 6 self-sufficient campers and there are no facilities besides picnic tables. Bring water and a gas/fuel stove. Reefs on the south-eastern and northern sides of the island are recommended for divers and snorkellers. **Map refs:** 171 F4

231 Middle Island (Northeastern Beach) camping area (boat-based camping)

Only 6 self-sufficient campers are permitted at any one time in this bush campsite behind the dunes of Middle Island's north-eastern beach. Reefs at

nearby Olive Point headland provide excellent snorkelling and diving. The only facilities on the island are picnic tables, so bring your own water, garbage bags and a gas/fuel stove. Note: fishing is prohibited in the waters around Middle Island. **Map refs:** 171 F4

232 Middle Island (Northwestern Beach) camping area (boat-based camping)

This bush campsite behind the dunes of Middle Island's north-western beach offers room for 6 self-sufficient campers. The only facilities on the island are picnic tables, so bring your own water, garbage bags and a gas/fuel stove. Note: fishing is prohibited in the waters around Middle Island. **Map refs:** 171 F4

233 Middle Island (Southeastern Beach) camping area (boat-based camping)

This campsite, behind the dunes of the smallest of Middle Island's 3 beaches, offers excellent access to the large reef to the west of the island. Picnic tables are the only facilities on the island, so this site suits self-sufficient campers only (maximum of 6 people); bring water, rubbish bags and a gas/fuel stove. Note: fishing is prohibited in the waters around Middle Island. **Map refs:** 171 F4

234 North Keppel Island (Considine Beach) Campground (boat-based camping)

This site with space for 75 self-sufficient campers is at the southern end of Considine Beach on the western side of North Keppel Island. Bring water, rubbish bags and a gas/fuel stove. Sandflies and mosquitoes are common so come prepared, and secure your food well to avoid attracting brushtail possums. **Map refs:** 171 F4

235 Pelican Island camping area (boat-based camping)

Camping is restricted to 6 people at any one time on rugged, isolated Pelican Island, and no facilities are provided. It is suitable for self-sufficient

campers only. Bring water and a gas/fuel stove.
Map refs: 171 F4

KROOMBIT TOPS NATIONAL PARK

Home to many rare and threatened plants and animals, Kroombit Tops National Park offers excellent bushwalks, a 4WD circuit, a lookout over the Boyne Valley, and day-use areas. The park is 85 km south-west of Gladstone, at the meeting point of the Dawes, Calliope and Milton ranges. Note: falling trees and branches pose a danger in this park, so avoid camping under dead or dying trees, and during periods of high winds. Advance bookings are required for camping.

How to book: NPRSR 13 7468 www.nprsr.qld.gov.au
Permits: camping permit required

236 The Barracks camping area (bush camping)

A clearing suitable for bush camping is located opposite the old forestry barracks (now a ranger station), 4 km south of the Tableland Rd entrance. It can be reached with 2WD only in dry weather. There is a maximum of 10 campers permitted at the site; no facilities are provided. Bring water, firewood and preferably a gas/fuel stove. While in the area, visit the lookout for excellent views over the Boyne Valley. **Map refs:** 168 D2

237 Bush camping areas

Bush camping is permitted in most areas of Kroombit Tops, excluding The Barracks, the lookout, and the intersection of Griffiths Creek and Tableland Rd. There are no facilities, so bring your own water, rubbish bags and milled firewood or a gas/fuel stove. **Map refs:** 168 D2

238 The Wall camping area (bush camping)

This grassy clearing on the south bank of Annie Creek can be reached on the 4WD loop road near the bomber crash site. There is a maximum of 20 campers allowed, but there are no defined sites and no facilities. Bring everything you will need. **Map refs:** 168 D2

LAKE MURPHY CONSERVATION PARK

Beneath Murphy's Range in the central highlands, Lake Murphy fills only when nearby Robinson Creek overflows. It's a peaceful, relaxing location – even when the lake is dry. The park is 13 km along Glenhaughton Rd, off the Leichhardt Hwy 18 km north of Taroom.

Who to contact: NPRSR 13 7468 www.nprsr. qld.gov.au *Permits:* camping permit required *Camping fees:* fees can be paid and permits acquired at the self-registration station

239 Lake Murphy camping area

This large camping area has plenty of space for motorhomes and large groups looking for a shady spot near the lake, which is a seasonal refuge for waterbirds. You'll need to bring firewood and drinking water. Access is via the main road into the park, near the picnic area. Note: this campsite can only be accessed by conventional vehicles during dry weather. **Map refs:** 168 B3

MOUNT WALSH NATIONAL PARK

Known for its exposed granite cliffs, the craggy landscape of Mt Walsh National Park offers excellent hiking for bushwalkers. It takes just 2.5 hrs to reach the summit of Mt Walsh, but the ascent should only be attempted by experienced walkers. Reach the park via the Biggenden–Maryborough Rd, 2 km east of Biggenden.

Who to contact: NPRSR 13 7468 www.nprsr. qld.gov.au *Permits:* camping permit required *Camping fees:* fees can be paid and permits acquired at QPWS Maryborough (07) 4121 1800

240 Bush camping areas (walk-in camping)

Bush camping is permitted at Mt Walsh for self-sufficient campers; no facilities are provided. It is recommended that walkers bring along a topographic map and compass. Campers are required to meet with the park ranger at QPWS Maryborough to discuss their itinerary before embarking; there are no self-registration facilities at Mt Walsh. **Map refs:** 156 D4, 169 F4

MOUTH OF BAFFLE CREEK CONSERVATION PARK

Mouth of Baffle Creek Conservation Park is on the northern shore of Rules Beach, 1 hr north of Bundaberg. Behind the sandy beaches are low, open she-oak woodlands and paperbark woodlands. The park is off Rules Beach Rd, from the Bundaberg–Agnes Water Rd. There is 4WD beach access at low tide only. Advance bookings are required for camping.

How to book: NPRSR 13 7468 www.nprsr.qld.gov.au *Permits:* camping permit required

 **Mouth of Baffle Creek camping area**

Visitors to this park can camp behind the dunes, 2 km south of the beach access point. There are no facilities and it is recommended for self-sufficient campers only: bring everything. Beware of marine stingers Oct–May. **Map refs:** 169 F2

MOUTH OF KOLAN RIVER CONSERVATION PARK

Located 25 km north-west of Bundaberg, Mouth of Kolan River Conservation Park protects a diverse array of wildlife and vegetation. Fragile saltplain plants line the river banks, and migratory birds – including pied oystercatchers, eastern curlews and red-necked stints – travel here annually to nest. Advance bookings are required for camping.

How to book: NPRSR 13 7468 www.nprsr.qld.gov.au *Permits:* camping permit required

 Mouth of Kolan River camping area (bush camping)

This bush camping area for self-sufficient campers lies behind the dunes at Moore Park Beach, and can be accessed by 4WD or private boat only. To get here, take the beach access road off Sylvan Dr in Moore Park at low tide. No facilities are provided and fires are prohibited, so bring all self-sufficient camping gear, including drinking water, rubbish bags and a gas/fuel cooker. **Map refs:** 169 F2

NUGA NUGA NATIONAL PARK

At the northern end of Arcadia Valley, Nuga Nuga National Park is a popular destination for fishing, canoeing, kayaking and bushwalking. It is about 400 km west of Gladstone, approximately 150 km north of Injune via Mulcahy Rd from the Carnarvon Developmental Rd. Check the road conditions, as there is access in dry weather only.

Who to contact: NPRSR 13 7468 www.nprsr. qld.gov.au *Permits:* camping permit required *Camping fees:* fees can be paid and permits acquired at the self-registration station

 Nuga Nuga camping area (bush camping)

Self-sufficient visitors can camp at this site on the banks of Lake Nuga Nuga. Access (in dry weather only) is via the main road to the park, 7 km from Arcadia Valley Access Rd. The surface is a combination of dirt and grass and there are no defined sites. Bring water, firewood and preferably a gas/fuel stove. **Map refs:** 168 A2, 183 H2

RUNDLE RANGE NATIONAL PARK

Approximately 40 km north-west of Gladstone, Rundle Range National Park protects areas of dry rainforest and open forests, with more than 280 plant species recorded. The park is about 60 km south-east of Rockhampton. Access is off the Bruce Hwy at Ambrose by 4WD in dry weather only.

Who to contact: NPRSR 13 7468 www.nprsr. qld.gov.au *Permits:* camping permit required *Camping fees:* fees can be paid and permits acquired at QPWS Gladstone (07) 4971 6500

 Sandfly Point camping area (bush camping)

This site for self-sufficient campers is on the western boundary of the national park. As the name suggests, sandflies and mosquitoes are a major problem here, so bring repellent and wear appropriate clothing. The boat ramp and creek

nearby are suitable for small vessels and fishing. Bring water, firewood and a gas/fuel stove.
Map refs: 168 D1, 171 F5

TOLDERODDEN CONSERVATION PARK

Beside the Burnett River, this small park is suitable for brief stays. Take the track from the camping area up a ridge (700 m) for a view over the park. It is on the Cracow Rd, just 4.5 km west of Eidsvold. Bookings are required in advance.

How to book: NPRSR 13 7468 www.nprsr.qld.gov.au
Permits: camping permit required

245 Tolderodden Conservation Park camping area (bush camping)

This grassy site beside the river has good accessibility for all types of vehicles. Tank water is available but should be boiled or treated before drinking. Bring your own firewood, as collecting wood in the park is not permitted.
Map refs: 156 A3, 168 D3

WILD CATTLE ISLAND NATIONAL PARK

Wild Cattle Island National Park takes up most of its eponymous island – a small, unspoiled sand island located near the sleepy hamlet of Tannum Sands, 15 km south-east of Gladstone. Access to this picturesque island is by boat, or on foot from Tannum Sands at low tide.

Who to contact: QPWS Gladstone (07) 4971 6500
Permits: camping permit required Camping fees: fees can be paid and permits acquired at QPWS Gladstone (07) 4971 6500

246 Bush camping areas (boat-based camping)

Camping is permitted at certain areas on Wild Cattle Island – check with QPWS Gladstone. There are no facilities provided and fires are prohibited, so bring all self-sufficient camping gear, including drinking water, rubbish bags and a gas/fuel stove.
Map refs: 169 E1, 171 F5

CAMPSITES LOCATED IN OTHER AREAS

247 1770 Camping Ground

Those looking for absolute beachfront access will adore this commercial camping area in the hamlet of Seventeen Seventy. All of the camp's 100 sites are within a short walk of the water and its activities, and 27 of them are absolute beachfront. The facilities here are basic but well maintained, and the lack of on-site cabins means that the 1770 Camping Ground is a favourite with seasoned campers. Bookings are recommended.
Map refs: 169 F1

How to book: 641 Captain Cook Dr, Seventeen Seventy (07) 4974 9286 www.1770campingground.com.au

248 BIG4 Cania Gorge

The friendly and welcoming folks at this tourist park offer a high standard of accommodation and facilities for the whole family. Campers have the option of powered and unpowered sites, or you can upgrade to a cabin or hillside villa. The park is very close to the spectacular cliffs, ancient caves and bright-coloured sandstone of Cania Gorge National Park. On-site activities include bird feeding, outdoor movies, a swimming pool, tennis court and even a 9-hole golf course. It is 4 km from Lake Cania, 25 km north of the Burnett Hwy and 35 km north of Monto. Bookings are recommended for peak periods. Map refs: 168 D2

How to book: Phil Marshall Dr, Monto (07) 4167 8188 www.caniagorge.com.au

249 Cania Gorge Tourist Retreat

In a sandstone gorge at the entrance to the Cania Gorge National Park, this excellent eco-friendly

tourist park packed with top-notch facilities has 40 powered sites, 20 unpowered sites and a modern amenities block. There's a pool, laundry, grocery shop, cabins, gas re-fills and a fish-cleaning area. Popular activities include taking a hike on the national park walking tracks, fishing in Lake Cania and taking a scenic drive on a 4WD track. From Monto, follow the Burnett Hwy for 12 km, then take the bitumen road a further 12 km to the national park. Bookings are recommended for peak periods. **Map refs:** 168 D2

How to book: 1253 Cania Rd, Monto (07) 4167 8110 www.caniagorgeretreat.com.au

250 Chain Lagoons camping area

This free campsite with no facilities is 15 km north-east of Taroom, reached via the Old Theodore Rd from the Leichhardt Hwy. Taroom, on the Dawson River, is 120 km north of Miles on the Warrego Hwy and 153 km south of Banana on the Dawson Hwy. **Map refs:** 168 B3

Who to contact: Banana Shire Council (07) 4992 9500

251 Discovery Holiday Parks – Lake Maraboon

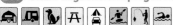

Said to be 3 times the size of Sydney Harbour, Lake Maraboon is a major destination for fishing and boating enthusiasts year-round. The caravan park has excellent facilities: swimming pool, cabins, licensed restaurant, boat hire and a kiosk for bait, ice, gas and fuel. Access to the lake is via Selma Rd from Emerald (18 km) or the Fairbairn Dam Access Rd from the Gregory Hwy. Bookings are recommended for peak periods. **Map refs:** 170 A5

How to book: Selma Rd, Emerald (07) 4982 3677, 1800 627 226 www.discoveryholidayparks.com.au/qld/central_highlands/lake_maraboon

252 Emerald Cabin and Caravan Village

Overlooking Emerald's 18-hole golf course, this caravan park has a range of facilities including drive-through powered sites, a laundry and a camp kitchen with gas BBQ, microwave and fridge. The camping area offers plenty of grass and shade. Visitors can get supplies in Emerald, go fossicking in the gem fields, or take a day trip to Carnarvon Gorge. **Map refs:** 170 A5

How to book: 64 Opal St, Emerald (07) 4982 1300 www.emeraldcabinandcaravanvillage.com.au

253 Glebe Weir camping area

A hugely popular spot for fishing and waterskiing, Glebe Weir is a 54 km drive from Taroom. To get to the campground, take the Leichhardt Hwy 28 km north of Taroom, turn right onto Glebe Weir Rd and travel for a further 26 km. Bring your own firewood and drinking water. Sites are allocated on a first-come, first-served basis. **Map refs:** 168 C3

Who to contact: Banana Shire Council (07) 4992 5900 *Camping fees:* fees can be paid at the self-registration station

254 Injune Caravan Park

This campground on Station St in Injune, about 90 km north of Roma, has laundry facilities, BBQs and other modern conveniences. Winter is the busiest period, so book ahead if you're travelling at this time. The Injune district is known for its natural wonders, including beautiful lakes and volcanic rocks, as well as Aboriginal paintings. **Map refs:** 183 H4

How to book: cnr Station St and Third Ave, Injune (07) 4626 1881 www.injunecaravanpark.com.au

255 Lake Awoonga Caravan Park

Catching huge barramundi is easy at Lake Awoonga – or so the locals say. If you fancy yourself as an angler, this caravan park provides a comfortable base. Set on the lake's edge, there are plenty of bonus extras such as a kiosk, laundry facilities, a bait and tackle shop, and a playground nearby. There's also the option of staying in permanent tents, a bunkhouse, canvas cabins or family cabins. You'll find the caravan park on Awoonga Dam Rd, 8 km west of the Bruce Hwy. Bookings are recommended for peak periods. **Map refs:** 169 E1, 171 F5

How to book: 865 Awoonga Dam Rd, Benaraby (07) 4975 0155 www.lakeawoonga.net

256 Lake Monduran Holiday Park

A fantastic spot for big barramundi fishing, Lake Monduran is 20 km north-west of Gin Gin and 4.5 km east of the Bruce Hwy. The campground, on Claude Wharton Dr, has free wireless internet, laundry facilities, a kiosk, fish-cleaning tables, a tackle shop and boat hire. There's also a golf course nearby at Gin Gin and it's less than an hour's drive to Bundaberg's distillery and shopping. Bookings are recommended for powered sites and cabins. **Map refs:** 156 C1, 169 E2

How to book: 1 Claude Wharton Dr, Lake Monduran (07) 4157 3881, 1800 228 754 www.lakem.com.au

257 Lilley's Beach camping area

A popular spot with locals, camping is permitted in the fenced enclosed area at the north end of Lilley's Beach on Boyne Island. No facilities are provided, so bring your own drinking water, rubbish bags, and firewood or a gas/fuel cooker. Wherever possible, camp in an existing site rather than creating a new one. Access is 4WD only

via Handley Dr and the Boyne Island Sewerage Treatment Plant. **Map refs:** 169 E1, 171 F5

Who to contact: Gladstone Regional Council (07) 4970 0700 *Permits:* 4WD access permit required

258 Mingo Crossing camping area

A popular spot for local anglers, Mingo Crossing camping area is located on the shores of Paradise Dam in Mt Perry. The park is recovering after damage incurred during the 2011 Qld floods, but progress has been swift. To get here, travel 30 km south of Mt Perry on Gayndah–Mt Perry Rd and turn left just before Mingo Crossing Bridge. **Map refs:** 156 C3, 169 E3

How to book: 2670 Gayndah–Mt Perry Rd, Mt Perry (07) 4161 6200

259 Neville Hewitt Weir camping area

Hugely popular in the winter months, this beautiful riverside campground in the town of Baralaba is a favourite with campers from southern Australian states looking to escape the cold weather in a picturesque spot. There's a dump point for caravan waste 500 m away at the showground. The town is on the Dawson River, 96 km north-west of Biloela and 141 km south-west of Rockhampton. You'll need to bring your own water and firewood. **Map refs:** 168 B1

Who to contact: Baralaba Land Care and Community Resource and Development Centre (07) 4998 1142

260 The Oaks camping area

This campground has 35 sites for self-sufficient campers within a skip of Oaks Beach on the north-west side of Facing Island. It is 2 km from the ferry drop-off point and suits self-sufficient campers. Bring a gas/fuel stove. The island is 12 km from the Gladstone mainland, accessible by private vessel or the Curtis Ferry Services barge; book ferry services on (07) 4972 6990. **Map refs:** 157 G5, 169 G4, 171 F5

How to book: Gladstone Visitor Information Centre (07) 4972 9000 www.gladstoneregion.info/ destinations/facing-island/accommodation/the-oaks-on-facing-island *Permits:* camping permit required

261 Rubyvale Caravan Park

This camping area is a short stroll from the Rubyvale town centre, and is located within easy distance of tourist mines and fossicking areas. There are powered and unpowered sites, and a range of good facilities. Rubyvale is about 60 km north-west of Emerald. **Map refs:** 170 A4, 185 H4

How to book: 16 Main St, The Gemfields (07) 4985 4118

262 South End Settlement

South End Settlement is just over 1 km from the ferry drop-off point on Curtis Island and is suitable for small caravans and camper trailers. It's an open grassy area with plenty of shade and 20 allocated campsites, just a short walk to Front Beach. On-site tank water needs to be treated before drinking. You need to bring a gas/ fuel stove. The island is 12 km from the Gladstone mainland, accessible by private vessel or the Curtis Ferry Services barge; pre-book the ferry trip if you're bringing a vehicle, (07) 4972 6990. **Map refs:** 169 E1, 171 F5

How to book: Gladstone Visitor Information Centre (07) 4972 9000 www.gladstoneregion. info/destinations/curtis-island/accommodation/ southend-at-curtis-island *Permits:* camping permit required

263 Takaru Bush Resorts Carnarvon Gorge

Located on the boundary of Carnarvon National Park's Carnarvon Gorge section, this commercial resort offers access to the natural wonders of the

gorge without having to battle for a spot in the school-holidays-only camping area or having to lug your gear to Big Bend. The modern facilities include a convenience store, gas bottle refills and a laundry. Note: there is no petrol for sale near Carnarvon Gorge; fill up at Injune or Rolleston before embarking. Advance bookings are recommended. **Map refs:** 183 G3

How to book: Carnarvon Gorge via Rolleston (07) 4984 4535 www.takaru.com.au/takaru

264 Workmans Beach Campsite

Just a short stroll to the unpatrolled surf beach, this campground is 1 km from the Agnes township and across the road from a skatepark. There are cold-water beach showers and free gas BBQs. Signposted access is off Springs Rd, just south of Agnes Water. The town is 57 km east of Miriam Vale on the Bruce Hwy and 130 km north of Bundaberg. **Map refs:** 169 F1

Who to contact: Agnes Water Rural Transaction Centre (07) 4902 1515

265 Wuruma Dam camping area

Well stocked with perch, bass and saratoga, Wuruma Dam is an angler's paradise. The dam is also popular for a range of watersports: canoeing, sailing, swimming and waterskiing. The area is 48 km north-west of Eidsvold along Wuruma Dam Rd. Note: watersports are permitted only when the dam is above 15% capacity. **Map refs:** 168 D3

Who to contact: (07) 4167 5177 *Permits:* a Stocked Impoundment Permit is required for fishing, from DAFF 13 7468 www.daff.qld.gov.au

Balancing Rock, Girraween National Park (p. 64)

DARLING DOWNS

The Darling Downs, on the western slopes of the Great Dividing Range, has long been known as the food bowl of southern Qld, with its rich soil for crops, livestock and magnificent gardens.

Look beyond the main centres of Toowoomba and Warwick and you'll find the green rolling hills, spectacular mountain scenery and lush rainforests that attract adventurous hikers and camping enthusiasts from far and wide. South of Toowoomba, Main Range National Park has some of the region's best known campgrounds and natural attractions: Cunninghams Gap, Spicers Gap, Mt Roberts, Goomburra and Queen Mary Falls. Collectively, these sections offer more than 20 bushwalking trails with various gradings and surfaces for easy strolls through to physically demanding hikes. The 2 km Queen Mary Falls circuit gives you the opportunity to watch Spring Creek plunge over the 40 m falls – a must-see for visitors.

Further west, the St George region is swiftly recovering from the effects of 3 devastating floods – in Mar 2010, Jan 2011 and Feb 2012 – and continues to offer lovely riverside campgrounds along the Barwon, Narran, Moonie and Bokhara rivers. East of St George, the border town of Goondiwindi – another major centre for agriculture – has some relaxing reserves ideal for overnight stays.

Watersports enthusiasts are spoilt for choice in the Darling Downs, with various lakes and dams across the region. Coolmunda Dam, Glenlyon Dam, Lake Broadwater, Lake Cressbrook, Lake Moogerah and Leslie Dam are popular destinations for fishing, canoeing, sailing, waterskiing and other activities.

If you prefer dry land, national parks and reserves such as Girraween, Sundown and Crows Nest offer secluded bush camping where you're likely to encounter rare and protected wildlife. Expect to see native species such as koalas, echidnas, possums and an array of colourful birdlife.

CAMPSITES LOCATED IN PARKS AND RESERVES

ALTON NATIONAL PARK

This undeveloped national park, approximately 100 km west of Moonie on the Moonie Hwy, protects 558 ha of brigalow-belah forest. It is remote and there are no facilities, so it is suited only to self-sufficient and experienced bush campers with 4WD vehicles.

Who to contact: QPWS Culgoa Floodplain (07) 4625 0942 *Permits:* camping permit required *Camping fees:* fees can be paid and permits acquired at any QPWS office

266 Bush camping areas

Self-sufficient campers are welcome to camp in Alton National Park, but be aware that there are no facilities or amenities and that open fires are prohibited. Bring all self-sufficient gear, including drinking water, rubbish bags and a gas/fuel stove. There is no self-registration facility in the park, so acquire your permit before camping. **Map refs: 166 A3**

CROWS NEST NATIONAL PARK

Crows Nest National Park, on the edge of the Great Dividing Range west of Brisbane, features the picturesque Crows Nest Falls with its 20 m drop into a granite rockpool. Downstream is the Valley of Diamonds, a deep gorge surrounded by cliffs up to 120 m high through which Crows Nest Creek flows. These natural attractions are set in a landscape of dry eucalypt forest, in which stringybarks, bloodwoods and ironbarks flourish. Advance bookings are required for camping.

How to book: NPRSR 13 7468 www.nprsr.qld.gov.au *Permits:* camping permit required

267 Crows Nest camping area

The eucalypt forests of Crows Nest provide a beautiful setting for wildlife-watching, hiking and bush camping. You can look for platypus in the creek, spot brush-tailed rock wallabies, or take a walk across the gorge to Crows Nest Falls. Other wildlife in the region include rosellas, sugar gliders and ringtail possums. The campground has showers operating on a self-serve donkey boiler system, and you should treat or boil the water before drinking. Follow the signs on Three Mile Rd, 6 km from Crows Nest. **Map refs: 152 C5, 154 C1, 167 F2**

DUNMORE STATE FOREST

This undeveloped state forest, about 15 km west of Cecil Plains on Cecil Plains–Tara Rd, exists primarily as a logging reserve, but can be accessed by intrepid bush campers. The forest fills with attractive wildflowers in spring, and the trails inside the forest are suitable for mountain-biking and horseriding. Advance bookings are required for camping.

How to book: NPRSR 13 7468 www.nprsr.qld.gov.au
Permits: camping permit required

268 Bush camping areas

Self-sufficient campers are welcome to camp in Dunmore State Forest, but be aware that there are no facilities or amenities and that open fires are prohibited. Bring all self-sufficient gear, including drinking water, rubbish bags and a gas/fuel stove. Exercise caution when driving in the forest, as logging trucks may be active. **Map refs: 166 D2**

GIRRAWEEN NATIONAL PARK

Situated between Stanthorpe and Tenterfield (NSW), Girraween National Park lies in Qld's Granite Belt and features pristine forests interspersed with towering granite outcrops. Picturesque creeks flow past teetering boulders, and there is an abundance of wildlife and wildflowers – Girraween is an Indigenous word meaning 'place of flowers'. Only a few

campsites, and markings on trees and rocks, remain as evidence of the Kambuwal people who once lived in this area. Girraween is signposted from Pyramids Rd off the New England Hwy, 11 km north of Wallangarra and 7 km south of Ballandean. Advance bookings are required for camping.

How to book: NPRSR 13 7468 www.nprsr.qld.gov.au
Permits: camping permit required

269 Bald Rock Creek camping area

Bald Rock Creek camping area is the first turning on the left as you enter the national park from the New England Hwy, and can be reached by conventional vehicle. The area is semi-grassed, has no designated sites and provides some shade. Firewood for BBQs can be purchased at the Ballandean Store, on the hwy 15 km from the park. **Map refs: 167 E4**

270 Bush camping areas (walk-in camping)

Self-sufficient and experienced walkers can make use of the remote walk-in bush campsites throughout the park. Open fires are prohibited and camping permits are required. You'll need to lodge a bush camping form in advance at the Girraween park office or by phoning QPWS Girraween on (07) 4684 5157. **Map refs: 167 E4**

271 Castle Rock camping area

Just 400 m from Bald Rock Creek, the forest setting at Castle Rock is suitable for walk-in or vehicle-based camping and there's plenty of room for large groups. You need to come equipped with firewood. Boil or treat the water provided before drinking. **Map refs: 167 E4**

GLEN ROCK PARK

This open park area at the head of the Tenthill Valley was purchased by the Qld state government in 1996 to provide open spaces for public use. It adjoins the World Heritage–listed Main Range National Park (whose Glen Rock outcrop gives the park its name) and offers riding trails for both bikes and horses, as well as walking trails. Fauna in the area include the brush-tailed rock wallaby, powerful owl and glossy black-cockatoo. Advance bookings are required for camping.

How to book: NPRSR 13 7468 www.nprsr.qld.gov.au
Permits: camping permit required

272 **Casuarina camping area**

This open, grassy campsite, close to a creek, offers excellent access to Glen Rock Park's network of walking, horseriding and biking trails. A horse corral is provided for riders. To get here, take Mt Sylvia Rd south from Gatton, through Tenthill, then continue south to Junction View. Turn left at Junction View Primary School and follow East Haldon Rd to its southern end in Glen Rock Park. Note: if you'd like to use the provided campfires, bring your own firewood.
Map refs: 154 D3, 167 F3

KUMBARILLA STATE FOREST

This undeveloped state forest, around 46 km south-west of Dalby on the Moonie Hwy, exists primarily as a logging reserve, but is open to intrepid bush campers. Fishing is permitted at Wilkie Creek. Advance bookings are required for camping.

How to book: NPRSR 13 7468 www.nprsr.qld.gov.au
Permits: camping permit required

273 **Bush camping areas**

Self-sufficient campers are welcome to camp in Kumbarilla State Forest, but be aware that there are no facilities or amenities and that open fires are prohibited. Bring all self-sufficient gear, including drinking water, rubbish bags and a gas/fuel stove. Exercise caution when driving in the forest, as logging trucks may be active.
Map refs: 166 D2

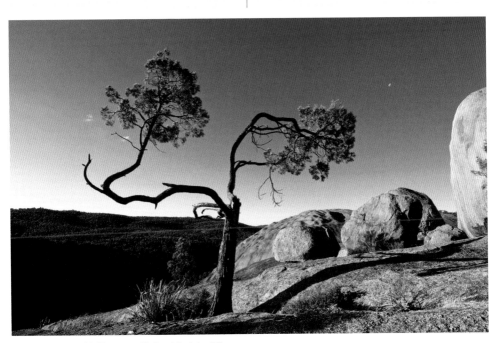

Tree on the Pyramid, Girraween National Park (p. 64)

LAKE BROADWATER CONSERVATION PARK

An important refuge for waterbirds and other wildlife, Lake Broadwater is surrounded by cypress pine, eucalypt and brigalow open woodland. The park, 30 km south-west of Dalby, preserves valuable remnants of the vegetation types that once covered the western Downs. Access to the lake is signposted off the Moonie Hwy, 20 km west of Dalby.

Who to contact: NPRSR 13 7468 www.nprsr.qld. gov.au *Permits:* camping and boating permits required; call Lake Broadwater on (07) 4663 3562 to arrange boating permit *Camping fees:* fees can be paid and permits acquired at the self-registration station

274 Lake Broadwater camping area

This camping area among the shady red and blue gums of Lake Broadwater Conservation Park lies 30 km south-west of Dalby. The lake is a popular watersports venue and the surrounding forests are great for birdwatching. The camping area is 10 km along Lake Broadwater Rd, off the Moonie Hwy. Bring your own firewood and treat or boil the water provided before drinking. **Map refs: 166 D2**

275 Wilga Bush camping area

On the northern side of Lake Broadwater, this secluded campground is linked to Lake Broadwater camping area via a 2 km track. You can learn about the park's vegetation along the walking track and see the remains of an old dingo fence built in the 1860s. The site is 8 km along Lake Broadwater Rd, off the Moonie Hwy. Treat or boil the water provided before drinking and bring your own firewood. **Map refs: 166 D2**

MAIN RANGE NATIONAL PARK

Covering 29 730 ha along the Great Dividing Range, World Heritage–listed Main Range National Park forms the western part of a crescent of mountains in south-east Qld known as the Scenic Rim. The park boasts impressive peaks and escarpments, and the delightful Queen Mary Falls. There are 3 main types of vegetation: rainforest in the moist, sheltered areas; open eucalypt forest on the high ridges and slopes; and mountain heath on the cliffs and rocky outcrops. Picnic spots are plentiful and there are spectacular views from Governors Chair (to the NSW border), and Sylvesters and Fassifern Valley lookouts. The park is divided into 3 sections with separate access routes: Cunninghams Gap, Goomburra and Queen Mary Falls. Advance bookings are required for camping.

Who to contact: QPWS Main Range (07) 4666 1133 for access information for bush camping areas *How to book:* NPRSR 13 7468 www.nprsr.qld.gov.au *Permits:* camping permit required

276 Bush camping areas (walk-in camping)

There are 11 bush campsites in Main Range National Park (Davies Ridge, Knoll E12, Knoll T30, Lizard South, Lower Panorama Point, Mt Huntley Saddle, Mt Steamer Saddle, Mt Superbus – South Peak, Panorama Point, Ramparts South and South Branch) for self-sufficient campers, located in remote areas of the park. These sites can only be reached by walking. For access instructions and locations, contact QPWS Main Range. **Map refs: 154 D4, 167 F3**

277 Double Top camping area (walk-in camping)

Thrillseekers and experienced climbers will delight in this tiny campsite (up to 4 people) on the edge of a razorback on the southern side of the north peak of Mt Spicer. There are no facilities provided and fires are prohibited, so bring all self-sufficient equipment, including drinking water, rubbish bags and a gas/fuel stove. Note: extreme caution should be taken in this area, owing to the site's proximity to unfenced clifftops. **Map refs: 154 D4, 167 F3**

278 Glen Rock camping area (walk-in camping)

Those looking for a scenic campsite will relish the views from this campsite (up to 8 people) on top of Glen Rock, in the far north of the Goomburra section. There are no facilities provided and fires are prohibited, so bring all self-sufficient equipment, including drinking water, rubbish bags and a gas/fuel stove. **Map refs:** 154 D3, 167 F3

279 Huntley – Sentinel Saddle camping area (walk-in camping)

This open forest site west of Mt Huntley in the Cunninghams Gap section offers camping for up to 8 experienced bush hikers. There are no facilities provided and fires are prohibited, so bring all self-sufficient equipment, including drinking water, rubbish bags and a gas/fuel stove. **Map refs:** 154 D4, 167 F3

280 Laidley Creek Falls camping area (walk-in camping)

This open forest site at the headwaters of Laidley Creek in the Goomburra section offers camping for up to 8 experienced bush hikers. There are no facilities provided and fires are prohibited, so bring all self-sufficient equipment, including drinking water, rubbish bags and a gas/fuel stove. **Map refs:** 154 D3, 167 F3

281 Manna Gum camping area

This large grassy campsite in the Goomburra section is shaded by manna gums, making it perfect for the warmer months. Many of the Goomburra section's walking trails begin at its eastern end. Bring your own firewood if you wish to use the wood BBQs (collecting firewood within the park is prohibited). Manna Gum is roughly 250 m past Poplar Flat at the end of Forestry Reserve Rd. **Map refs:** 154 D3, 167 F3

282 Mount Huntley camping area (walk-in camping)

This elevated open forest site next to rainforest in the Cunninghams Gap section offers camping for up to 8 experienced bush hikers. There are no facilities provided and fires are prohibited, so bring all self-sufficient equipment, including drinking water, rubbish bags and a gas/fuel stove. **Map refs:** 154 D4, 167 F3

283 Mount Superbus – North Peak camping area (walk-in camping)

This rough rainforest campsite on the north peak of Mt Superbus offers camping for up to 8 experienced bush hikers. There are no facilities provided and fires are prohibited, so bring all self-sufficient equipment, including drinking water, rubbish bags and a gas/fuel stove. Note: there is limited protection from the elements in windy weather. **Map refs:** 154 D4, 167 F3

284 Mount Superbus – Raspberry Saddle camping area (walk-in camping)

This pleasant, sheltered rainforest site in the saddle between the peaks of Mt Superbus offers camping for up to 8 experienced bush hikers. There are no facilities provided and fires are prohibited, so bring all self-sufficient equipment, including drinking water, rubbish bags and a gas/fuel stove. **Map refs:** 154 D4, 167 F3

285 Paddy's Knob camping area (walk-in camping)

This newly created site, 400 m from Paddy's Knob in the Queen Mary Falls section, offers expansive views of the Condamine Gorge for up to 8 experienced bush hikers. There are no facilities provided and fires are prohibited, so bring all self-sufficient equipment, including drinking water, rubbish bags and a gas/fuel stove. **Map refs:** 154 D4, 167 F4

286 Point Pure camping area (walk-in camping)

This newly created site in the Goomburra section, near Glen Rock, offers good views to the west over Glen Rock Park. There are no facilities provided and fires are prohibited, so bring all self-sufficient equipment, including drinking water, rubbish bags and a gas/fuel stove. **Map refs:** 154 D3, 167 F3

287 Poplar Flat camping area

On the banks of Dalrymple Creek in the Goomburra section, this large grassy campsite is big enough for 100 campers. You'll need to bring your own firewood if you want to use the BBQs, or purchase it locally, as firewood must not be collected from the park or roadside (fines apply). The site is on Forestry Reserve Rd, 35 km east of Allora, reached from the New England Hwy via Inverramsay Rd. **Map refs:** 154 D3, 167 F3

288 Spicers – Double Top Saddle camping area (walk-in camping)

This open forest site in the saddle between the peaks of Mt Spicer offers more room – and less risk – than the nearby Double Top camping area. There are no facilities provided and fires are prohibited, so bring all self-sufficient equipment, including drinking water, rubbish bags and a gas/fuel stove. **Map refs:** 154 D4, 167 F3

289 Spicers Gap camping area (walk-in camping)

Spicers Gap is a small walk-in campground on the eastern side of the gap, with good walking trails nearby. A maximum of 50 campers is allowed, but there's the freedom of setting up anywhere in the mown area. Boil or treat water before drinking and bring your own firewood or a gas/fuel stove. It is on East Spicers Gap Rd, 17.5 km south-west of Aratula. **Map refs:** 154 D4, 167 F3

290 Spicers Peak (East) camping area (walk-in camping)

Climbers tackling Mt Spicer can rest at this small site (up to 4 people) on the margin between rainforest and heath. There are no facilities provided and fires are prohibited, so bring all self-sufficient equipment, including drinking water, rubbish bags and a gas/fuel stove. **Map refs:** 154 D4, 167 F3

291 Spicers Peak (West) camping area (walk-in camping)

Climbers tackling Mt Spicer can rest at this site (up to 8 people) on the margin between rainforest and heath. There are no facilities provided and fires are prohibited, so bring all self-sufficient equipment, including drinking water, rubbish bags and a gas/fuel stove. **Map refs:** 154 D4, 167 F3

292 Stern camping area (walk-in camping)

This newly created campsite in the Cunninghams Gap section offers bush camping for up to 8 experienced hikers. There are no facilities provided and fires are prohibited, so bring all self-sufficient equipment, including drinking water, rubbish bags and a gas/fuel stove. **Map refs:** 154 D4, 167 F3

293 Swan Knoll camping area (walk-in camping)

This open forest site in the Cunninghams Gap section offers bush camping for up to 8 experienced hikers. There are no facilities provided and fires are prohibited, so bring all self-sufficient equipment, including drinking water, rubbish bags and a gas/fuel stove. Note: there is limited protection from the elements in windy weather. **Map refs:** 154 D4, 167 F3

MOOGERAH PEAKS NATIONAL PARK

This small national park includes a number of isolated mountain peaks, such as Mt Edwards (632 m), Mt French (579 m), Mt Greville (770 m) and Mt Moon (784 m), the result of volcanic activity in the area some 22 million years ago. The vegetation on the mountains is mainly open eucalypt forest, with spotted gum, grey gum and stringybark. Advance bookings are required for camping.

How to book: NPRSR 13 7468 www.nprsr.qld.gov.au
Permits: camping permit required

294 Frog Buttress camping area (walk-in camping)

This small campground in Moogerah Peaks, suitable for walk-in camping only, is located 11 km west of Boonah on Mt French Rd, signposted 1 km south of Boonah off the Boonah–Rathdowney Rd. Bring your own firewood. There is a carpark and day-use area close to the campsites.
Map refs: 155 E3, 167 F3

295 Mount French camping area

Although Frog Buttress is unsuited to vehicular camping, 2 vehicle campsites suitable for caravans or camper trailers (but not tents) are available in the carpark of the Mt French section of the park. No facilities are provided, but the carpark is a short stroll from the Mt French day-use area's facilities, which include BBQs, toilets and picnic tables. Bring your own firewood for use in the wood BBQs or a gas/fuel cooker. Note: this camping area is allocated on a first-come, first-served basis and you need to book a permit in advance for Frog Buttress to access it.
Map refs: 155 E3, 167 F3

SUNDOWN NATIONAL PARK

South-west of Brisbane on the Qld–NSW border, Sundown National Park is known for its rugged gorge scenery around the Severn River and its wilderness trails for experienced walkers. The park is popular for swimming, fishing and canoeing, and there's access for conventional vehicles signposted off Glenlyon Dam Rd. Advance bookings are required for camping.

How to book: NPRSR 13 7468 www.nprsr.qld.gov.au
Permits: camping permit required

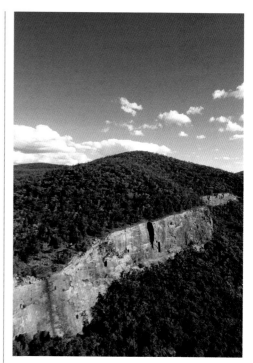

Cliffs in Sundown National Park

296 The Broadwater camping area

These grassy sites on the banks of the Severn River are on Permanents Rd, signposted from Glenlyon Dam Rd. Visitors with caravans longer than 4 m are recommended not to attempt entering the site due to narrow sections of track. There are donkey boiler hot-water showers on site. **Map refs:** 167 E4

297 Burrows Waterhole camping area

This site has a maximum capacity of 60 people, with a maximum group size of 6. It is reached from the park's eastern boundary, 18 km from the park entrance gate and signposted along the Sundown National Park access road. Bring drinking water, firewood or a gas/fuel stove. **Map refs:** 167 E4

298 Bush camping areas (walk-in camping)

Bush campsites throughout the park are for experienced and self-sufficient walkers only. Campers should discuss their planned itinerary with the park ranger and check conditions before setting out. Open fires are permitted with firewood brought in from outside the park, but a gas/fuel stove is recommended. **Map refs:** 167 E4

299 Nundubbermere Falls camping area (bush camping)

Bush camping for self-sufficient campers is available at Nundubbermere Falls, at the northernmost point of Sundown. There are no facilities provided, but you can swim, fish and canoe along the Severn River. Access is via Stanthorpe–Texas and Nundubbermere rds and is suitable for conventional vehicles. Bring your own water and firewood or a gas/fuel stove. **Map refs:** 167 E4

300 Red Rock Gorge camping area

There are few facilities other than pit toilets at Red Rock Gorge, but this remote campsite is close to a marvellous lookout over the gorge. Access is 4WD only via Curr and Sundown rds from Ballandean. Bring your own drinking water and firewood or a gas/fuel stove. **Map refs:** 167 E4

301 Reedy Waterhole camping area (bush camping)

This campsite on the Severn River offers no facilities and is suitable for self-sufficient campers only. Campers can swim, fish and canoe in the Severn, or take a walk up to the natural lookout at Rats Castle. It is 18 km into Sundown, accessible by 4WD only via Curr and Sundown rds from Ballandean. Bring your own drinking water and firewood or a gas/fuel cooker. **Map refs:** 167 E4

WESTERN CREEK STATE FOREST

This undeveloped state forest, about 30 km west of Millmerran on the Gore Hwy, exists primarily as a logging reserve but can be accessed by intrepid bush campers. The forest was previously a grazing selection; curious explorers may find abandoned log huts and other historical artefacts here. Advance bookings are required for camping.

How to book: NPRSR 13 7468 www.nprsr.qld.gov.au
Permits: camping permit required

302 Bush camping areas

Self-sufficient campers are welcome to camp in Western Creek State Forest, but be aware that there are no facilities or amenities and that open fires are prohibited. Bring all self-sufficient gear, including drinking water, rubbish bags and a gas/fuel stove. Exercise caution when driving in the forest, as logging trucks may be active. **Map refs:** 166 D3

CAMPSITES LOCATED IN OTHER AREAS

303 Archers Crossing camping area

A great spot for fishing, Archers Crossing has a boat ramp on the southern side of the Condamine River. Suitable for self-sufficient campers, the only facilities are the shelter shed, tables and BBQs. The site is 24 km south-east of Chinchilla, reached by Hopelands Rd. **Map refs:** 166 D1, 168 D5

Who to contact: Chinchilla Visitor Information Centre (07) 4679 4491

304 Balonne Minor Bridge camping area (bush camping)

Self-sufficient campers can stay at this site, 3 km west of Dirranbandi on Dirranbandi–Bollon Rd, around 94 km south of St George. **Map refs:** 181 G4

Who to contact: Balonne Visitor Information Centre (07) 4620 8877

305 Barney's Beach camping area (bush camping)

You'll find this campground beside the Moonie River, on Thallon–Dirranbandi Rd, 3 km west of Thallon. There are no facilities at the site. Thallon is 76 km south-east of St George. **Map refs:** 166 A4, 181 H4

Who to contact: Balonne Visitor Information Centre (07) 4620 8877

306 Barwon River camping area (bush camping)

This basic camping area is set on the north bank of the Barwon River in Mungindi, 118 km south-east of St George. **Map refs:** 166 A4, 181 H4

Who to contact: Balonne Visitor Information Centre (07) 4620 8877

307 Beardmore Dam Turnoff camping area (bush camping)

This campground is 13 km north of St George, on the turn-off to Beardmore Dam. You'll need to bring drinking water, as there are no facilities. St George is at the junction of the Carnarvon, Balonne and Moonie hwys, 200 km west of Goondiwindi and 290 km east of Cunnamulla. **Map refs:** 166 A3, 181 H3

Who to contact: Balonne Visitor Information Centre (07) 4620 8877

308 Bengalla Reserve camping area (bush camping)

This area is about 34 km from Goondiwindi, with good river access for dropping in a line. You need to bring firewood and water. From the Goondiwindi post office, travel east on Marshall St to the large roundabout. Take the Border Rivers Tourist Dr exit, then travel 33 km to the reserve sign and follow the bush track to the river. Note: conventional vehicle access is only possible in dry weather. **Map refs:** 166 C4

Who to contact: Goondiwindi Regional Council (07) 4671 7400

309 BIG4 Toowoomba Garden City Holiday Park

Toowoomba is known as the 'Garden City', and this holiday park certainly takes that reputation to heart, offering award-winning landscaped gardens to its guests. Other facilities include a library, laundry, baby-care facilities and a fresh herb garden for guests to add a little zest to their cooking. The attractions of Toowoomba's central district are nearby. Advance bookings are recommended. **Map refs:** 154 C2, 167 E2

How to book: 34A Eiser St, Harristown (07) 4635 1747, 1800 333 667 www.big4toowoombagchp.com.au

310 Bingi Crossing camping area (bush camping)

This site, suitable for self-sufficient campers (bring drinking water), is 45 km east of the town of Surat. Take the Surat–Tara Rd from the Carnarvon Hwy. Surat is 78 km south of Roma and 116 km north of St George. **Map refs:** 166 B1

Who to contact: Surat Visitor Information Centre (07) 4626 5136

311 Bokhara River camping area (bush camping)

This site with no facilities is set beside the Bokhara River in Hebel, 162 km south of St George and 65 km south of Dirranbandi. **Map refs:** 181 F4

Who to contact: Balonne Visitor Information Centre (07) 4620 8877

312 Boonanga Reserve camping area (bush camping)

This site is just over 90 km from Goondiwindi near Talwood. You can camp beside the Barwon River, but you'll need to bring your own drinking water and firewood. From Talwood, travel 15 km

on the Talwood–Boomi Rd to Barwon River.
Map refs: 166 B4

Who to contact: Goondiwindi Regional Council
(07) 4671 7400

313 **Bowenville Reserve camping area**

This large, shady campground is on the southern
banks of Oakey Creek – perfect for fishing or
taking a dip. Bring your own drinking water. To get
here, follow Bowenville–Norwin Rd, 4 km south of
the Warrego Hwy. **Map refs:** 152 A5, 154 A1, 167 E2

Who to contact: Toowoomba Regional Council
13 1872

314 **Caliguel Lagoon camping area**

Very popular with waterskiers, this site is 7 km
south of Condamine and 33 km south of Miles.
Bring your own firewood and water (or boil/
treat the tank water provided) to the camping
area, reached from Condamine–Meandarra Rd.
Map refs: 166 C1

Who to contact: Miles Visitor Information Centre
(07) 4627 1492

315 **Cecil Plains Rural Retreat
Caravan Park**

This basic campground with a toilet block and hot
showers is on Taylor St in Cecil Plains, opposite
Henry Stuart Russell Park. There is a black-water
dump here but you need to bring your own
drinking water. From Toowoomba, take the Cecil
Plains–Toowoomba Rd west for about 90 km.
Map refs: 166 D2

Who to contact: Toowoomba Regional Council
13 1872

316 **Cecil Plains Weir camping area**

The Condamine River flows through the
Millmerran area, where a number of campsites
are available, ideal for fishing and boating. This

site is 1 km east of Cecil Plains, reached via Cecil
Plains–Toowoomba Rd. Millmerran is on the
Gore Hwy, 82 km south-west of Toowoomba.
Map refs: 166 D2

Who to contact: Toowoomba Regional Council
13 1872

317 **Chinchilla Weir camping area**

Catch some perch, catfish or Murray cod in the
Condamine River near this campsite, where a
maximum 2-night stay applies. There is a boat
ramp on site but fishing is not permitted within
200 m of the weir wall. BYO firewood and drinking
water. From Chinchilla, travel 8 km south on
Chinchilla–Tara Rd. **Map refs:** 166 C1, 168 C5

Who to contact: Chinchilla Visitor Information
Centre (07) 4679 4491

318 **Cow Paddocks camping area
(bush camping)**

This site with no facilities is 2 km east of Surat on
Sawmill Rd. Surat is on the Carnarvon Hwy, 78 km
south of Roma and 116 km north of St George. Bring
all necessary supplies. **Map refs:** 166 A2, 181 H2

Who to contact: Surat Visitor Information Centre
(07) 4626 5136

319 **Fishermans Park camping area**

This basic campground with toilets and picnic
tables is on the Carnarvon Hwy at the Balonne
River, on the north side of the town of Surat.
You need to bring firewood and drinking water.
It's 78 km south of Roma and 116 km north of
St George. **Map refs:** 166 A2, 181 H2

Who to contact: Surat Visitor Information Centre
(07) 4626 5136

320 **Gil Weir camping area**

This basic campsite by the Gil Weir, south of Miles,
offers good fishing opportunities. Bring your own

drinking water and firewood for the BBQs. The campsite is located on the Leichhardt Hwy, 4 km south of Miles. **Map refs:** 166 C1, 168 C5

Who to contact: Miles Visitor Information Centre (07) 4627 1492

321 Glenlyon Dam Tourist Park

A popular destination for watersports, Glenlyon Dam is also a top spot for fishing for perch, eel-tailed catfish and Murray cod. The tourist park has laundry facilities, a kiosk, boat hire and fuel. Follow the signs off the Glenlyon–Texas Rd, 93 km south of Stanthorpe, or the Bruxner Hwy, 67 km north-west of Tenterfield. Bookings are advised for peak periods. **Map refs:** 167 E5

How to book: Glenlyon–Texas Rd, Glenlyon Dam (02) 6737 5266

322 Grays Reserve camping area (bush camping)

This small site has no facilities and suits self-sufficient campers only. From Chinchilla, travel 16 km south along Chinchilla–Tara Rd. After a large dip in the road, travel 200 m and turn right onto the bush track that leads to the river, opposite the property called Chinta. **Map refs:** 166 C1, 168 C5

Who to contact: Chinchilla Visitor Information Centre (07) 4679 4491

323 Green Timbers camping area (bush camping)

This site is for self-sufficient campers only, as there are no facilities. It is 18 km south of Surat off the Carnarvon Hwy, and is accessible in dry weather only. Surat is 78 km south of Roma and 116 km north of St George. **Map refs:** 166 A2, 181 H2

Who to contact: Surat Visitor Information Centre (07) 4626 5136

324 Jack Taylor Weir camping area (bush camping)

This site is on the western side of the weir in St George. There are no facilities but it is close to town. St George is at the junction of the Carnarvon, Balonne and Moonie hwys, 200 km west of Goondiwindi and 290 km east of Cunnamulla. **Map refs:** 181 H3

Who to contact: Balonne Visitor Information Centre (07) 4620 8877

325 Jandowae Accommodation Park

You'll find a good range of facilities at this park, 50 km north of Dalby, but bring your own firewood. There's a swimming pool, camp kitchen, laundry facilities, kiosk and the option of self-contained cabins. It's on High St in Jandowae. The nearby dam is ideal for picnicking, boating and fishing. **Map refs:** 166 D1, 168 D5

How to book: 104 High St, Jandowae (07) 4668 5071

326 Judd's Lagoon camping area

Great for fishing, this quiet and tidy campsite is on Mongool Rd, 5 km south-east of Yuleba. There are few facilities on site, so bring drinking water and firewood. Yuleba is on the Warrego Hwy, 60 km east of Roma and 80 km west of Miles. Note: the signage on the hwy is poor. **Map refs:** 166 B1, 168 B5

Who to contact: Maranoa Regional Council 1300 007 662

327 Keetah Reserve camping area (bush camping)

This campsite, close to the NSW border, offers great fishing. Take the Border Rivers Tourist Dr exit from Goondiwindi, then travel 52 km to an intersection. Follow the road marked Yelarbon to the camping area in an open paddock on your right. **Map refs:** 166 D4

Who to contact: Miles Visitor Information Centre (07) 4627 1492

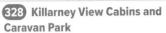 Killarney View Cabins and Caravan Park

This award-winning caravan park outside the quiet hamlet of Killarney offers remarkably modern amenities, including a laundry and camp kitchen. It is a short distance from Queen Mary Falls and the natural splendour of Main Range National Park. Advance bookings are recommended. **Map refs:** 154 D4, 167 F4

How to book: cnr O'Maras and Claydons rds, Killarney (07) 4664 1522, 0418 789 531 www.killarneyview.com.au

 Lake Coolmunda Caravan Park

Waterskiing and fishing for silver perch, cod and catfish are popular pursuits on Coolmunda Dam, on the dam access road 13 km east of Inglewood. The caravan park has drive-through campsites, 8 cabins and an excellent range of facilities, including a swimming pool and tennis courts. Bookings are recommended at peak periods. **Map refs:** 166 D4

How to book: 38 Access Rd, Coolmunda (07) 4652 4171

 Lake Cressbrook camping area

With excellent fishing, canoeing, kayaking, sailing and windsurfing on offer, it's a watersports wonderland at Lake Cressbrook. For walkers, a 5 km circuit starts at the camping ground and loops around the lake shore. The camping ground has a self-registration system and no bookings are taken at any time. It is suitable for small caravans and trailers and is situated 13 km north-east of Pechey and 50 km north of Toowoomba. There is signposted access off the New England

Hwy from Crows Nest and Pechey. Note: there is an access fee, to be paid at the boomgate. **Map refs:** 152 D5, 154 D1, 167 F2

Who to contact: Toowoomba Regional Council 13 1872

 Lake Moogerah Caravan Park

On the shores of Lake Moogerah, this large caravan park is packed with top-grade facilities for a comfortable stay in the region. There's a kiosk, 2 boat ramps, laundry, campfire pits, 2 amenities blocks, cabins and a playground, plus it's close to the tennis courts, restaurants, pubs and cafes at Boonah. Local attractions include wineries, scenic drives and rock climbing. To get here, follow the signs from the Cunningham Hwy and turn off near Aratula. **Map refs:** 155 E4, 167 F3

How to book: 1 Muller Park Rd, Moogerah (07) 5463 0141 www.moogerah.com

 Lees Reserve camping area (bush camping)

Another anglers' favourite, this free campsite on the Dumaresq River is pet-friendly and allows open fires. Take the Border Rivers Tourist Dr exit from Goondiwindi, then travel 29 km east. A narrow access road takes you to the campsite and the banks of the Dumaresq. **Map refs:** 166 C4

Who to contact: Miles Visitor Information Centre (07) 4627 1492

 Lemontree Weir

The lack of facilities ensures this spot is suitable for self-sufficient campers only. It's 20 km north of Millmerran. Access is via Lemon Tree Rd, off the Gore Hwy, in dry weather only. **Map refs:** 154 A2, 166 D3

Who to contact: Toowoomba Regional Council 13 1872

334 Moonie River camping area (bush camping)

There are no facilities at this site beside the Moonie River in Nindigully, 44 km south-east of St George. St George is at the junction of the Carnarvon, Balonne and Moonie hwys, 200 km west of Goondiwindi and 290 km east of Cunnamulla. **Map refs: 166 A3, 181 H3**

Who to contact: Balonne Visitor Information Centre (07) 4620 8877

335 Narran River camping area (bush camping)

This campground beside the Narran River has no facilities. To get here, take Dirranbandi–Hebel Rd, 37 km south of Dirranbandi. **Map refs: 181 G4**

Who to contact: Balonne Visitor Information Centre (07) 4620 8877

336 Old Yuleba Town camping area

Suitable for self-sufficient stopover camping, there are no facilities at this site 13 km east of Yuleba. From the Warrego Hwy, go south onto Forestry Rd, then right onto Mongool Rd and right again after the fourth grid. Yuleba is 60 km east of Roma and 80 km west of Miles. **Map refs: 166 B1, 168 B5**

Who to contact: Maranoa Regional Council 1300 007 662

337 Pialaway Reserve camping area

This no-frills site is 85 km north of Surat. From the Surat–Condamine Rd, head along the Warkan Rd for 18 km. Surat is on the Carnarvon Hwy, 78 km south of Roma and 116 km north of St George. **Map refs: 166 B1**

Who to contact: Maranoa Regional Council 1300 007 662

338 Queen Mary Falls Caravan Park and Cabins

Great for kids, you can handfeed king parrots, take a twilight animal-viewing walk or stroll to beautiful Queen Mary Falls opposite this caravan park. The office has an adjoining cafe, there's a laundry and campfires are allowed in designated areas. The caravan park is on Spring Creek Rd, 11 km east of Killarney. Bookings are recommended for powered sites. **Map refs: 154 D5, 167 F4**

How to book: 676 Spring Creek Rd, Killarney (07) 4664 7151 www.queenmaryfallscaravanpark.com.au

339 Rainbow Reserve camping area (bush camping)

Camp by the McIntyre River at this site just outside Goondiwindi, a great spot for fishing and camping, with a boat ramp too. From the Goondiwindi post office, travel east on Marshall St to the large roundabout. Take the Border Rivers Tourist Dr exit and travel 17 km to the site. **Map refs: 166 C4**

Who to contact: Goondiwindi Regional Information Centre (07) 4671 2653 www.goondiwindi.qld.au

340 Rocklands Camping Reserve

This 8 ha campground is a little more secluded than nearby Washpool Camping Reserve, and is suitable for tents, camper trailers and small caravans. It is 18 km west of Washpool on Rocklands Rd, off Glen Rd. Campers are encouraged to use existing fire sites; bring your own firewood and drinking water. **Map refs: 154 B4, 167 E3**

Who to contact: (07) 4661 7844, 0418 870 354
Camping fees: pay fees at the self-registration station

341 Walpole Park camping area

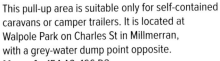

This pull-up area is suitable only for self-contained caravans or camper trailers. It is located at Walpole Park on Charles St in Millmerran, with a grey-water dump point opposite.
Map refs: 154 A3, 166 D3

Who to contact: Toowoomba Regional Council 13 1872

342 Warroo Bridge camping area (bush camping)

Camping is permitted on the north side of the bridge at this site 60 km north of St George. Bring your own drinking water. To get here, follow the Wycombe School–Warroo Bridge Rd from the Carnarvon Hwy, then travel 9 km to the bridge.
Map refs: 166 A2, 181 H2

Who to contact: Balonne Visitor Information Centre (07) 4620 8877

343 Washpool Camping Reserve

Washpool's 25 ha campground is well grassed, shady and has 40 powered sites. The scenic Leslie Dam nearby is well known as a good fishing spot for golden perch and is popular for canoeing and sailing. The camping area is on Leslie Dam Rd, off the Cunningham Hwy, 13 km west of Warwick.
Map refs: 154 C4, 167 E3

Who to contact: (07) 4661 7844, 0418 870 354
Camping fees: fees can be paid at the camp office or self-registration station

344 Yarramalong Camping and Outdoor Recreation Centre

There's no shortage of space for comfortable camping at this 65 ha property, with 2 campgrounds: The Main and The Island. Both have private fireplaces (bring your own wood) and shady trees. There are 8 hot showers on site and a kiosk, and Aratula's bakery, pub and service

station is close by. Reynold's Creek nearby is ideal for swimming, canoeing and fishing. Yarramalong, on Lake Moogerah Rd, is signed from the Aratula turn-off adjacent to the pub and from the road to Boonah, Kalbar and Aratula. Pets are permitted except during public holidays and long weekends.
Map refs: 155 E3, 167 F3

How to book: 688 Lake Moogerah Rd, Kalbar (07) 5463 7369

345 Yarramalong Weir

Camp on the riverbank at this basic site, 30 km east of Millmerran on the Condamine River; bring along firewood and drinking water. It's on Shire Rd (No. 96) off the Millmerran–Leyburn Rd. Millmerran is 82 km south-west of Toowoomba.
Map refs: 154 A3, 167 E3

Who to contact: Toowoomba Regional Council 13 1872

346 Yellowbank Reserve camping area (bush camping)

This campsite by the Dumaresq River is a little more difficult to access than others in the region, but it offers excellent fishing. Take the Border Rivers Tourist Dr exit from Goondiwindi and travel 25 km east. The campsite is on a bush track that leads towards the Dumaresq (dry-weather access only for conventional vehicles). **Map refs:** 166 C4

Who to contact: Miles Visitor Information Centre (07) 4627 1492

OUTBACK AND THE GULF

Remote and revered, picturesque and pristine, isolated and iconic – camping in Qld's outback and gulf country is a unique experience. Historic country towns such Mt Isa, Birdsville, Charleville, Longreach and Blackall are a springboard for campers to discover numerous national parks, reserves and fossicking fields. Winton, Cunnamulla, Cloncurry, Hughenden, Barcaldine and Normanton are the other major centres to use as bases for trekking into this vast region.

In the north-west corner, Boodjamulla (Lawn Hill) National Park is spectacular gorge country, shaped by sandstone ranges and laden with World Heritage–listed fossils. Campgrounds such as Adels Grove and Lawn Hill Gorge have excellent facilities and are heavily booked Apr–Aug.

Further south in the Channel Country lie the red sand dunes of Diamantina National Park, which has 2 campgrounds close to waterholes for excellent fishing and canoeing. Closer to Winton is Bladensburg National Park, known for its scenic

drives and spectacular views at Scrammy Gorge.

South-east of Winton, campers can pitch a tent by the waterhole at Longreach and discover Australia's aviation history at the Qantas Founders Museum or visit the Stockman's Hall of Fame. Birdsville – home of the famous Birdsville Races every Sept – is in the south-west corner of the state.

Further west is Qld's largest national park, at 1 million ha: Munga-Thirri National Park, where bush camping is permitted within 500 m of the unsealed QAA Line track. In the southern pocket, history buffs can follow the footsteps of explorers Burke and Wills at the Dig Tree camping area on Cooper Creek. Other popular camping destinations across the region include the Barcoo Riverside Camp in Blackall (home to legendary shearer Jackie Howe), bush camping by the Thompson River in Lochern National Park near Longreach, and the Normanton Tourist Park in the Carpentaria Shire.

CAMPSITES LOCATED IN PARKS AND RESERVES

BLACKBRAES RESOURCES RESERVE

This resources reserve is part of a larger complex of reserves that, combined with Blackbraes National Park, protects 52 000 ha of outback highlands. The scenery in these reserves and parks includes sandstone plateaus and escarpments, granite hills and woodlands of lemon-scented gums and ironbarks. It is 520 km north-east of Mt Isa or 380 km west of Townsville, on the Kennedy Developmental Rd.

Who to contact: NPRSR 13 7468 www.nprsr. qld.gov.au **Permits:** camping permit required **Camping fees:** fees can be paid and permits acquired at the self-registration station

347 Emu Swamp camping area (bush camping)

Bush camping is permitted beside Emu Swamp dam, 20.5 km from the park entrance on the

Kennedy Developmental Rd. There are no facilities or amenities and open fires are prohibited, so bring all self-sufficient gear, including drinking water, rubbish bags and a gas/fuel stove. **Map refs:** 187 E2

BLADENSBURG NATIONAL PARK

Situated 17 km south-west of Winton, Bladensburg National Park is a great place for a scenic drive along the River Gum route or Scrammy Dr to the spectacular lookout. Conventional vehicles can access Bladensburg during dry weather only; a high-clearance 4WD is recommended. Most of the driving roads in the park are suitable for mountain-bikers. Advance bookings are required for camping.

How to book: NPRSR 13 7468 www.nprsr.qld.gov.au **Permits:** camping permit required

348 Bough Shed Hole camping area

This campground is accessed via the Route of River Gums. Campers are encouraged not to tie ropes

Hunters Gorge, near Hunters Gorge camping area, Diamantina National Park (p.81)

to trees or drape things over vegetation, and to set up camp away from animal nests and burrows. Bring self-sufficient supplies, including drinking water and a gas/fuel stove. The campsite offers good access to Scrammy Lookout and Bladensburg Homestead. **Map refs:** 184 A3, 195 H3

BOODJAMULLA (LAWN HILL) NATIONAL PARK

In Qld's arid far north-west lies a place of such unexpected and arresting beauty that its remoteness appears to be no impediment to travellers. Lawn Hill Gorge, with its multicoloured sandstone cliffs towering over a palm-fringed, emerald-green river, is the oasis-like centrepiece of Boodjamulla National Park. The park also contains the Riversleigh World Heritage Site, an important trove of fossils. Advance bookings are required for camping.

How to book: NPRSR 13 7468 www.nprsr.qld.gov.au
Permits: camping permit required

349 **Lawn Hill Gorge camping area**

This campground for self-sufficient campers has 20 campsites adjacent to Lawn Hill Creek, about 4 km from the park entrance. Conventional vehicles can access the park May–Oct, but 4WD is recommended at all times. Only 1 vehicle per campsite is permitted; the campground is not suitable for vehicles wider than 6 m. **Map refs:** 190 C2

350 **Miymba camping area (bush camping)**

On the banks of the Gregory River, Miymba is 3.5 km south of Riversleigh D Site. Conventional vehicles can access the Riversleigh section May–Sept, but 4WD is recommended at all times. Open fires and generators are prohibited; bring a gas/fuel stove and drinking water, as the tank-water supply is unreliable. **Map refs:** 190 D2

CAMOOWEAL CAVES NATIONAL PARK

The traditional country of the Indjilandji people, Camooweal Caves National Park lies about

180 km north-west of Mt Isa, 8 km south of Camooweal along Urandangi Rd. The caves, or sinkholes as they're known, are not accessible to visitors and there are only 2 short walking tracks in the park. The park is dry-weather access only and a 4WD is recommended. Advance bookings are required for camping.

How to book: NPRSR 13 7468 www.nprsr.qld.gov.au
Permits: camping permit required

351 **Caves Waterhole camping area**

Set beside Nowranie Waterhole, about 14 km from the park entrance, the Caves Waterhole campground can be reached by conventional vehicle with difficulty – a 4WD is strongly recommended. Open fires and generators are prohibited. Bring all self-sufficient supplies, including rubbish bags, drinking water and a gas/fuel stove. **Map refs:** 190 C4

CULGOA FLOODPLAIN NATIONAL PARK

Lying on the Qld–NSW border about 130 km south-west of Dirranbandi, this national park is known for its diverse woodlands, flood plains and stony ridges. Wildlife-watchers can spot kangaroos, goannas and various bird species. Access to the park is via Goodooga in NSW.

Who to contact: NPRSR 13 7468 www.nprsr. qld.gov.au *Permits:* camping permit required
Camping fees: fees can be paid and permits acquired at the park office *Road conditions:* call Culgoa Floodplains (07) 4625 0942 before embarking

352 **Bush camping areas**

For self-sufficient campers only, bush camping is permitted at various sites throughout the park. To get here from St George, travel 160 km south to Hebel on a sealed road then 45 km south to Goodooga (impassable after rain). From Goodooga, turn right into Brenda Rd then take the left fork after the cattle grid and follow the 'Byra 7 km' sign. **Map refs:** 181 E4

CURRAWINYA NATIONAL PARK

Currawinya National Park, set in rugged mulga country, protects a significant wetland system. There are 2 large lakes, Numalla and Wyara which, together with the Paroo River and its seasonal waterholes and other smaller semi-permanent lakes, are a significant bird habitat and a wildlife refuge during drought. More than 200 bird species have been recorded here – around 280 000 birds have been recorded on the lakes at one time. In this national park you can canoe and swim in the lakes, picnic on the shores of Lake Numalla and fish at sites specified by the ranger (it is an 85 km, 4WD return trip from the ranger station to the lakes). Farming relics dot the landscape, reminders of the 1860s when the area was a pastoral property.

Who to contact: NPRSR 13 7468 www.nprsr. qld.gov.au *Permits:* camping permit required *Camping fees:* fees can be paid and permits acquired at the self-registration station

353 Caiwarro Waterhole camping area (bush camping)

This bush camping area on the south bank of the Paroo River, west of the Caiwarro Homestead ruins, is suitable only for self-sufficient and experienced bush campers. Bring your own water, rubbish bags and firewood or a gas/fuel stove. To access Caiwarro Waterhole, turn right after reaching Caiwarro Homestead from Hungerford Rd, cross the Paroo River, then turn right once more and follow the road south-west. **Map refs:** 180 B4

354 Corni Paroo Waterhole camping area (bush camping)

This bush campsite is located next to the ruins of Caiwarro Homestead, and it offers some modest facilities, such as toilets (located in the ruins) and picnic tables. Bring your own water, rubbish bags and firewood or a gas/fuel stove. Access to Corni Paroo is via Hungerford Rd, 20 km north of Hungerford, then a further 3 km east. **Map refs:** 180 B4

355 Ourimperee Waterhole camping area

Behind the Currawinya Woolshed, the Ourimperee Waterhole is accessed off the Hungerford Rd, 20 km north of Hungerford. The campground, for self-sufficient campers only, is accessible by 2WD in dry weather only. **Map refs:** 180 B4

Currawinya Woolshed, near Ourimperee Waterhole camping area, Currawinya National Park

356 Pump Hole camping area (bush camping)

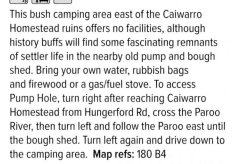

This bush camping area east of the Caiwarro Homestead ruins offers no facilities, although history buffs will find some fascinating remnants of settler life in the nearby old pump and bough shed. Bring your own water, rubbish bags and firewood or a gas/fuel stove. To access Pump Hole, turn right after reaching Caiwarro Homestead from Hungerford Rd, cross the Paroo River, then turn left and follow the Paroo east until the bough shed. Turn left again and drive down to the camping area. **Map refs:** 180 B4

DIAMANTINA NATIONAL PARK

Shaped by sandstone ranges, grass plains, waterholes and wetlands, this 500 000 ha national park lies about 300 km south-west of Winton. The scenic Warracoota Circuit drive (around 150 km) takes in historic sites and birdwatching and fishing hot spots. Travel via the Kennedy Developmental Rd if you're coming from the north; from the south, take the Diamantina Developmental Rd.

Who to contact: NPRSR 13 7468 www.nprsr. qld.gov.au *Permits:* camping permit required *Camping fees:* fees can be paid and permits acquired at the self-registration stations

357 Gum Hole camping area

This campground is 11 km past the turn-off to Hunters Gorge, about 21 km west of the ranger station on Boulia Rd. A pit toilet and self-registration station are the only facilities; pick up a drive guide brochure from the self-registration station. Bring your own drinking water and a gas/fuel stove. **Map refs:** 195 E5, 196 C1

358 Hunters Gorge camping area

The turn-off to this campground is 10 km along the Boulia–Springvale Rd from the Diamantina

National Park HQ. A further 4 km along is the Mundewerra Waterhole, a channel of the Diamantina River. A pit toilet and self-registration station are the only facilities. This is a great spot for fishing, canoeing and birdwatching. Bring your own drinking water and a gas/fuel stove. **Map refs:** 195 E5, 196 D1

FOREST DEN NATIONAL PARK

The grass plains and woodlands of Forest Den National Park are 100 km north of Aramac, reached via the Corinda turn-off from Torrens Creek Rd. The Four Mile Waterhole camping area, accessible by 4WD, is a great spot for viewing wildlife. Forest Den is relatively small by national park standards, at only 6000 ha. Advance bookings are required for camping.

How to book: NPRSR 13 7468 www.nprsr.qld.gov.au *Permits:* camping permit required

359 Four Mile Waterhole camping area

Campers must be totally self-sufficient to use this site near the banks of Torrens Creek; there are no facilities. Take the Corinda turn-off from Torrens Creek Rd; travel for 5 km to the park entrance, plus a further 5 km north to the camping area. A 4WD is strongly recommended. **Map refs:** 184 D2

IDALIA NATIONAL PARK

Set in the Gowan Range in central western Qld, Idalia National Park is a dry, remote wilderness. Although the park encompasses the headwaters of the Bulloo River and the tributaries of the Barcoo River, the waterways have wide, sandy beds that are usually dry, except following big rains. There are a number of pastoral relics, including Old Idalia, the site of an abandoned musterer's hut and stockyards. Visitors must be self-reliant. Advance bookings are recommended for camping.

How to book: NPRSR 13 7468 www.nprsr.qld.gov.au *Permits:* camping permit required *Camping fees:* if you have not booked ahead, fees can be paid and permits acquired at the self-registration station

360 Monks Tank camping area (bush camping)

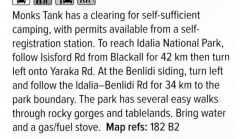

Monks Tank has a clearing for self-sufficient camping, with permits available from a self-registration station. To reach Idalia National Park, follow Isisford Rd from Blackall for 42 km then turn left onto Yaraka Rd. At the Benlidi siding, turn left and follow the Idalia–Benlidi Rd for 34 km to the park boundary. The park has several easy walks through rocky gorges and tablelands. Bring water and a gas/fuel stove. **Map refs: 182 B2**

LOCHERN NATIONAL PARK

Protecting more than 24 000 ha of habitat rich with lagoons and waterholes, Lochern National Park is 150 km south-west of Longreach and 330 km south of Winton. Take a drive along the 40 km (2–4 hr) scenic route through woodlands to the flood plains of the Thomson River. To get here, follow the signposted access off Longreach–Jundah Rd, 100 km south of Longreach.

Who to contact: NPRSR 13 7468 www.nprsr. qld.gov.au *Permits:* camping permit required *Camping fees:* fees can be paid and permits acquired at the self-registration station

361 Broadwater Waterhole camping area (bush camping)

Camping for self-sufficient campers is permitted at Broadwater Waterhole, 2 km north of the access road. There are no walking tracks, but the waterhole is a great spot for watching wildlife such as birds and turtles. Fires are prohibited; bring drinking water and a gas/fuel stove. **Map refs: 184 A5, 195 H5, 197 G1**

MARIALA NATIONAL PARK

Mariala, 128 km north-west of Charleville, is a small, remote national park known for its abundance of birdlife. Walking trails are not marked in the park, so bushwalkers need to be well equipped with a compass and maps. 4WDs are recommended on the unsealed roads.

Who to contact: NPRSR 13 7468 www.nprsr. qld.gov.au *Permits:* camping permit required *Camping fees:* fees can be paid and permits acquired at QPWS Charleville (07) 4654 4777

362 Bush camping areas

Bush camping is permitted for self-sufficient campers along Adavale–Charleville Rd in the park. Be aware that there is no ranger in the park (a permit is required before entering), the local water supply is unsuitable for drinking, and there are no facilities. Bring drinking water and a gas/fuel stove. **Map refs: 182 B4**

MOORRINYA NATIONAL PARK

Shaped by dry, flat plains and crucial water catchments, Moorrinya National Park is about 90 km south of Torrens Creek or 180 km north of Aramac on Torrens Creek–Aramac Rd. It is accessible only by 4WD during dry weather. Expect to see plenty of wildlife in the region including kangaroos, koalas, emus and dingoes. Note: the park may be closed Nov–Apr.

Who to contact: NPRSR 13 7468 www.nprsr. qld.gov.au *Permits:* camping permit required *Camping fees:* fees can be paid and permits acquired at the self-registration station

363 Moorrinya camping area (bush camping)

Self-sufficient bush camping (with a permit) is allowed near the old shearing shed, about 4.5 km from the homestead, accessible by 4WD only. Open fires and generators are not permitted. Bring water and a gas/fuel stove. **Map refs: 184 D1, 187 G5**

MUNGA-THIRRI NATIONAL PARK

The largest national park in Qld, Munga-Thirri National Park is part of the remote and unforgiving Simpson Desert, a destination for experienced outback adventurers only. Covering the intersecting borders of 3 states – Augustus Poeppel in 1884 established the corner point now known as Poeppel Corner – the park is characterised by huge sand dunes up to 50 m high, which run parallel to each other, around 1 km apart, and extend for up to 200 km. The park is closed 1 Dec–15 Mar annually due to high temperatures. Note: visitors must keep to the QAA Line. Advance bookings are required for camping.

How to book: NPRSR 13 7468 www.nprsr.qld.gov.au *Permits:* camping permit required

364 Bush camping areas

Camping is permitted in the national park only within 500 m either side of the QAA Line. Munga-Thirri is extremely remote: visitors must take a 2-way radio, spare vehicle parts, fuel and a week's worth of food and water in case of emergency. Only very experienced, self-sufficient visitors should explore the Simpson Desert. The park boundary is about 75 km west of Birdsville. **Map refs:** 193 B3

NARKOOLA NATIONAL PARK

This recently gazetted national park consists of 11 799 ha of mulga and brigalow scrub 20 km west of Bollon near the Balonne Hwy. Several sections of the park are currently recovering from their former use as farming land, and park facilities, including access roads, are still being developed.

Who to contact: QPWS Culgoa Floodplain (07) 4625 0942 *Permits:* camping permit required *Camping fees:* fees can be paid and permits acquired at any QPWS office *Road conditions:* QPWS Culgoa Floodplain (07) 4625 0942

365 Bush camping areas

Self-sufficient campers are welcome to camp in Narkoola National Park, but be aware that there are no facilities or amenities. Fires are prohibited. Bring drinking water, rubbish bags and a gas/fuel stove. **Map refs:** 181 E3

PORCUPINE GORGE NATIONAL PARK

Appearing like an oasis in the dry, flat plains north of Hughenden, Porcupine Gorge National Park features towering sandstone cliffs and a ribbon of greenery lining Porcupine Creek.

Over millions of years, this stream has eroded the surrounding basalt-capped sandstone into the deep gorge we see today; it changes from a string of pools in winter to a cascade in the wet season. The best time to visit this national park is in the cooler months of the year, as the summers can be extremely hot. Come with a 4WD in wet weather. Advance bookings are recommended for camping.

How to book: NPRSR 13 7468 www.nprsr.qld.gov.au *Permits:* camping permit required *Camping fees:* if you have not booked ahead, fees can be paid and permits acquired at the self-registration station

366 Pyramid Campground

Over time, Porcupine Creek has carved sculptures and potholes in the natural rock, the most famous of which is the Pyramid, an isolated monolith of multicoloured sandstone rising from the floor of the gorge. Pyramid Campground, with 22 sites for self-sufficient campers, is in the upper level of the gorge at the starting point for the 2.4 km return Pyramid track that leads down into the gorge. It is 500 m from the park entrance and 2.5 km from Mt Emu Plains Rd. Bring drinking water. Note: open fires and generators are not permitted. Half of the sites can be booked in advance; the other half are first-come, first-served. **Map refs:** 187 F4

THRUSHTON NATIONAL PARK

About 40 km north-east of Bollon in southern Qld, Thrushton National Park is a popular reserve for nature lovers. About 130 km north-west of St George and 190 km south of Mitchell, the park is accessible only in dry weather, and 4WD vehicles are recommended.

Who to contact: QPWS Culgoa Floodplain (07) 4625 0942 *Permits:* camping permit required *Camping fees:* fees can be paid and permits acquired at any QPWS office

367 Bush camping areas

Self-sufficient campers are welcome to camp in Thrushton National Park, but be aware that there

are no facilities or amenities and it is very rarely patrolled. Come equipped with drinking water and a gas/fuel stove, as fires are prohibited. There are no self-registration facilities at this park. **Map refs: 181 F3**

WELFORD NATIONAL PARK

On the Barcoo River, Welford National Park protects 124 000 ha and can be accessed from either Jundah, Windorah, Blackall or Quilpie. Access roads are unsealed and a 4WD is recommended; the roads are impassable when wet. The park's northern boundary is 30 km south-east of Jundah. Advance bookings are required for camping.

How to book: NPRSR 13 7468 www.nprsr.qld.gov.au
Permits: camping permit required

368 Little Boomerang Waterhole camping area

On the banks of the Barcoo River, this is a remote campground for experienced, self-sufficient campers. To get here, turn west off the Jundah–Quilpie Rd; the campground is about 10 km from the turn-off. Conventional vehicles can access this campsite in dry weather only, and 4WD is recommended at all times. Open fires are prohibited, so bring a gas/fuel stove and drinking water. **Map refs: 197 G3**

CAMPSITES LOCATED IN OTHER AREAS

369 Adels Grove

Most sites at this campground, 10 km north of Boodjamulla (Lawn Hill) National Park, have water, a fireplace and a BBQ plate, but no power is available. There is a modern amenities block and a laundry with 2 machines. Other on-site accommodation options include permanent tents and rooms with beds and linen provided. Popular

activities in the area include swimming, canoeing, fishing, birdwatching and bushwalking. Note: the bar and restaurant on site are open for breakfast, lunch and dinner. **Map refs: 190 D2**

How to book: Lot 3 Lawn Hill Rd, Lawn Hill (07) 4748 5502 www.adelsgrove.com.au

370 Albert River camping area (bush camping)

Bush camping for self-sufficient campers is permitted on the banks of the Albert River north-east of Burketown; there are no designated sites and no facilities. The Western Gulf region of Qld has a mixture of sealed and maintained unsealed roads; checking with local authorities for road conditions is recommended. The best time to travel is during the dry season (May–Oct). **Map refs: 188 D4**

Who to contact: Burketown Visitor Information Centre (07) 4745 5111

371 Aramac Caravan Park

This campground is next to the Aramac Showgrounds on Booker St in Aramac. There are some powered sites and laundry facilities are available. Aramac is part of the Barcaldine Regional Council, 440 km west of Rockhampton, one of the largest cattle-producing regions in central west Qld. **Map refs: 184 D4**

Who to contact: Barcaldine Regional Council (07) 4651 3311 *Camping fees:* fees can be paid at the council offices in Gordon St, Aramac

372 Barcaldine Tourist Park

About 1.5 km from the centre of town on Box St (Matilda Hwy), this tourist park with drive-through grassy sites has an excellent range of facilities including wireless internet, and free use of the washing machines and iron. The town centre offers plenty of restaurants and shops. Barcaldine is about 100 km east of Longreach and about

100 km north of Blackall. Ensuite cabins are also available on site. **Map refs: 184 D5**

How to book: 51-65 Box St, Barcaldine (07) 4651 6066, 1300 658 251 www.barcaldinetouristpark.com.au

373 Barcoo River camping area

Camping is permitted beside the Barcoo River in Isisford. The camping area has a toilet block; the nearby park has an amenities block with showers. The Barcoo River offers excellent fishing, camping, canoeing and birdwatching. Isisford is about 120 km west of Blackall and about 85 km south of Ilfracombe. **Map refs: 182 A1**

Who to contact: Longreach Regional Council, Isisford branch (07) 4658 8900

374 Barcoo Riverside Camp

Caravan-based campers with self-contained facilities can use the clearing on the northern side of the Barcoo River, about 500 m from the centre of Blackall. All visitors must register at the information centre on Shamrock St. On the Landsborough Hwy, 108 km south of Barcaldine, Blackall features a statue of sheep shearer Jackie Howe, who in 1892 set a world record by shearing 321 sheep with hand shears in under 8 hours. **Map refs: 182 C2**

Who to contact: Blackall Visitor Information Centre (07) 4657 4637 *Camping fees:* fees can be paid at the visitor centre, 145A Shamrock St, or at the self-registration station

375 Birdsville Caravan Park

Make sure to book well ahead (at least 6 months) for powered sites at this caravan park during the Birdsville Races in Sept, and bookings are recommended Mar–Nov. The park, on Florence St, covers an area of about 12 ha, with plenty of unpowered sites if you miss out. The internet

cafe has 2 computers; BBQs are coin-operated. No pets are allowed during race week. Birdsville is reached from the north via Bedourie (187 km), from the east via Windorah (380 km) and from the south along the Birdsville Track from Marree in SA (519 km). **Map refs: 193 D4, 196 A4**

How to book: 1 Florence St, Birdsville (07) 4656 3214 www.birdsvillecaravanpark.com

376 Boulia Caravan Park

This spacious, grassy caravan park with 40 powered sites is on the eastern banks of the Burke River, on the Diamantina Developmental Rd. In addition to caravan and camping sites, the park offers unit accommodation with ensuites, 1 self-contained cabin and laundry facilities. Bring your own firewood. Boulia is 288 km south of Mt Isa and 363 km west of Winton. **Map refs: 192 D4, 194 C4**

How to book: Winton Rd, Boulia (07) 4746 3320

377 Burke and Wills Roadhouse

This roadhouse with 12 powered sites sits at the junction of Wills Developmental Rd and Burke Developmental Rd, about 180 km north of Cloncurry and about 200 km south of Normanton. The camping surface is a mixture of grass and dirt. Bring your own firewood. **Map refs: 191 G2**

Who to contact: Burke Developmental Rd, Four Ways (07) 4742 5909

378 Burketown Caravan Park

This caravan park in Burketown, about 225 km west of Normanton, has excellent facilities: tourist and fishing information, 2 amenities blocks, laundry facilities, EFTPOS and a kiosk. There are also self-contained air-conditioned units and standard rooms for 4–6 people. Crocodiles make the waterways dangerous for all activities except fishing, but you can cool off in the council-owned pool. The Western Gulf region of Qld has a mixture of sealed and maintained unsealed roads; check road conditions before heading off. **Map refs:** 188 D4

How to book: Sloman St, Burketown (07) 4745 5118

379 Cameron Corner camping area

An expansive camping area covering about 240 ha, Cameron Corner fees go to the Royal Flying Doctor Service. Firewood and other basic supplies are available at the on-site store. Cameron Corner is where the Qld, NSW and SA borders meet. A 4WD is recommended. **Map refs:** 198 D5

How to book: Cameron Corner Store (08) 8091 3872

380 Cooper Creek camping area (bush camping)

Bush camping for self-sufficient campers is offered 6 km east of the Thomson Developmental Rd, north-east of Windorah in Barcoo Shire. The shire's primary river systems are the Thomson and Barcoo, which join above Windorah to flow into Cooper Creek. This site can be accessed by conventional vehicles in dry weather only. **Map refs:** 197 F3

Who to contact: Windorah Visitor Information Centre (07) 4656 3063

381 Dajarra Campground

This basic campground with an amenities block including hot showers is on the Diamantina Developmental Rd at Dajarra, a small community 140 km south of Mt Isa. Bring in your own drinking water. **Map refs:** 192 D2, 194 C2

Who to contact: Jimberella Co-Op (07) 4748 4828

382 Dig Tree camping area

Hugely popular with tourists passing through, this historic site is where explorers Burke and Wills were expecting to meet the remainder of their 1861 expedition party; however, all they found was a blazed tree and a limited amount of supplies buried. Burke later died under the tree. The campground is beside Cooper Creek with signposted access off the Adventure Way. For supplies, including drinking water, travel 55 km south-west to Innamincka, SA. Dogs are permitted if you advise the ranger in advance. **Map refs:** 198 D2

Who to contact: Dig Tree Ranger (07) 4655 4323

383 Discovery Holiday Parks – Cloncurry

Those looking for a taste of outback history will revel in Cloncurry, the town famous for launching the first-ever Royal Flying Doctor Service flight. This hoiday park offers a range of modern conveniences, including a kiosk, laundry and swimming pool. Advance bookings are recommended. **Map refs:** 191 G5

How to book: McIlwraith St (Flinders Hwy), Cloncurry (07) 4742 2300, 1800 635 559 www.discoveryholidayparks.com.au/qld/outback_queensland/cloncurry

384 Discovery Holiday Parks – Mount Isa

This caravan park in the heart of Mt Isa, with a swimming pool, internet access and laundry, offers a refreshing slice of civilisation deep in the outback. Nearby attractions include mine tours and the Riversleigh Fossil Centre. Advance bookings are recommended. **Map refs:** 191 E5

How to book: 185–195 Little West St, Mt Isa (07) 4743 4676, 1800 456 661 www.discoveryholidayparks.com.au/qld/outback_queensland/mount_isa

385 Duck Creek camping area (bush camping)

Self-sufficient bush camping is permitted in the opal fields of Duck Creek, about 60 km south-east of Toompine and 130 km south of Quilpie. Check road conditions before setting off, as access is dry weather only for conventional vehicles. **Map refs:** 180 B2

Who to contact: Quilpie Visitor Information Centre (07) 4656 0540 *Permits:* camping and fossicking permits required *Camping fees:* fees can be paid and permits acquired from the Quilpie Visitor Information Centre

386 Explorers Caravan Park

This campground has 25 powered sites, more than 20 unpowered sites, plus the option of 6 ensuite cabins or 4 standard rooms. The camp kitchen is well equipped, but you need to bring firewood. Laundry facilities are available. Thargomindah is 185 km west of Cunnamulla and 195 km south of Quilpie. **Map refs:** 180 A3, 199 H3

How to book: 88 Dowling St, Thargomindah (07) 4655 3307

387 Fishermans Rest camping area

This riverside campground for self-sufficient campers is 4 km west of Mitchell, 500 m off the Warrego Hwy. Mitchell is on the Maranoa River, 90 km west of Roma and 180 km east of Charleville. **Map refs:** 181 G1, 183 G5

Who to contact: Mitchell Visitor Information Centre (07) 4624 6923

388 Hells Gate Roadhouse

Open only during the dry season (Apr–Sept/Oct), this roadhouse is 180 km west of Burketown and 48 km east of the NT border. The Western Gulf region has a mixture of sealed and maintained

John Dick's carving of Burke's face in the Face Tree, near Dig Tree camping area (p. 86)

unsealed roads; check with the roadhouse for road conditions. Visitors have access to laundry facilities. **Map refs:** 188 B4

How to book: Savannah Way (07) 4745 8258
Road conditions: (07) 4745 8258

389 Hughenden Allan Terry Caravan Park

This charming council-owned caravan park in the small town of Hughenden offers modern, clean amenities and facilities, including a laundry, kiosk and even carwash facilities. Resolution St is off the Flinders Hwy. **Map refs:** 187 E5

How to book: Resolution St, Hughenden (07) 4741 1190

390 Jericho Showground Caravan Park

Campers passing through the hamlet of Jericho will be delighted to find a campsite with comprehensive facilities at the showground. It is on Showground Rd, off the Capricorn Hwy. **Map refs:** 185 F5

Who to contact: Barcaldine Regional Council, Jericho office (07) 4651 4188 *Camping fees:* fees can be paid at the self-registration station

391 Jundah Caravan Park

You'll find this caravan park on Miles St in Jundah, near the town park and swimming pool. There are on-site laundry facilities; a dump point is availble 800 m away on Longreach Rd. Jundah is part of Barcoo Shire, a remote council in central western Qld. **Map refs:** 197 G2

Who to contact: Jundah Visitor Information Centre (07) 4658 6930

392 Karumba Point Tourist Park

This caravan park has an excellent range of facilities, including a swimming pool, craft shop,

2 amenities blocks, fish-cleaning areas and laundry facilities. Air-conditioned, on-site caravans are available. You'll find it on Col Kitching Dr (the road to Karumba Point) in Karumba, a popular destination for barramundi fishing at the mouth of the Norman River. Bookings are required for May–Aug. **Map refs:** 189 F4

How to book: 2 Col Kitching Dr, Karumba (07) 4745 9306 www.karumbapoint.com.au

393 Kingfisher Camp

Kingfisher Camp is 42 km west of the Savannah Way, and a further 126 km from Burketown. The campground has 30 grassed, shaded sites at one end of a 5 km waterhole. Each campsite has its own fireplace and water tap (boil or treat before drinking). Generators are permitted. The Western Gulf region of Qld has a mixture of sealed and maintained unsealed roads; checking with local authorities for road conditions is recommended. The best time to travel is during the dry season. **Map refs:** 188 B5

How to book: Bowthorn Station Rd, Lawn Hill (07) 4745 8212 www.kingfisherresort.com.au

394 Leichhardt Camping Park

About 800 m from the Norman River on the Normanton–Croydon Rd (Savannah Way), 26 km east of Normanton. There are no powered sites here but campers are encouraged to bring their own generators. You need to boil or treat water before drinking. Normanton, the major commercial centre of the Carpentaria Shire, is popular with barramundi anglers. The town is about 380 km north of Cloncurry and 680 km west of Cairns. **Map refs:** 189 F4

How to book: Savannah Way (07) 4745 1330, 0487 675 173

395 Long Waterhole camping area (bush camping)

Self-sufficient campers can stay at this site, but be aware that there is no power, water or facilities.

The camping area is reached from the Winton–Jundah Rd, about 2 km south of Winton. While you're here, head into town to visit the Waltzing Matilda museum. **Map refs:** 184 A3, 195 H3

Who to contact: Winton Visitor Information Centre (07) 4657 1466

396 Longreach Caravan Park

This holiday park provides a comfortable stay in one of central Qld's popular tourist towns. Facilities include 2 swimming pools, 3 spas, a mini mart, wireless broadband internet or internet kiosks, free electric BBQs and 3 amenities blocks. Caravan sites have electricity, water and sullage points. Also, check out the Stockman's Hall of Fame and the Qantas Founders Museum. **Map refs:** 184 C4

How to book: 180 Ibis St, Longreach (07) 4658 1770 www.longreachcaravanpark.com.au

397 Longreach Waterhole camping area

The Longreach Waterhole is reached from the Landsborough Hwy, about 4 km north-west of Longreach. There's a toilet block, picnic tables and shelters in the adjacent day-use area, but you need to be totally self-sufficient to stay here. To get here from Longreach, take the hwy towards Winton, then turn east to the motorcross track; the camping area is north, by the river. **Map refs:** 184 C4

Who to contact: Longreach Visitor Information Centre (07) 4658 3555

398 Major Mitchell Campground

This campsite, 45 km north of Mitchell on Forestvale Rd, is of tremendous historical significance to the Maranoa region, as it is where Sir Thomas Livingstone Mitchell based his camp while exploring the region during his fourth expedition. Toilet facilities and sheltered

wood BBQs are provided, but you will need to bring your own drinking water and firewood. **Map refs:** 183 G4

Who to contact: Mitchell Visitor Information Centre (07) 4624 6923

399 Major Mitchell Caravan Park

This caravan park has a total of 67 sites, including 47 powered sites and 16 ensuite sites. On the Warrego Hwy in Mitchell, close to town, the park's other on-site accommodation options include 3 cabins and 2 overnight vans. Mitchell is beside the Maranoa River, 90 km west of Roma and 180 km east of Charleville. **Map refs:** 181 G1, 183 G5

How to book: Warrego Hwy, Mitchell (07) 4623 6600 www.majormitchellcaravanpark.com.au

400 Muttaburra Caravan Park

Muttaburra Caravan Park is on Bridge St in Muttaburra, about 85 km north-west of Aramac. Muttaburra is part of the Barcaldine Regional Council, one of the largest cattle-producing regions in central western Qld. **Map refs:** 184 C3

Who to contact: Barcaldine Regional Council (07) 4658 7191 *Camping fees:* pay at the Muttaburra Library, Bridge St

401 Neil Turner Weir camping area

This camping area is on River St in Mitchell by the Maranoa River. If you're a keen angler, check out Fishermans Rest. Mitchell is 90 km west of Roma and 180 km east of Charleville on the Warrego Hwy. **Map refs:** 181 G1, 183 G5

Who to contact: Maranoa Regional Council 1300 007 662

402 Normanton Tourist Park

This park has 55 powered sites, 25 unpowered sites, 12 ensuite cabins and 5 budget rooms. Facilities include a lap pool, artesian spa bath and 3 amenities blocks. Normanton is about 380 km north of Cloncurry and 680 km west of Cairns. Bookings are recommended for Apr–Aug. **Map refs:** 189 F4

How to book: 14 Brown St, Normanton (07) 4745 1121, 1800 193 469 www.normantontouristpark.com.au

403 Oma Waterhole camping area

The Oma Waterhole for self-sufficient campers is set beside the Barcoo River on Yaraka Rd, 13 km south of Isisford. The river offers excellent fishing, camping, canoeing and birdwatching. Isisford is about 120 km west of Blackall and 85 km south of Ilfracombe. **Map refs:** 182 A1, 197 H1

Who to contact: Longreach Regional Council, Isisford branch (07) 4658 8900

404 Opalton Field camping area

The Opalton Field is one of the largest and most extensively worked opal deposits in Qld. The camping area is about 110 km south of Winton; the turn-off is signposted on Jundah Rd, 15 km south of Winton (dry-weather access only for conventional vehicles). Bring firewood and drinking water. If you wish to fossick, obtain a permit through Queensland Mining and Safety's Winton office, (07) 4657 1727. **Map refs:** 195 H4

Who to contact: Opalton Outpost (07) 4657 1418 *Permits:* fossicking permit required *Camping fees:* fees can be paid at the honesty box

405 Redbank Park camping area

Jericho's free campsite is by the banks of the Jordan Creek. Turn onto Davy St from Edison St (Blackall–Jericho Rd) and follow it over the levee. A donation system helps cover the cost of maintaining the facilities. **Map refs:** 185 F5

Who to contact: Barcaldine Regional Council, Jericho office (07) 4651 4188

406 Sheep Station Creek camping area (bush camping)

Self-sufficient bush camping is permitted in the opal fields of Sheep Station Creek, about 60 km south-east of Toompine and 130 km south of Quilpie. Check road conditions before arriving, as access is dry weather only. **Map refs:** 180 B2

Who to contact: Quilpie Visitor Information Centre (07) 4656 0540 *Permits:* camping and fossicking permits required *Camping fees:* fees can be paid and permits acquired from the Quilpie Visitor Information Centre

407 Southern Cross Caravan Park

Southern Cross Caravan Park is in the tiny settlement of Hungerford, on the Qld–NSW border. The campground is in the centre of town near the pub, which doubles as a general store and fuel station. Hungerford is about 120 km south of Eulo on the Thargomindah–Cunnamulla Rd and about 100 km north of Wanaaring in NSW. **Map refs:** 180 A4

Who to contact: Royal Mail Hotel, Hungerford (07) 4655 4093

408 Stonehenge Caravan Park

This caravan park is on the corner of Salisbury and Stratford sts in Stonehenge, part of Barcoo Shire, a remote council in central western Qld. Bring your own firewood. **Map refs:** 197 G2

Who to contact: Stonehenge Visitor Information Centre (07) 4658 5857

409 Thomson River camping area (bush camping)

This site for self-sufficient campers is beside the Thomson River, west of Jundah on Thomson Developmental Rd. **Map refs:** 197 G2

Who to contact: Jundah Visitor Information Centre (07) 4658 6930

410 Top Six Mile camping area (bush camping)

This bush site for self-sufficient campers is beside the Thomson River, 14 km north of Jundah on the Thomson Developmental Rd. **Map refs:** 197 G2

Who to contact: Jundah Visitor Information Centre (07) 4658 6930

411 Wallam Creek camping area

This campground for self-sufficient campers is by the creek in Bollon, on the Balonne Hwy, 112 km west of St George. Hot showers are located a short walk away, opposite the Bollon pub. **Map refs:** 181 F3

Who to contact: St George Shire Visitor Information Centre (07) 4625 4996

412 Ward River camping area (bush camping)

The Ward River bush camping area is on the east side of the river on Quilpie Rd, about 20 km west of Charleville. Visitors must be totally self-sufficient; there are no amenities block and no powered sites. To get here, follow Quilpie Rd west from Charleville for 19 km, then turn right onto the dirt track to the camping area (dry-weather access only for conventional vehicles). **Map refs:** 182 D5

Who to contact: Charleville Visitor Information Centre (07) 4654 3057

413 Wilson River camping area

This campground is beside the Wilson River, just across the road from the Noccundra Hotel, 141 km west of Thargomindah. The amenities block with toilet and hot showers is next to the hotel. Campers must be totally self-sufficient. **Map refs:** 199 F3

Who to contact: Thargomindah Information Centre (07) 4655 3399 *Camping fees:* gold-coin donation for use of amenities block

414 Windorah Caravan Park

There are laundry facilities at this caravan park on Diamantina Developmental Rd (Maryborough St) in Windorah, part of Barcoo Shire. There is a dump point 800 m away. The primary river systems here are the Thomson and Barcoo, which merge above Windorah to become Cooper Creek. **Map refs:** 197 F3

Who to contact: Windorah Visitor Information Centre (07) 4656 3063

415 Yaraka Town Caravan Park

This small caravan park for self-sufficient visitors is behind the Yaraka Town Hall, next to the Yaraka Hotel. There are 3 sites available (free of charge) with concrete slabs, power and water. Yaraka is about 100 km south-west of Isisford and 160 km west of Blackall. **Map refs:** 182 A2, 197 H2

Who to contact: Longreach Regional Council, Isisford branch (07) 4658 8900

Crystal Creek, Paluma Range
National Park (p. 111)

THE MID-TROPICS

Grab your snorkel and flippers – the Mid-Tropics is the jumping-off point for the magical tropical islands of the Whitsundays and Great Barrier Reef. Plush resorts and hotels are scattered along the coastline, but many campgrounds in this region have prime positions even closer to the beaches and offshore reefs that you'll be exploring. Campers can pitch a tent behind the dazzling white silica sands of Whitehaven Beach on Whitsunday Island – a completely undeveloped beach typically visited via a boat or helicopter daytrip – or set up camp on Hinchinbrook Island, Australia's largest island national park.

Visitors to the region can go snorkelling amid kaleidoscopic corals, brightly coloured fish, turtles and dugongs, or take a daytrip to the outer reef for once-in-a-lifetime scuba diving. The beaches are sensational for soaking up the sunshine, and sailboat cruises take you around the islands to some of the best snorkelling locations. Beach camping clearings such as those on Hook Island

are quiet, secluded, mostly free from tourist traffic and offer sensational snorkelling just metres from your tent. Other national parks with island-based campgrounds include Family, Gloucester, Goold, Hinchinbrook, Lindeman, Molle, Newry and Orpheus islands.

On the mainland, the southern section of Eungella National Park near Mackay is a popular destination for daytrippers and campers. Visitors can set up camp beside Broken River, go bushwalking or try spotting a platypus in the river. North-west of Eungella is the large Eungella Dam, a popular camping and fishing venue for barramundi. About 50 km north of Mackay, Cape Hillsborough National Park has scenic walking tracks to lookouts, picnic areas and broad beaches. Other highly recommended camping spots on the mainland include Mission Beach Caravan Park south of Innisfail, Ball Bay Campground north of Mackay and Platypus Bush Camp at Finch Hatton Gorge.

CAMPSITES LOCATED IN PARKS AND RESERVES

ABERGOWRIE STATE FOREST

The tropical rainforests and pine plantations of Abergowrie State Forest, in the Herbert River Valley, lie about 45 km west of Ingham via Trebonne. Visitors enjoy the 1.6 km return Rainforest Walk (30 min) and the 3 km return Creek Walk (1 hr), where you can cool off in pools along Broadwater Creek near the Wet Tropics World Heritage Area boundary. Advance bookings are required for camping.

How to book: NPRSR 13 7468 www.nprsr.qld.gov.au
Permits: camping permit required
Road conditions: 13 1905

416 Broadwater camping area

Endangered riparian rainforest lines the clear waters of Broadwater Creek, and open eucalypt

forest dominates the visitor areas in Broadwater campground, 47 km west of Ingham and 16 km of unsealed road from the forest entrance. This is a cool and pleasant place for family camping, with a large grassy picnic area and plenty of wildlife, including the vulnerable rufous owl and the spectacular, but endangered, southern cassowary. Bring old sneakers if you want to take a dip – poisonous bullrout fish inhabit the creek. You need to treat or boil the water before use, and bring firewood. Check road conditions during the wet season (Dec–Apr), when roads may be closed temporarily, and drive carefully, as logging trucks also use access roads. **Map refs:** 160 D2, 172 A1, 175 G5, 187 H1

BOWLING GREEN BAY NATIONAL PARK

A spectacular nature reserve with more than 55 000 ha of rugged landscapes, Bowling Green Bay National Park is 28 km south of Townsville. Highlights include the Alligator Creek area, a popular spot for family picnics, and for serious hikers there's the challenging 17 km return track to Alligator Falls, with stunning mountain views along the way. Advance bookings are required for camping.

How to book: NPRSR 13 7468 www.nprsr.qld.gov.au
Permits: camping permit required

417 Alligator Creek camping area

Just 600 m from the main access gate, near the day-use picnic area, this site is a great base to explore around the creek area, hike along the Alligator Falls track, or go fishing – all the while keeping an eye out for wildlife such as rock wallabies and brush-tail possums. The campground is only suitable for tents and small campervans. Gas BBQs are located in the day-use picnic area. Tap water needs to be boiled or treated before use. This camping area can be very crowded in holiday periods. Note: the main gate to the camping and picnic area is open 6.30am to 6.30pm daily. **Map refs:** 172 B2

418 Alligator Falls camping area (walk-in camping)

This bush camping site, 8 km from the main Alligator Creek camping area in the Mt Elliot section, is suitable for self-sufficient campers only. It has room for a maximum of 6 campers. Bring water and a gas/fuel stove. **Map refs:** 172 B3

419 Barratta Creek camping area (bush camping)

This bush camping site, near the town of Jerona in the Bowling Green Bay section, is suitable for self-sufficient campers only. There are 7 campsites, and 8 campers are permitted per site. It can only be accessed by 4WD. Check tide times before embarking and avoid travelling 2 hrs either side of high tide. Bring water and a gas/fuel stove. **Map refs:** 172 C3

420 Bush camping areas (walk-in camping)

Remote bush camping in undefined spots is available for experienced and self-sufficient hikers in the Mt Elliot and Mt Cleveland areas of the park. There is a limit of 6 hikers per group and hikers must set up camp at least 1 km from other camping areas and other groups. Bring water and a gas/fuel stove. **Map refs:** 172 B3

421 Cockatoo Creek camping area (walk-in camping)

This bush camping site, 2 km from the main Alligator Creek camping area in the Mt Elliot section, is suitable for self-sufficient campers only. It has room for a maximum of 6 campers. Bring water and a gas/fuel stove. **Map refs:** 172 B2

422 Cocoa Creek camping area (bush camping)

This bush camping area, off Cape Cleveland Rd in the Cape Cleveland section, is suitable for self-sufficient campers only. There are 7 campsites, and 8 campers are permitted per site. It can be accessed by conventional vehicles only during dry weather. Bring water and a gas/fuel stove. **Map refs:** 161 H5, 172 B2

423 Salmon Creek camping area (bush camping)

This bush camping area, 6 km along the beach from the town of Cungulla in the Cape Cleveland section, is suitable for self-sufficient campers only. There are 6 campsites, and 8 campers are permitted per site. It can only be accessed by 4WD. Check tide times before embarking and avoid travelling 2 hrs either side of high tide. Bring water and a gas/fuel stove. **Map refs:** 161 H5, 172 C2

BRAMPTON ISLANDS NATIONAL PARK

Located 32 km north of Mackay, Brampton Islands National Park encompasses 2 islands, Brampton and Carlisle. From open eucalypt forests on the islands' ridges to the fringing coral reefs, these traditional lands of the Indigenous Ngaro people are rich with wildlife. Beware of marine stingers Oct–May. Advance bookings are required for camping.

How to book: NPRSR 13 7468 www.nprsr.qld.gov.au
Permits: camping permit required

424 **Neils camping area**
(boat-based camping)

Bush camping is permitted on Carlisle Island, at the entrance to the Whitsunday Passage. Toilets and picnic shelters are the only facilities, so bring all self-sufficient supplies. The surrounding coral reefs provide excellent snorkelling but beware of marine stingers Oct–May. **Map refs:** 159 E4, 173 F5

BROAD SOUND ISLANDS NATIONAL PARK

The 116 km long string of 48 islands that comprises Broad Sound Islands National Park stretches east from Flock Pigeon Island, which is 129 km south-east of Mackay. The park protects a variety of wildlife and environments, including most of the flatback turtle's east coast nesting habitat. Access to Broad Sound Islands is by private boat only; the more far-flung islands are rarely patrolled and should be tackled only by seasoned sailors. Advance bookings are required for camping.

How to book: NPRSR 13 7468 www.nprsr.qld.gov.au
Permits: camping permit required

425 **Aquila Island camping area**
(boat-based camping)

Camping is permitted on Aquila Island, 16 km north-east of the town of Clairview. There are no facilities provided and fires are prohibited, so bring all self-sufficient camping gear, including drinking water, rubbish bags and a gas/fuel stove. **Map refs:** 170 D2

426 **Flock Pigeon Island camping area**
(boat-based camping)

Camping is permitted on Flock Pigeon Island, 3 km east of Clairview. There are no facilities provided and fires are prohibited, so bring all self-sufficient camping gear, including drinking water, rubbish bags and a gas/fuel stove. **Map refs:** 170 D2

427 **Hexham Island camping area**
(boat-based camping)

Camping is permitted on Hexham Island, 35 km north-east of Stanage Bay, adjacent to Shields Island. There are no facilities provided and fires are prohibited, so bring all self-sufficient camping gear, including drinking water, rubbish bags and a gas/fuel stove. Note: as this campsite is remote, bring extra supplies and plan for all eventualities. **Map refs:** 171 E2

428 **High Peak Island camping area**
(boat-based camping)

Camping is permitted on High Peak Island, 180 km south-east of Mackay. There are no facilities provided and fires are prohibited, so bring all self-sufficient camping gear, including drinking water, rubbish bags and a gas/fuel stove. Note: as this campsite is very remote, bring extra supplies and plan for all eventualities. **Map refs:** 171 E2

429 **Shields Island camping area**
(boat-based camping)

Camping is permitted on Shields Island, 35 km north-east of Stanage Bay, adjacent to Hexham Island. There are no facilities provided and fires are prohibited, so bring all self-sufficient camping gear, including drinking water, rubbish bags and a gas/fuel stove. Note: as this campsite is remote, bring extra supplies and plan for all eventualities. **Map refs:** 171 E2

BYFIELD CONSERVATION PARK

Adjacent to Byfield National Park, this conservation park is noted for its coastal scenery, enormous sand dunes and eucalypt woodlands.

It is accessible by 4WD through Byfield National Park's main section. A popular walking activity is the Five Rocks track (up to 2 hr return) that follows Findlays Creek and leads to the beach. Advance bookings are required for camping.

How to book: NPRSR 13 7468 www.nprsr.qld.gov.au
Permits: camping permit required

430 Five Rocks camping area

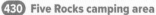

This is the only campground in both the Byfield National Park and Conservation Park with facilities; generators are permitted. There are 12 numbered campsites; timber pallets are available to use as a camp surface. It is 28 km east of Water Park Creek and accessed through the national park's main section; a 4WD vehicle is required. From here you can go fishing or take a dip in the surf. The water should be boiled or treated before drinking. **Map refs: 171 F3**

BYFIELD NATIONAL PARK

Known for its massive sand dunes that stretch up to 6 km inland, Byfield National Park protects 15 000 ha of scenic and diverse landscapes. It is about 70 km north-east of Rockhampton and 43 km north of Yeppoon. Experienced bushwalkers have a range of signed trails to explore, and fishing enthusiasts can throw a line in at Nine Mile Beach, Water Park Point or at the end of Sandy Point Rd. Advance bookings are required for camping.

How to book: NPRSR 13 7468 www.nprsr.qld.gov.au
Permits: camping permit required

431 Nine Mile Beach camping area (bush camping)

Nile Mile Beach is a top spot for fishing, but there are no facilities at this campground so you need to be totally self-sufficient. Accessible by 4WD or boat, it is 27 km east of Water Park Creek and about 6 km south of the Nine Mile Access Track. Small generators (65 dBA or quieter) are permitted between 8am and 7pm. **Map refs: 171 E4**

432 Scouts camping area (bush camping)

Accessible only by boat or walking at low tide from Corio Bay carpark, this small campground on the northern side of Corio Bay has room for just 20 campers and no facilities. It's suitable for self-sufficient campers only; small generators (65 dBA or quieter) are permitted between 8am and 7pm. Note: if you're walking along the beach, it takes about 2 hrs to reach the campground. **Map refs: 171 F4**

BYFIELD STATE FOREST

Go bushwalking through magnificent rainforests, view rare wildlife or have a relaxing picnic by the creek – Byfield State Forest offers a beautiful natural setting for a range of recreational activities. About 34 km north of Yeppoon, the forest has scenic easy-to-moderate walking tracks, some good spots for fishing, and excellent day-use areas. Note: swimming is not permitted in some areas, as estuarine crocodiles have been seen in Water Park Creek. Advance bookings are required for camping.

How to book: NPRSR 13 7468 www.nprsr.qld.gov.au
Permits: camping permit required

433 Red Rock camping area

Camp under the pine trees at this grassy campground 1 km along the turn-off signed on Byfield Rd, just before the Byfield Forestry office. Small generators (65 dBA or quieter) are permitted between 8am and 7pm and open fires are allowed in existing fireplaces – bring your own wood. Water is available here but must be boiled or treated before drinking. Note: this is the only campground in the forest that allows pets; dogs must be on a leash at all times. **Map refs: 171 E4**

434 Upper Stony camping area

Adjacent to Stony Creek, this campground is in a great location, close to swimming areas and bushwalking tracks. There are 18 numbered sites and some are suitable for vans and camper trailers. Automated BBQs are in the day-use area or you can use the built-in fireplaces (bring your own milled timber). The campground is 11 km from Byfield Rd, along a gravel road turn-off. Bring plenty of insect repellent and sunscreen, and treat or boil the water before drinking. **Map refs:** 171 E4

435 Water Park Creek camping area

Water Park Creek has 14 secluded walk-in campsites close to the Bowenia rainforest bushwalking circuit (1.2 km return, 2 hrs). Swimming is not permitted here. The campground is 4 km from the turn-off signed on Byfield Rd, and a short walk from the carpark area. Small generators (65 dBA or quieter) are permitted between 8am and 7pm. Bring your own firewood as well as a gas/fuel stove. The water should be boiled or treated before use. The nearest shop is

in Byfield township, 2 km north of the turn-off to Water Park Creek. **Map refs:** 171 E4

CAPE HILLSBOROUGH NATIONAL PARK

Cape Hillsborough National Park is renowned for its beautiful beaches nestled between rocky headlands. Rhyolite boulders are scattered over the sand, the result of volcanic activity millions of years ago. Home to the Yuipera people for thousands of years, the cape got its European name in 1770 when Captain James Cook named it after the Earl of Hillsborough. Advance bookings are required for camping at Smalleys Beach.

How to book: Cape Hillsborough Nature Resort (07) 4959 0152 www.capehillsboroughresort.com.au; or NPRSR 13 7468 www.nprsr.qld.gov.au for Smalleys Beach camping area *Permits:* camping permit required for Smalleys Beach

436 Cape Hillsborough Nature Resort

This private enterprise tucked away inside Cape Hillsborough National Park offers a pocket of modern amenities and creature comforts while surrounded by wilderness. There's a laundry, internet access and book exchange, as well as

Dawn at Cape Hillsborough National Park

unparalleled access to the park's walking trails. To get here, turn off the Bruce Hwy at Yakapari, Kuttabul or Mt Ossa and follow the signs. **Map refs:** 158 D4, 170 C1, 173 F5

437 Smalleys Beach camping area

The gravel road to Smalleys Beach is signposted about 6 km along Cape Hillsborough Rd, 50 km north-west of Mackay. The campground offers plenty of shade under eucalypt trees and there are 11 numbered sites. The nearby Great Barrier Reef Marine Park permits boating and fishing, but beware of estuarine crocodiles, box jellyfish and marine stingers, which are common Oct–May. Generators are not permitted at the campground. Fires are allowed in off-ground fire containers only – bring your own wood – but a gas/fuel stove is preferred. **Map refs:** 158 D4, 173 F5

CAPE PALMERSTON NATIONAL PARK

The rocky headlands, rainforests and sand dunes of Cape Palmerston National Park lie 115 km south-east of Mackay. There are 3 bush campgrounds in the park, some great spots for fishing, and you can walk to Cape Palmerston for beautiful views of Northumberland Isles and Mt Funnel. Access is by 4WD only via Cape Palmerston Rd, off Greenhill Rd from Ilbilbie, on the Bruce Hwy. Advance bookings are required for camping.

How to book: NPRSR 13 7468 www.nprsr.qld.gov.au
Permits: camping permit required

438 Bush camping areas

Bush camping is permitted in the fore dunes along the eastern coast of Cape Palmerston. There are no facilities or amenities provided, so bring all self-sufficient camping gear, including drinking water, rubbish bags and a raised fire container/brazier – bring your own wood – or a gas/fuel stove. **Map refs:** 170 D1

439 Cape Creek campsite

Cape Creek is to the south-west of Cape Palmerston. For self-sufficient campers, it is accessible by 4WD only via a sandy track. Fires are permitted if you bring your own raised fire container/brazier – bring your own wood; gas/fuel stoves are recommended. **Map refs:** 170 C2

440 Windmill Bay campsite

This basic site for self-sufficient campers is south of Cape Palmerston on the eastern edge of the park. Access is by 4WD only via a sandy track. Fires are permitted in raised fire containers/braziers – bring your own wood – but gas/fuel stoves are preferred. **Map refs:** 170 C2

CAPE UPSTART NATIONAL PARK

Known for its granite outcrops and sandy beaches, Cape Upstart National Park is a large headland north of Bowen and south of Ayr. With no access for vehicles, camping is boat-based only. There are ramps at Elliot River near Guthalungra and at Molongle Creek, south of Gumlu. Advance bookings are required for camping.

How to book: NPRSR 13 7468 www.nprsr.qld.gov.au
Permits: camping permit required

441 Coconut Beach camping area (boat-based camping)

Coconut Beach has no facilities and suits self-sufficient campers. Access is by boat only; beware of marine stingers Oct–May and beware of estuarine crocodiles year-round. The campground is surrounded by the waters of the Great Barrier Reef Marine Park; anglers should check zoning and regulations before casting off. **Map refs:** 172 D3

CATHU STATE FOREST

Take a scenic drive to the Clarke Range Lookout, enjoy a relaxing bush picnic or simply sit back and enjoy views of the Whitsunday islands – Cathu State Forest has much to offer campers and daytrippers. Cathu is 72 km north of Mackay or 51 km south of Proserpine, and Jaxut is 12 km off the Bruce Hwy.

Who to contact: NPRSR 13 7468 www.nprsr.qld. gov.au **Permits:** camping permit required **Camping fees:** fees can be paid and permits acquired at the self-registration station

442 Jaxut camping area

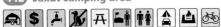

This camping area is next to Pandanus Creek at Jaxut, about 200 m past the old forest station. Access is via the Cathu–O'Connell River Rd, a very steep road suitable for small caravans and camper trailers only. Campers should bring firewood and water, or treat/boil the tap water provided. Cathu State Forest is known as a particularly good location for birdwatching, with more than 100 species inhabiting the area. **Map refs:** 158 B4, 173 E5

CHARON POINT CONSERVATION PARK

Located 44 km north of Marlborough, Charon Point Conservation Park encompasses the southern side of the mouth of the Styx River, famous for its massive tides and fast tidal currents. These features make it an attractive spot for professional fishers and crabbers. Advance bookings are required for camping.

How to book: NPRSR 13 7468 www.nprsr.qld.gov.au **Permits:** camping permit required

443 Beach camping area (bush camping)

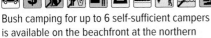

Bush camping for up to 6 self-sufficient campers is available on the beachfront at the northern tip of Charon Point. No facilities are provided, so bring your own drinking water, rubbish bags and firewood or (preferably) a gas/fuel stove. **Map refs:** 170 D3

444 Boat Ramp camping area (bush camping)

As its name might suggest, Boat Ramp camping area is located near the beach next to one of Charon Point's 2 boat ramps. Up to 6 self-sufficient campers can stay here. No facilities are provided, so bring your own drinking water, rubbish bags and firewood or (preferably) a gas/fuel stove. **Map refs:** 170 D3

445 Meadow Camp (bush camping)

Meadow Camp is located slightly inland, to the south of Boat Ramp campsite, but still very close to its own boat launch. Up to 6 self-sufficient campers can stay here. No facilities are provided, so bring your own drinking water, rubbish bags and firewood or (preferably) a gas/fuel stove. **Map refs:** 170 D3

CONWAY NATIONAL PARK

Bushwalking trails through beautiful, lush rainforests and beach tracks with scenic ocean views can be explored in Conway National Park. In particular, the Mt Rooper track has excellent views of the Whitsunday Passage; allow 2.5 hrs for the 5.4 km circuit. To reach the national park from Airlie Beach, follow Shute Harbour Rd south-east for 6.5 km. Conway State Forest was incorporated into Conway National Park in July 2012, and the park now contains the entirety of the Whitsunday Great Walk, a challenging 30 km, 3-day, 1-way walk for experienced hikers and campers. Advance bookings are required for camping.

How to book: NPRSR 13 7468 www.nprsr.qld.gov.au **Permits:** camping permit required

446 Swamp Bay camping area (walk-in camping)

Walk 2.1 km from the Swamp Bay/Mt Rooper carpark to this campground overlooking

Daydream Island (accessible only by foot or boat). A pit toilet, shelter shed and picnic tables are the only facilities, so you need to bring all self-sufficient goods and equipment. Keen bushwalkers should check out the Swamp Bay walking track (2.1 km, 1 hr), which links to the scenic Mt Rooper track. Beach fishing is permitted at Swamp Bay and Coral Beach (check the regulations). **Map refs:** 158 C2, 173 E4

Whitsunday Great Walk

///// *Please note that campsites are listed in alphabetical order, not track order. Refer to the map on p. 158 for further information.*

447 **Bloodwood camping area** (walk-in camping)

Hikers on the Whitsunday Great Walk can camp at this site, 11.5 km (5–6 hrs) from Repulse Creek camp and 8.5 km from the end of the walk at Airlie Beach. The track from Repulse Creek follows a ridge to the summit of Mt Hayward and continues to Bloodwood Camp, with picturesque views beyond Jubilee Pocket to the Whitsunday islands. Bring a gas/fuel stove. **Map refs:** 158 C2, 173 E4

448 **Bush camping areas** (walk-in camping)

Experienced and self-sufficient hikers looking for a little extra challenge on the Whitsunday Great Walk can camp at 2 bush campsites, 1.8 and 3 km beyond Repulse Creek campsite (or 11.3 and 10.1 km respectively from Bloodwood campsite). No facilities are supplied, so bring your own water and a gas/fuel stove. **Map refs:** 158 C2, 173 E4

449 **Repulse Creek camping area** (walk-in camping)

Experienced hikers and campers can walk 8.3 km from the Brandy Creek carpark along the Whitsunday Great Walk to reach this site (allow 3.5–4.5 hr). Along the way, look out for

rare wildlife such as the buff-breasted paradise-kingfisher and leaf-tail gecko. Toilets, picnic tables and tank water are the only facilities; bring all self-sufficient goods and equipment. **Map refs:** 158 C2, 173 E4

CREDITON STATE FOREST

Protecting stately rose gums and relics of gold mining from the 1880s, Crediton State Forest possesses a quiet rural charm. The Mackay Highlands Great Walk passes through this forest. Crediton is 80 km west of Mackay and 8 km south of Eungella. Advance bookings are required for camping.

How to book: NPRSR 13 7468 www.nprsr.qld.gov.au
Permits: camping permit required

450 **Crediton Hall camping area**

This spacious campsite on a grassy hill, 14.7 km south-east of Eungella, offers camping for up to 24 people. To reach it, turn off Eungella Dam Rd 8 km south of Eungella and follow Crediton Loop Rd 6.7 km to the camping area. Crediton Hall is a designated campsite on the Mackay Highlands Great Walk, and is 11.2 km from Fern Flat camping area (Eungella National Park) and 19.5 km from Denham Range camping area. The water must be boiled or treated before drinking. **Map refs:** 158 B5, 170 B1, 173 E5

451 **Denham Range camping area**

This camping area, near the border of Homevale National Park, offers cooling breezes and excellent views from its ridge-top location. There are few facilities, so bring self-sufficient camping equipment, including water (or boil/treat the water provided) and a gas/fuel stove. To reach it, turn off Eungella Dam Rd 14.7 km south of Eungella and follow Cockies Creek Rd 23.7 km to the campsite. Denham Range is a designated campsite on the Mackay Highlands Great Walk, and is 19.5 km from Crediton Hall camping area and 16.2 km from Moonlight Range camping area (Homevale National Park). **Map refs:** 158 B5, 170 B1, 173 E5

452 The Diggings camping area

The forest here still contains relics from goldmining exploration during the 1880s. Self-sufficient campers can use this site near Eungella Dam Rd. There are no facilities, so bring drinking water, rubbish bags and firewood or a gas/fuel stove. **Map refs:** 158 B5, 170 B1, 173 E5

DALRYMPLE NATIONAL PARK

Situated 42 km north of Charters Towers, Dalrymple National Park's main feature is the Burdekin River, which provides a seasonal habitat for waterbirds and makes the spot ideal for birdwatchers. The old Dalrymple township, one of the first inland settlements in northern Australia, can also be found in the park. Advance bookings are required for camping.

How to book: NPRSR 13 7468 www.nprsr.qld.gov.au
Permits: camping permit required

453 Burdekin River camping area (bush camping)

Camp on the banks of the Burdekin River here, just 700 m from the entrance to the park. This site suits self-sufficient campers only; there are no facilities. Open fires are prohibited and generators are not permitted. Note: the road is often impassable for conventional vehicles in wet weather, Nov–Mar. **Map refs:** 172 A3, 187 H3

DRYANDER NATIONAL PARK

Accessible by boat from Airlie Beach or Dingo Beach, this national park overlooks the Whitsunday islands and Great Barrier Reef Marine Park. Visitors should check fishing and boating permissions in the marine park and beware of marine stingers Oct–May. Advance bookings are required for camping.

How to book: NPRSR 13 7468 www.nprsr.qld.gov.au
Permits: camping permit required

454 Grimstone Point camping area (boat-based camping)

This low-key, quiet campground is accessible by boat only. Pit toilets and picnic tables are the only facilities here so bring all self-sufficient goods and equipment (including insect repellent). **Map refs:** 158 C1, 173 E4

EUNGELLA NATIONAL PARK

In the rugged Clarke Range, high above the surrounding plains, this mountainous national park is rent by deep gorges and contains large tracts of both tropical and subtropical rainforest. Isolated from similar forests for at least 30 000 years, this important rainforest refuge supports around 860 plant species and some unique wildlife, including the critically endangered Eungella day frog, the rare Eungella tinkerfrog and the Eungella honeyeater. Advance bookings are required for camping.

How to book: NPRSR 13 7468 www.nprsr.qld.gov.au
Permits: camping permit required

455 Fern Flat camping area (walk-in camping)

This campground, 5 km south of Eungella, is just 600 m from the carpark and picnic area at Broken River. The site has toilets and water (which must be boiled or treated before use), but you'll need to visit the picnic area for information, BBQs and picnic tables. It is a designated campsite on the Mackay Highlands Great Walk, 10 km from Pine Grove carpark, the walk's trailhead, and 11.2 km from Crediton Hall camping area (Crediton State Forest). **Map refs:** 158 B5, 170 B1, 173 E5

FAMILY ISLANDS NATIONAL PARK

Part of the Great Barrier Reef World Heritage Area, this national park embraces a group of islands off the coast north of Cardwell, and is accessible via boat from Mission Beach. The park is about 130 km south-east of Cairns. The Bandjin and Djiru people are the traditional owners of the land. Advance bookings are required for camping.

How to book: NPRSR 13 7468 www.nprsr.qld.gov.au
Permits: camping permit required

456 Coombe Island camping area (boat-based camping)

Fancy staying at your own exclusive, secluded bush campground? This site, about 13 km east of Tully Heads, only permits 1 group at a time. There are, however, no facilities here so you'll need to be completely self-sufficient. Note: private boat access is from Mission Beach. **Map refs: 161 E1, 163 G5, 175 G5**

457 Dunk Island camping area

This campground is on the west coast of Dunk Island, with 9 designated sites provided. Dunk has 13 km of scenic walking tracks; you can trek through rainforests, complete a circuit of the island or enjoy beautiful views from the summit of Mt Kootaloo. The island also offers excellent swimming and snorkelling opportunities. Note: at the time of printing this campsite was closed owing to cyclone damage. The NPRSR website will advise when the site has re-opened. **Map refs: 163 G5, 175 G4**

458 Wheeler Island camping area (boat-based camping)

Located 12 km east of Tully Heads, Wheeler Island is accessible by private boat from Mission Beach. The campground's only facilities are pit toilets and picnic tables, so campers will need to bring all self-sufficient goods and equipment, including drinking water and a gas/fuel stove. **Map refs: 161 E1, 163 G5, 175 G5**

GIRRAMAY NATIONAL PARK

Girramay National Park lies in the foothills of the Kirrama Range, and consists of 2 sections: Edmund Kennedy, 5 km north of Cardwell, and Murray Falls, 41 km north-west of Cardwell. One of the region's prettiest waterfalls, the 10 m Murray Falls can be admired from a river boardwalk leading from the camping area. The campground is signposted off the Bruce Hwy, 14 km south of Tully. Advance bookings are required for camping.

How to book: NPRSR 13 7468 www.nprsr.qld.gov.au
Permits: camping permit required

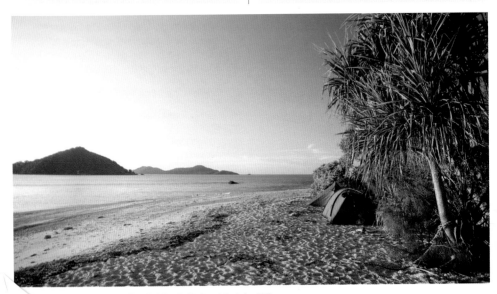

~ing on Coombe Island, Family Islands National Park (p. 101)

459 Murray Falls camping area

Campers here can enjoy the 930 m walk through a rainforest gully that leads into open forest and finishes with amazing views over the falls and Murray Valley. The first 75 m section of the boardwalk at the top end of the campground is wheelchair accessible. There is swimming at the day-use area. Bring drinking water and firewood. **Map refs:** 160 C1, 163 F5, 175 F5

GIRRINGUN NATIONAL PARK

Girringun National Park, part of the traditional lands of the Warrgamaygan people, comprises 4 sections: Wallaman Falls, Mt Fox, Blencoe Falls and Dalrymple Gap Walking Track. The Wallaman Falls section in the Herbert River Valley is the most accessible; Wallaman Falls plunges 300 m off the Seaview Range, making it the longest single-drop waterfall in Australia. The gorge here supports rainforest with palms, umbrella trees and figs, while around the rim grow casuarinas, eucalypts and grasstrees. Camping is not permitted along Dalrymple Gap Walking Track; the nearest campsite is Broadwater camping area in Abergowrie State Forest. The Wet Tropics Great Walk, a network of 5 connected walking tracks, winds through this park. Advance bookings are required for camping.

How to book: NPRSR 13 7468 www.nprsr.qld.gov.au
Permits: camping permit required

460 Blencoe Falls camping area

This remote site for totally self-sufficient campers is set beside Blencoe Creek, 81 km west of Cardwell. 4WD is recommended, but stay on the marked tracks, as damaging vegetation can incur penalties. Bring drinking water and firewood. To get here, travel along Kirrama Range Rd, off Kennedy Creek Rd from the Bruce Hwy at Kennedy. Blencoe Falls is a designated campsite on the Wet Tropics Great Walk; it is 10.5 km from Blanket Creek camping area on the Juwun and Jambal walks. **Map refs:** 160 B1, 175 F5, 187 G1

461 Wallaman Falls camping area

This campground is beside the Stony Creek picnic area – a great place for spotting platypus. It's 51 km west of Ingham, off the Abergowrie Rd at Trebonne. Check out the Banggurru circuit walk while you're here, an easy 1 km track, or try the 4 km Djyinda walk. Bring your own firewood or, preferably, a gas/fuel stove. Water here must be boiled or treated before use. **Map refs:** 160 C3, 172 A1, 175 F5, 187 H1

Wet Tropics Great Walk

Please note that campsites are listed in alphabetical order, not track order. Refer to the map on p. 160 for further information.

462 Blanket Creek camping area (walk-in camping)

This bush campsite for self-sufficient hikers by the Herbert River is shaded by she-oaks. No facilities are provided and open fires are prohibited, so bring all self-sufficient gear, including drinking water, rubbish bags and a gas/fuel stove. It is 10.5 km from Blencoe Falls camping area and 33.5 km from Yamanie camping area on the Juwun and Jambal walks. Note: do not swim in the river, as crocodiles inhabit it. **Map refs:** 160 C1, 175 F5, 187 H1

460 Blencoe Falls camping area
  See opposite.

463 Herbert River Gorge camping area (walk-in camping)

Intrepid hikers taking the strenuous Juwun walk can camp anywhere along the 26.5 km stretch of the Herbert River Gorge between Blanket Creek and Orange Tree. No facilities are provided and open fires are prohibited, so bring all self-sufficient gear, including drinking water, rubbish bags and a gas/fuel stove. Note: do not swim in the river, as crocodiles inhabit it. **Map refs:** 160 C2, 175 F5, 187 H1

464 Pack Trail camping area
(walk-in camping)

This campsite on the Buujan Quiinbiira and Djagany walks offers sweeping views over the Herbert River Valley, but few facilities aside from composting toilets. Bring all self-sufficient gear, including drinking water, rubbish bags and a gas/fuel stove. Open fires are prohibited. It is 13.9 km from Stony Creek camping area, 15.2 km from Yamanie camping area and 23.3 km from Wallaman Falls camping area. **Map refs:** 160 C2, 172 A1, 175 F5, 187 H1

465 Stony Creek camping area
(walk-in camping)

This campsite on the Djagany and Gugigugi walks is in open woodland beside Stony Creek. There are no facilities except for a composting toilet and open fires are prohibited, so bring all self-sufficient gear, including drinking water, rubbish bags and a gas/fuel stove. It is 13.9 km from Pack Trail camping area, 18.7 km from Yamanie camping area and 19.6 km from the Henrietta gate pick-up point. **Map refs:** 160 C2, 172 A1, 175 F5, 187 H1

461 Wallaman Falls camping area

See p. 103.

466 Yamanie camping area
(bush camping)

Bush camping along the banks of the Herbert River is permitted at this site, 54 km west of Ingham. Access to the area is by 4WD or via the Wet Tropics Great Walk, and campers need to be completely self-sufficient. Fires and generators are not permitted and no rubbish bins are provided. The campsite functions as a collection point for hikers on the Wet Tropics Great Walk, and is 7 km from the southern end of Herbert River Gorge camping area at Orange Tree on the Juwun walk, 15.2 km from Pack Trail camping area on the Buujan Quiinbiira walk and 18.7 km from Stony Creek camping area on the Gugigugi walk. Note: estuarine crocodiles inhabit the waters surrounding this camping area. **Map refs:** 160 C2, 175 F5, 187 H1

GLOUCESTER ISLANDS NATIONAL PARK

One of the most remote national parks in the Whitsunday region, the Gloucester Islands are east of Bowen and north of Airlie Beach. Camping is allowed at 3 of the islands – Gloucester, Saddleback and Armit. To get here, catch a commercial or private boat from Shute Harbour at Airlie Beach or Dingo Beach. Advance bookings are required for camping.

How to book: NPRSR 13 7468 www.nprsr.qld.gov.au
Permits: camping permit required

467 Armit Island camping area
(boat-based camping)

This campground in the south-west corner of the island has space for 12 totally self-sufficient campers. Access to the southern beach and Little Armit Island is prohibited Oct–Mar each year, for regeneration. Remember to go slow when boating, report marine strandings and not collect coral or shells. **Map refs:** 158 B1, 173 E4

468 Bona Bay camping area
(boat-based camping)

This large shaded campground, with beach views, is on the south-west side of Gloucester Island. The site can hold up to 36 campers, making it suitable for large groups, but you need to be completely self-sufficient. The surrounding waters are part of the Great Barrier Reef World Heritage Area; some fishing and collecting activities are not permitted. **Map refs:** 158 B1, 173 E3

469 East Side Bay camping area
(boat-based camping)

This site is on the east side of Gloucester Island between 2 rocky headlands and adjacent to a seasonal freshwater lagoon. It's a small campground suitable for a maximum of 6 people and there are no facilities. **Map refs:** 158 B1, 173 E3

470 Saddleback Island camping area (boat-based camping)

On the western side of Saddleback Island, this campground has space for 12 people. The only facilities are picnic tables, so you need to bring all self-sufficient goods and equipment. **Map refs:** 158 B1, 173 E3

GOOLD ISLAND NATIONAL PARK

Goold Island's close proximity to Cardwell (17 km north-east) makes it a good choice for camping. The surrounding waters are great for waterskiing and boating, but be wary, as estuarine crocodiles are present in the area. Fishing is not permitted in the freshwater creeks on the island. Access to Goold Island is by private boat or ferry service from Cardwell. Advance bookings are required for camping.

How to book: NPRSR 13 7468 www.nprsr.qld.gov.au
Permits: camping permit required

471 Southern Beach camping area (boat-based camping)

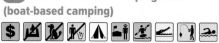

Intrepid adventurers can reach this secluded spot (up to 6 campers) on the east side of Goold Island only by sea kayak – there are no ferry services and powered boats are forbidden. There are no facilities and open fires are prohibited, so bring all self-sufficient gear, including drinking water, rubbish bags and a gas/fuel stove. **Map refs:** 161 E1, 163 G5, 175 G5

472 The Spit (Western Beach) camping area (boat-based camping)

This site on the island's west coast has a maximum capacity of 50 campers; the surface is sand and grass and there are some shady trees. Walkers can attempt the beach walk around the coastline of Goold Island, extending for 13 km (5 hr), at low tide only. Generators are not permitted at the campground. Bring drinking water and a gas/fuel stove, as the BBQ should not be relied upon. **Map refs:** 161 E1, 163 G5, 175 G5

473 Wilderness Cove camping area (boat-based camping)

Boaties will relish this secluded beach campsite, accessible only to private boats (no ferry services). There's room for 12 campers on the dunes here, but there are no facilities and open fires are prohibited, so bring all self-sufficient gear, including drinking water, rubbish bags and a gas/fuel stove. **Map refs:** 161 E1, 163 G5, 175 G5

HINCHINBROOK ISLAND NATIONAL PARK

A tropical island with stunning postcard-perfect scenery, Hinchinbrook is Australia's largest island national park. Off the north Qld coast, 8 km east of Cardwell, Hinchinbrook is home to sweeping sandy beaches, rainforests and rugged mountains, dugongs, green turtles and other marine life. For hikers, one of the main attractions is the 32 km (3–5 day) Thorsborne Trail on the island's east coast. Advance bookings are required for camping.

How to book: NPRSR 13 7468 www.nprsr.qld.gov.au
Permits: camping permit required

474 Agnes Beach camping area (boat-based camping)

This campsite for self-sufficient campers and accessible only by boat, lies between Little Ramsay Bay and Zoe Bay. It is closed Apr–Sept to protect nesting seabirds. There are no facilities and fires are prohibited; bring all self-sufficient camping gear, including drinking water, rubbish bags and a gas/fuel stove. **Map refs:** 161 E2, 172 A1, 175 G5

475 Banksia Bay camping area (bush camping)

This campsite for self-sufficient campers and accessible only by boat or via the Thorsborne Trail, lies between Little Ramsay Bay and Zoe Bay, close to Agnes Beach. There are no facilities and fires are prohibited; bring all self-sufficient camping gear, including drinking water, rubbish bags and a gas/fuel stove. **Map refs:** 161 E2, 172 A1, 175 G5

476 Banshee Bay camping area (boat-based camping)

This campsite for self-sufficient campers and accessible only by boat, is on the north-east of the island, just south of Cape Sandwich. There are no facilities and fires are prohibited; bring all self-sufficient camping gear, including drinking water, rubbish bags and a gas/fuel stove. **Map refs:** 161 E1, 172 A1, 175 G5

477 Blacksand Beach camping area (boat-based camping)

This campsite for self-sufficient campers and accessible only by sea kayak, is at the southern end of Ramsay Bay, near Nina Peak. There are no facilities and fires are prohibited; bring all self-sufficient camping gear, including drinking water, rubbish bags and a gas/fuel stove. **Map refs:** 161 E2, 172 A1, 175 G5

478 George Point camping area

This campground for self-sufficient campers is 7.5 km south of Mulligan Falls at the southern trackhead of the Thorsborne Trail. It can also be accessed by private boat or sea kayak. Water can be collected from Mulligan Falls. A maximum 2-night stay applies. **Map refs:** 161 E2, 172 A1, 175 G5

479 The Haven (Scraggy Point) camping area (boat-based camping)

The Haven is on the west coast of the island in Hinchinbrook Channel. Access is by charter or private boat and there is a maximum 7-night stay. Bring all supplies for self-sufficient camping. **Map refs:** 160 D2, 172 A1, 175 G5, 187 H1

480 Mulligan Bay camping area (boat-based camping)

This campsite for self-sufficient campers and accessible only by boat, is on the south-east of the island, north of George Point. There are no facilities and fires are prohibited; bring all self-sufficient camping gear, including drinking water, rubbish bags and a gas/fuel stove. **Map refs:** 161 E2, 172 A1, 175 G5

481 North Macushla camping area (boat-based camping)

This campsite, on the north of the island, is a 100 m walk away from South Macushla, and has less well-developed facilities. It can only be accessed by boat. Bring drinking water, rubbish bags and a gas/fuel stove. **Map refs:** 161 E1, 172 A1, 175 G5

482 North Zoe Bay camping area (boat-based camping)

The North Zoe Bay camping area has no facilities and there is a maximum 2-night stay. Access is by private boat only, subject to weather conditions. Bring all self-sufficient supplies. **Map refs:** 161 E2, 172 A1, 175 G5

483 South Macushla camping area (boat-based camping)

North and South Macushla camping areas are just 100 m apart in the north of the island, on the east coast of Missionary Bay, and are accessed by boat. A maximum 7-night stay applies here. Bring drinking water and a gas/fuel stove. **Map refs:** 161 E1, 172 A1, 175 G5

484 South Zoe Bay camping area

South Zoe Bay is 10.5 km south of Little Ramsay Bay and 7.5 km north of Mulligan Falls on the Thorsborne Trail. There is a maximum 2-night stay. Water from the nearby creek must be boiled or treated before use. Bring all self-sufficient supplies with you. **Map refs:** 161 E2, 172 A1, 175 G5

485 Sunken Reef Bay camping area (bush camping)

There are no facilities at this campground, on the Thorsborne Trail between South Zoe Bay and Mulligan Falls, so be prepared to be self-sufficient. Sunken Reef Bay can also be accessed by sea kayak. Water from the nearby creek must be boiled or treated before drinking. The maximum stay is 2 nights. **Map refs:** 161 E2, 172 A1, 175 G5

486 Sunset Beach camping area (boat-based camping)

This campsite on the north-east of the island, just west of Cape Sandwich, is accessible only by boat. There are no facilities and fires are prohibited; bring all self-sufficient camping gear, including drinking water, rubbish bags and a gas/fuel stove. **Map refs:** 161 E1, 172 A1, 175 G5

Thorsborne Trail

Please note that campsites are listed in alphabetical order, not track order. Refer to the map on p. 161 for further information.

475 Banksia Bay camping area (bush camping)

See p. 105.

478 George Point camping area

See p. 106.

487 Little Ramsay Bay camping area (walk-in camping)

This site on the Thorsborne Trail is 2.5 km south of Nina Bay camping area and 10.5 km north of South Zoe Bay camping area. Water from the nearby creek must be boiled or treated before drinking. The site is gas/fuel stove only. A maximum 2-night stay applies. **Map refs:** 161 E2, 172 A1, 175 G5

488 Mulligan Falls camping area (walk-in camping)

With a 1-night maximum stay, Mulligan Falls campground is 7.5 km south of South Zoe Bay camping area, 1 km south of Diamantina Creek and 7.5 km north of George Point camping area on the Thorsborne Trail. Water from the nearby creek must be boiled or treated before drinking. Bring all self-sufficient supplies. **Map refs:** 161 E2, 172 A1, 175 G5

489 Nina Bay camping area (walk-in camping)

Nina Bay has a maximum 2-night stay. It is 4 km south of the Ramsay Bay trackhead for the Thorsborne Trail and 2.5 km north of Little Ramsay Bay. Creek water must be boiled or treated before drinking. **Map refs:** 161 E2, 172 A1, 175 G5

484 South Zoe Bay camping area

See opposite.

485 Sunken Reef Bay camping area (bush camping)

See opposite.

HOMEVALE NATIONAL PARK

The dramatic landscape of Homevale National Park – full of cliffs, peaks and spires – was formed through volcanic activity over 30 million years ago. Older still are the fossil sites from the Permian period (225–280 million years ago) that the park protects. The park currently houses dry softwood scrub, open eucalypt forests and brigalow trees. Advance booking is required for camping.

How to book: NPRSR 13 7468 www.nprsr.qld.gov.au
Permits: camping permit required

490 Moonlight Dam camping area

This tranquil camping area lies at the edge of Moonlight Dam, 70 km south-west of Mackay. There are few facilities besides pit toilets and tap water (treat or boil before drinking), but it offers spectacular wildlife-watching as birds descend on the dam at dusk to drink. To get here, head north 6 km along the Peak Downs Hwy from Nebo, turn left onto Nebo–Glenden Rd, then right onto Turrawulla Rd, and follow this to the signed intersection for Moonlight Dam. Moonlight Dam is a designated campsite on the Mackay Highlands Great Walk and is 16.2 km from Denham Range camping area (Credition State Forest) and 5.5 km to the Great Walk entry at Mt Britton. **Map refs:** 170 B1

LINDEMAN ISLANDS NATIONAL PARK

With humpback whales and dolphins often spotted from the shore, Lindeman Island is a tropical paradise surrounded by waters with stunning marine life that is sure to make your stay memorable. Lindeman Islands National Park is within the Great Barrier Reef Marine Park and is accessible via boat from Shute Harbour or Laguna Quays. Advance bookings are required for camping.

How to book: NPRSR 13 7468 www.nprsr.qld.gov.au
Permits: camping permit required

491 Boat Port camping area (boat-based camping)

Once used as a location for cleaning sailing vessels, this quiet campground on Lindeman Island with room for 12 campers is a world away from Club Med. Backing onto rainforest, there are no facilities here, so you'll need to bring all self-sufficient supplies, including drinking water and a gas/fuel stove, with you on the 25 km boat

ride from Shute Harbour. There is, however, 20 km of walking tracks to explore – perfect for keen hikers. **Map refs:** 158 D2, 173 F4

492 Neck Bay camping area (boat-based camping)

A good stopover for kayakers, this small campground on the north-west side of Shaw Island has space for about 12 campers. All visitors must be completely self-sufficient, as there are no facilities at the site; bring drinking water and a gas/fuel stove. Shaw Island is approximately 40 km south-east of Shute Harbour. **Map refs:** 158 D2, 173 F4

MIA MIA STATE FOREST

Scenic drives, trail-bike tracks, creek swimming and peaceful bush camping are some of the attractions in Mia Mia State Forest, in the foothills of the Clarke Range west of Mackay. Access is by 4WD only; the gravel access road is closed in wet weather and high fire-danger periods.

Who to contact: QPWS Mackay (07) 4944 7800
Permits: camping permit required *Camping fees:* fees can be paid and permits acquired at QPWS Mackay

493 Captain's Crossing camping area

Camp beside lovely Teemburra Creek at this campground and picnic spot. There are no facilities; bring all self-sufficient supplies, including drinking water, rubbish bags and a gas/fuel stove. Access is by 4WD only. **Map refs:** 158 C5, 170 B1, 173 E5

MOLLE ISLANDS NATIONAL PARK

Lying 10 km from Airlie Beach off the Qld coast, Molle Islands National Park has superb walking tracks and circuits with beautiful views and lookouts, picturesque swimming spots and, best of all, excellent snorkelling, particularly off South Molle Island. Access is by private or commercial boat from Airlie Beach or Shute Harbour. Advance bookings are required for camping.

How to book: NPRSR 13 7468 www.nprsr.qld.gov.au
Permits: camping permit required

494 Cockatoo Beach camping area
(boat-based camping)

This campground is at the southern end of North Molle Island. The site holds a maximum of 24 people and suits self-sufficient campers only; bring water and a gas/fuel stove.
Map refs: 158 C2, 173 E4

495 Denman Island camping area
(boat-based camping)

Denman Island, east of South Molle Island, has a small campsite with a sand and rubble surface, and is suitable for a maximum for 4 people. The island is 6.5 km east-north-east of Shute Harbour and can be accessed at low or high tide. Bring water and a gas/fuel stove. Note: fishing is not permitted. **Map refs:** 158 C2, 173 E4

496 Paddle Bay camping area
(boat-based camping)

Overlooking Daydream Island, Paddle Bay is a well-shaded site connected to the 11.5 km walking track system at the north-western tip of South Molle Island, 500 m from Bauer Bay resort. The maximum number of campers is 12. Generators are not permitted; bring a gas/fuel stove and water. South Molle Island's Mt Jeffreys walk is 5.6 km return (3 hr) taking you to the island's highest point. **Map refs:** 158 C2, 173 E4

497 Planton Island camping area
(boat-based camping)

Planton Island, east of South Molle Island, has a small campground for 4 people behind the beach. Composting toilets are the only facilities, so you need to bring all self-sufficient supplies. **Map refs:** 158 C2, 173 E4

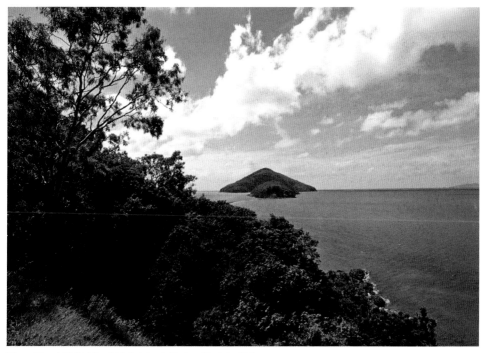

View of South Molle Island, Molle Islands National Park (p. 108)

498 Sandy Bay, Long Island camping area (boat-based camping)

Not to be confused with the Sandy Bay campground on South Molle Island, this small campground on Long Island is close to a mangrove creek – bring insect repellent! Also bring all self-sufficient supplies, including drinking water and a gas/fuel stove. **Map refs:** 158 C2, 173 E4

499 Sandy Bay, South Molle Island camping area (boat-based camping)

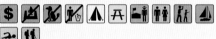

Reachable only by boat at mid-high tide, this campground on the west side of South Molle Island is connected to the rest of the island by a 11.5 km walking track system. One of South Molle's most popular walks is the Spion Kop track, a 2 hr, 4.4 km return walk taking you through rainforest to spectacular lookouts. The clearing can hold a maximum of 36 self-sufficient campers; bring water and a gas/fuel stove. Generators are not permitted. **Map refs:** 158 C2, 173 E4

500 Tancred Island camping area (boat-based camping)

Just 1 km from Shute Harbour, this campground has no facilities and suits self-sufficient campers only. A maximum of 6 campers per night is permitted. **Map refs:** 158 C2, 173 E4

NEWRY ISLANDS NATIONAL PARK

The exposed headlands, sandstone cliffs and sandy beaches of Newry Islands National Park lie off the coast of Seaforth, about 48 km north of Mackay. The islands are teeming with wildlife and its surrounding waters, home to dugongs, are part of the Great Barrier Reef World Heritage Area. Access to the park is via private boat only, with nearby boat ramps located at Seaforth, Mackay Marina, Murray Creek and Laguna Keys. Advance bookings are required for camping.

How to book: NPRSR 13 7468 www.nprsr.qld.gov.au
Permits: camping permit required

501 Newry Island camping area (boat-based camping)

This open campsite had a past life as the grounds of a resort, but now offers splendid camping for up to 36 people. Visitors can explore the remains of the resort or use the campsite as a base for exploring the other islands of the Newry group. Campers should take drinking water, rubbish bags and a gas/fuel stove. **Map refs:** 158 C4, 173 E5

502 Outer Newry Island camping area (boat-based camping)

This campground is on Outer Newry Island's south-west coast. If you're lucky you might see some amazing birdlife on the island, including brahminy kites, ospreys and white-bellied sea eagles. Campers should take fresh water, a gas/ fuel stove and insect repellent. Generators are prohibited and all rubbish should be taken back to the mainland. **Map refs:** 158 C4, 173 F5

503 Tug's Point camping area (boat-based camping)

Camping is permitted on Rabbit Island's south-east coast, where you'll find a gas BBQ and a few other basic facilities such as picnic tables and a shelter shed. Bring drinking water. There's excellent wildlife-watching on the island – try spotlighting for possums at night. Note: insect repellent is a must for Rabbit Island; beware of marine stingers and estuarine crocodiles. **Map refs:** 158 C4, 173 E5

NORTHUMBERLAND ISLANDS NATIONAL PARK

Ranging 45–90 km off the coast of Mackay, this undeveloped and little-known national park protects several islands of the Northumberland Islands group (which also includes the Percy Isles and Broad Sound Islands). Access is via private boat only, and should only be attempted

by those with high levels of seagoing ability –
there are significant navigational challenges.
Advance bookings are required for camping.

How to book: NPRSR 13 7468 www.nprsr.qld.gov.au
Permits: camping permit required

504 North Beach camping area (boat-based camping)

This site on Curlew Island, 82 km south-east of
Mackay, offers camping for up to 6 self-sufficient
campers. There are no facilities, so bring all self-
sufficient gear, including drinking water, rubbish
bags and a gas/fuel stove. **Map refs:** 170 D2

505 Prudhoe Island camping area (boat-based camping)

This site on Prudhoe Island, 54 km south-east of
Mackay, offers camping for up to 6 self-sufficient
campers. There are no facilities, so bring all self-
sufficient gear, including drinking water, rubbish
bags and a gas/fuel stove. **Map refs:** 159 F5,
170 D1, 173 G5

ORPHEUS ISLAND NATIONAL PARK

The caves, headlands and rock formations in
Orpheus Island National Park, 110 km north of
Townsville and 45 km east of Ingham, have been
a source of fascination for geologists for many
years. The park offers picturesque picnic and
day-use areas, superb wildlife-watching and
lovely camping areas. The closest boat ramp
is at Taylors Beach, 25 km from Ingham, and
charter boat access is from Dungeness (Lucinda),
23 km to the north-west. Advance bookings are
required for camping.

How to book: NPRSR 13 7468 www.nprsr.qld.gov.au
Permits: camping permit required

506 Pioneer Bay camping area (boat-based camping)

This small campground on the north-west coast
has a clearing for up to 12 people. Composting
toilets and picnic tables are the only facilities,

so bring all self-sufficient supplies, including
drinking water and a gas/fuel stove. Fishing is not
permitted in certain areas. Note: stinging jellyfish
may be present in the surrounding waters during
the warmer months. **Map refs:** 161 F3, 172 B1,
175 G5

507 South Beach camping area (boat-based camping)

This campground on the south-east coast has no
facilities and suits self-sufficient campers only.
Generators and open fires are not permitted: bring
everything necessary. Note: the reefs and waters
surrounding Orpheus Island National Park are
protected within the Great Barrier Reef Marine
Park, so check for permission before boating or
fishing. **Map refs:** 161 F3, 172 B1

508 Yanks Jetty camping area (boat-based camping)

Yanks Jetty campground is just north of Harrier
Point on the south-west coast of the island. The
gas BBQ is free but open fires are prohibited;
bring a gas/fuel stove and drinking water. The
campground has space for up to 30 self-sufficient
campers. **Map refs:** 161 F3, 172 B1

PALUMA RANGE NATIONAL PARK

Lying within the Wet Tropics World Heritage
Area, Paluma Range National Park offers
mountain-top views and picturesque waterfalls.
The Mt Spec section encompasses the summit
and escarpment of the Paluma Range, while
the Jourama Falls section, in the foothills of the
Seaview Range, features cascades, rapids and
the impressive Jourama Falls on Waterview
Creek. Both sections offer picnic areas, lookouts,
bushwalks and campsites. Advance bookings
are required for camping.

How to book: NPRSR 13 7468 www.nprsr.qld.gov.au
Permits: camping permit required

509 Big Crystal Creek camping area

This popular swimming and picnic area is off the Old Bruce Hwy; the 4 km road to the campground is partially unsealed. Bring a gas/fuel stove and drinking water, or treat the creek water before drinking. The summit of Mt Spec, rising 1000 m above the Big Crystal Creek flood plain, receives 3 times the average rainfall of the surrounding area and is often cloaked in mist or low cloud. Vegetation changes from open eucalypt forests in the park's lower areas to dense rainforest on the higher slopes. **Map refs: 161 E4, 172 A2**

510 Jourama Falls camping area

This campground, beside Waterview Creek, is about 300 m from the entrance to the national park. Nearby Jourama Falls Lookout Walk (3 km return, 1 hr) leads through dry open forest of poplar gum, bloodwood and Moreton Bay ash. Rainforest grows on the higher slopes and lines the banks of Waterview Creek. Wildlife-watchers may spot the azure kingfisher, satin flycatcher and northern fantail during the day and the southern boobook, large-tailed nightjar and tawny frogmouth by torchlight at night. Other nocturnal residents include sugar gliders and endangered mahogany gliders. Note: the camping area can flood during heavy rain. **Map refs: 160 D4, 172 A2, 187 H2**

PERCY ISLES NATIONAL PARK

The Percy Isles, 128 km south-east of Mackay, have long been known as a yachties' paradise and are famous in the sailing world for their stunning beaches, unspoilt waters and isolation. The isles found fame outside the sailing world recently after several legal battles over ownership of Middle Percy Island, which is now firmly part of the Percy Isles National Park, with the exception of the Middle Percy Island Conservation Park, a small, privately managed section.

Who to contact: NPRSR 13 7468 www.nprsr.qld. gov.au **Permits:** camping permit required

511 North West Beach camping area (boat-based camping)

This site on South Percy Island offers camping for up to 12 campers. There are no facilities, so bring all self-sufficient gear, including drinking water, rubbish bags and a gas/fuel stove. Owing to South Percy Island's distance from the mainland and the navigational challenges posed, sailing there should only be attempted by seasoned sailors. Note: as this campsite is very remote, bring extra supplies and plan for all eventualities. **Map refs: 171 E2**

REPULSE ISLANDS NATIONAL PARK

Repulse Islands National Park protects 3 small islands south of Cape Conway, about 35 km south-east of Airlie Beach. The deep blue waters surrounding the islands are ideal for boating and fishing. Private boat access is from Shute Harbour or Abel Point Marina. Advance bookings are required for camping.

How to book: NPRSR 13 7468 www.nprsr.qld.gov.au **Permits:** camping permit required

512 South Repulse Island camping area (boat-based camping)

This sheltered campground for self-sufficient campers – a maximum of 12 – is on the west side of the island, with views of Conway Range. Generators are not permitted and the site is gas/fuel stove only; also bring drinking water. There is good anchorage at the site; remember to go slow when boating, report marine strandings and not collect coral or shells. **Map refs: 158 C3, 173 E4**

SHOALWATER BAY CONSERVATION PARK

Located at the northern end of Shoalwater Bay, 23 km south-east of the hamlet of Stanage and 62 km north-east of Marlborough, Shoalwater Bay Conservation Park is a remote area protecting coastal heathland. Access to the park is by boat only; owing to its remoteness, the voyage should only be tackled by experienced sailors.

Who to contact: NPRSR 13 7468 www.nprsr.qld. gov.au **Permits:** camping permit required

513 Chips Hut camping area
(boat-based camping)

There are no facilities provided at Chips Hut and fires are prohibited, so bring all self-sufficient camping gear, including drinking water, rubbish bags and a gas/fuel stove. Note: as this campsite is remote, bring extra supplies and plan for all eventualities. **Map refs:** 171 E3

514 Macdonalds Point camping area
(boat-based camping)

There are no facilities provided at Macdonalds Point and fires are prohibited, so bring all self-sufficient camping gear, including drinking water, rubbish bags and a gas/fuel stove. Note: as this campsite is remote, bring extra supplies and plan for all eventualities. **Map refs:** 171 E3

SMITH ISLANDS NATIONAL PARK

For a truly secluded mid-tropics experience, head to Smith Islands National Park, 45 km north of Mackay. This isolated group of 16 islands lies halfway between Mackay and the Lindeman Islands of the Whitsundays. The Smith Islands share many of the features of the Whitsundays, but without the hordes of tourists. Access to the islands is by boat only; the nearest boat ramp is in Seaforth. Advance bookings are required for camping.

How to book: NPRSR 13 7468 www.nprsr.qld.gov.au
Permits: camping permit required

515 Roylen Bay camping area
(boat-based camping)

Camping is permitted on Goldsmith Island, part of the Great Barrier Reef World Heritage Area off the coast of Mackay. Toilets and picnic tables are the only facilities, so you'll need to bring all self-sufficient supplies. The surrounding coral reefs provide excellent snorkelling but beware of marine stingers Oct–May. **Map refs:** 158 D3, 173 F4

SOUTH CUMBERLAND ISLANDS NATIONAL PARK

Located 60 km north-east of Mackay and 50 km from Seaforth by boat, the 9 islands that comprise South Cumberland Islands National Park are characterised by rugged, hoop pine–clad headlands, long sandy beaches and hidden pockets of remnant dry rainforest. The islands are an important breeding site for flatback and green turtles. Access to the islands is by private or charter boat only. Advance bookings are required for camping.

How to book: NPRSR 13 7468 www.nprsr.qld.gov.au
Permits: camping permit required

516 Cockermouth Island camping area
(boat-based camping)

Bush camping is permitted for up to 12 people at Cockermouth Island's south-western bay. There are no facilities provided, so bring all self-sufficient camping gear, including drinking water, rubbish bags and a gas/fuel stove. **Map refs:** 159 E3, 173 F5

517 Refuge Bay camping area
(boat-based camping)

Bush camping is permitted at Refuge Bay on Scawfell Island. Toilets and a shelter shed are the only facilities, so you'll need to bring all self-sufficient supplies, including drinking water and a gas/fuel stove. The island is an important turtle rookery, and the surrounding coral reefs provide excellent snorkelling but beware of marine stingers Oct–May. **Map refs:** 159 F4, 173 G5

518 Turtle Beach camping area
(boat-based camping)

Bush camping is permitted for up to 24 people at this camping area, on the north shore of the steep and rugged St Bees Island. There are no facilities provided, so bring all self-sufficient camping gear, including drinking water, rubbish bags and a gas/fuel stove. **Map refs:** 159 E4, 173 F5

WHITE MOUNTAINS NATIONAL PARK

The white sandstone gorges of White Mountains National Park lie 140 km south-west of Charters Towers and 80 km north-west of Hughenden. Lovers of flora and fauna will be attracted by the flowering native vegetation and various reptiles, birds and wallabies found in the park. Note: there are no signed walking trails in the park. Advance bookings are required for camping.

How to book: NPRSR 13 7468 www.nprsr.qld.gov.au
Permits: camping permit required

519 **Canns Camp Creek camping area (bush camping)**

This campground is 11 km west of the Burra Range Lookout and 19 km east of Torrens Creek. The road is sometimes closed to conventional vehicles between Dec–Apr due to wet weather. Generators and fires are not permitted; bring drinking water and a gas/fuel stove. **Map refs: 187 G4**

WHITSUNDAY ISLANDS NATIONAL PARK

Protecting one of Qld's most beautiful and popular holiday destinations, this national park features 32 islands, including Whitsunday Island and its famous Whitehaven Beach. Whitsunday Island has 2 excellent walking trails well worth exploring. The Tongue Point track (400 m, 15 min) leads to a beautiful view of Whitehaven Beach, and the Dugong Beach to Sawmill Beach track (1.5 km, 45 min) features gorgeous bay outlooks. Other protected islands include Hook Island, with its stunning coral reef just metres offshore from 2 campgrounds, and Black and Langford islands. Access to various islands is via Shute Harbour or Airlie Beach. If boating in the region, remember to go slow, report marine strandings, not collect coral or shells, and check for permissions before fishing. Advance bookings are required for camping.

How to book: NPRSR 13 7468 www.nprsr.qld.gov.au
Permits: camping permit required

520 **Chance Bay camping area (boat-based camping)**

The sandy Chance Bay campground is on the south coast of Whitsunday Island, about 27 km east-south-east of Shute Harbour. A composting toilet and picnic tables are the only facilities, so bring all self-sufficient supplies. The site can only be reached at mid-high tide. **Map refs: 158 D2, 173 F4**

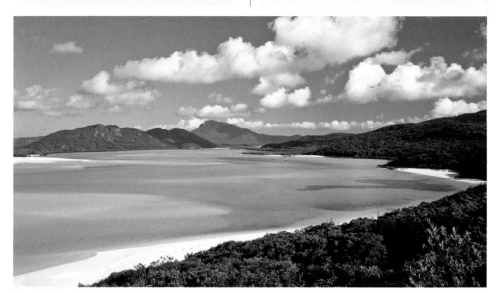

Beautiful blue waters of Hill Inlet, Whitsunday Islands National Park

521 Crayfish Beach camping area
(boat-based camping)

This campground on the east coast of Hook Island is sheltered by a large rocky headland to the east, and mountains to the north and west. Hook Island has some of the Whitsundays' most accessible coral reefs, just metres from the shore, providing magnificent snorkelling. The site suits self-sufficient campers; bring drinking water and a gas/fuel stove. **Map refs: 158 D1, 173 F4**

522 Curlew Beach camping area
(boat-based camping)

This small campground on the south coast of Hook Island at Macona Inlet has space for 12 campers. Open fires and generators are not permitted, and you need to bring drinking water and a gas/fuel stove. **Map refs: 158 C1, 173 E4**

523 Dugong Beach camping area
(boat-based camping)

Ideal for larger groups, Dugong Beach campground on the west coast of Whitsunday Island has space for up to 36 people. A 1 km walking track links it to nearby Sawmill Beach. Access is best at mid-high tide. Bring drinking water and a gas/fuel stove. **Map refs: 158 D2, 173 F4**

524 Joe's Beach camping area
(boat-based camping)

The reef off Joe's Beach on Whitsunday Island is ideal for snorkelling and there are superb views of nearby islands. The campground has space for 12 campers. Generators and open fires are not permitted; bring a gas/fuel stove and drinking water. **Map refs: 158 C2, 173 F4**

525 Maureen's Cove camping area
(boat-based camping)

Maureen's Cove is a coral rubble beach on the north coast of Hook Island with excellent snorkelling opportunities at the fringing coral reef. The site, for a maximum of 24 people, has great views of the Coral Sea, and a small creek runs behind the campground. Bring all self-sufficient supplies. **Map refs: 158 C1, 173 F3**

526 Nari's Beach camping area
(boat-based camping)

Nari's Beach is a small campground on the west coast of Whitsunday Island with space for 6 self-sufficient campers. The area has magnificent views of Cid Island. The site is gas/fuel stove only; bring drinking water. **Map refs: 158 C2, 173 F4**

527 Northern Spit camping area
(boat-based camping)

This campground for totally self-sufficient campers is in a secluded spot behind the beach on the northern side of Henning Island, overlooking Whitsunday and Hamilton islands. Open fires and generators are not permitted. **Map refs: 158 C2, 173 F4**

528 Peter Bay camping area
(boat-based camping)

This picturesque campground on the north-east coast of Whitsunday Island has views across the bay to Border and Dumbell islands. It can only be reached at mid-high tide and is for a maximum of 12 totally self-sufficient campers. **Map refs: 158 D1, 173 F4**

115

...ch camping area
...ping)

This campground on the north-west coast of Hook Island overlooks Hayman Island. The fringing coral reef provides excellent snorkelling. Bring drinking water and a gas/fuel stove. **Map refs:** 158 C1, 173 E3

530 Whitehaven Beach camping area (boat-based camping)

Famous for its postcard-perfect white sandy beach and azure waters, Whitehaven on Whitsunday Island is one of Qld's most beautiful protected camping spots. The area is busy with hundreds of tourists during the day, but campers at this site can enjoy being the only visitors with permission to stay overnight – there are no hotels, bars or restaurants at Whitehaven. Set in the eucalypt woodland behind the beach, there are 7 defined sites for a maximum of 36 people. A new toilet block was recently built on site. Open fires and generators are prohibited. Bring all self-sufficient supplies. **Map refs:** 158 D2, 173 F4

CAMPSITES LOCATED IN OTHER AREAS

531 Ball Bay Campground

Ball Bay is a basic campground (no powered sites) off Cape Hillsborough Rd, about 48 km north of Mackay. Camping attendants visit the site daily to collect fees. Mackay is on the Bruce Hwy, about 125 km south of Proserpine, with more than 30 sandy beaches and access to several tropical islands in the Great Barrier Reef World Heritage Area. **Map refs:** 158 D4, 173 F5

Who to contact: (07) 4959 0695

532 BIG4 Adventure Whitsunday Resort

This modern 26 ha camping and caravan park is located in Cannonvale, 4 km from Airlie Beach's town centre. The facilities are top class: ensuite powered sites, plenty of shade, concrete slabs, and 3 amenities blocks with coin-operated laundry facilities. Other features include free electric BBQs and a large undercover camp kitchen with microwave and fridge. **Map refs:** 158 C2, 173 E4

How to book: 25–29 Shute Harbour Rd, Cannonvale (07) 4948 5400, 1800 640 587
www.adventurewhitsunday.com.au

533 BIG4 Airlie Cove Resort Van Park

This modern tourist park with excellent facilities is located 2.5 km from Airlie Beach town centre on Shute Harbour Rd. The campground features a Polynesian-style camp kitchen with fridge, microwave, hotplates and other conveniences. Other benefits include a pool with waterslide and spa, a mini market, television room, laundry and free gas BBQs. All caravan sites have cement slabs, sullage, water and electricity points. **Map refs:** 158 C2, 173 E4

How to book: Lot 2, Shute Harbour Rd, Jubilee Pocket (07) 4946 6727, 1800 653 445
www.airliecove.com.au

534 Bingil Bay camping area

This campground is about 3 km north of Mission Beach on Bingil Bay Rd. There is no power available here. Mission Beach is a 2 hr drive from Cairns or a 3 hr drive from Townsville, and is known for its 14 km stretch of sandy beaches. Note: take precautionary measures against marine stingers Oct–May. **Map refs:** 163 G4, 175 G4

Who to contact: Tully Visitor Information Centre (07) 4068 2288

535 Burdekin Falls Dam Caravan Park

Well stocked with barramundi for excellent fishing, Burdekin Falls Dam on Lake Dalrymple is 120 km south of Mingela on the Flinders Hwy, with signposted access via Ravenswood Rd. The caravan park has good facilities and gets very busy in holiday periods, as the dam is also a popular spot for canoeing, sailing and waterskiing. **Map refs:** 172 C4

How to book: SunWater Burdekin Dam (07) 4770 3177

536 Camp Kanga

Powered sites are available at this campground, 24 km north-west of Proserpine on Crystal Brook Rd. It's just 1.5 km from Lake Proserpine (also known as Peter Faust Dam) and offers handy extras such as laundry facilities and a camp kitchen. The lake is well stocked with fish for excellent sport fishing, and is also a popular spot for waterskiing and boating. **Map refs:** 158 B2, 173 E4

How to book: 2396 Crystal Brook Rd, Crystal Brook (07) 4947 2600 www.campkanga.com.au

537 Eungella Dam camping area

Eungella Dam, 40 km north-west of Eungella, is a popular place for all manner of watersports. The fishing is good too, as the dam is well stocked with sooty grunter and barramundi. You need to be totally self-sufficient if you are camping here; bring your own firewood and drinking water. **Map refs:** 158 A5, 170 B1, 173 E5

Who to contact: SunWater Mackay (07) 4954 2220 *Permits:* a permit is required to fish in Eungella Dam *Camping fees:* fees can be paid at the ranger station

538 Ferns Hideaway Resort

The camping facilities at this resort, 39 km north of Yeppoon, are relatively basic, but the lush rainforest surrounds more than make up for that. Campers looking for a touch of civilisation will find the resort's pool, restaurant and bar a godsend, while outdoors adventurers can paddle down Sandy Creek in a canoe (provided free of charge to camping guests). Bookings are essential at peak periods. **Map refs:** 171 E4

How to book: 67 Cahills Rd, Byfield (07) 4935 1235 www.fernshideaway.com.au

539 Fletcher Creek Camping Reserve

This camping reserve is beside Fletcher Creek, 45 km north of Charters Towers near the entrance to Dalrymple National Park; access is via Gregory Developmental Rd from the Flinders Hwy. The Charters Towers region is noted for its diverse landscapes, with rainforests in the north-east and desert plains in the south-west. **Map refs:** 172 A3, 187 H3

Who to contact: Charters Towers Regional Council (07) 4761 5300

540 Hull Heads camping area

Estuary and reef fishing from an all-weather boat ramp and pontoon makes Hull Heads an excellent destination for anglers. The campground is next to the coastguard on Luff St in Hull Heads, 15 km east of the Bruce Hwy. There are 7 sites with a 4-night maximum stay, and generators are permitted during the day. The access road is 6 km south of Tully at Silky Oak, on the Bruce Hwy. **Map refs:** 160 D1, 163 G5, 175 G4

Who to contact: Tully Visitor Information Centre (07) 4068 2288

nt Waters Leisure Resort

Popular with waterskiers and anglers, the Kinchent Waters Leisure Resort includes a 4 ha camping area, offering a range of accommodation options including cabins and backpacker rooms, plus a bar, restaurant and laundry facilities. Kinchant Dam is about 40 km west of Mackay, off the Peak Downs Hwy at Eton. Fishing permits are available on site. **Map refs:** 158 C5, 170 C1, 173 E5

How to book: 841 Kinchant Dam Rd, Eton North (07) 4954 1453

542 Lake Paluma camping area

Surrounded by World Heritage rainforest, Lake Paluma (12 km north-west of Paluma) is a popular spot for swimming, canoeing and kayaking, so bookings are essential. The lake is a well-known wildlife-watching area, with opportunities to see platypus, peregrine falcons and eastern water dragons. The day-use area has BBQs and weatherproof shelters, and there's a drinking-water storage area. Heavy rain and strong winds can lead to road closures, and the gravel access road is unsuitable for caravans. Note: motorised boating is not permitted on the lake. **Map refs:** 161 E4, 172 A2, 187 H2

How to book: Townsville City Council 1300 878 001 www.townsville.qld.gov.au *Camping fees:* fees can be paid online, at a Townsville City Council customer service centre or at the self-registration station

Mackay Highlands Great Walk

This 56 km, 3–5 day walk allows experienced and self-sufficent hikers to see everything from rugged cliffs and cool rainforests to open eucalypt woodland and an 1880s gold-mining hamlet. Some sections of the track require a high level of physical fitness, and the track is easier to manage if approached north to south, from Pine Grove in Eungella National Park to Mt Britton township. Advance bookings are required for all camping on the walk.

Please note that campsites are listed in alphabetical order, not track order. Refer to the map on p. 170 for further information.

How to book: NPRSR 13 7468 www.nprsr.qld.gov.au
Permits: camping permit required

450 Crediton Hall camping area
See p. 100.

451 Denham Range camping area
See p. 100.

455 Fern Flat camping area
(walk-in camping)
See p. 101.

490 Moonlight Dam camping area
See p. 108.

543 Magnetic Gateway Holiday Village

Situated on the Bruce Hwy at Cluden, just 8 km from Townsville, this tourist park has plenty of shady tent sites and an excellent range of facilities. Visitors can enjoy the swimming pool, spa, TV room and book exchange, laundry, internet facilities and a kiosk with gas refills and ice. Air-conditioned ensuite cabins are also available on site. Access is from Racecourse Rd via Abbott St. **Map refs:** 161 G5, 172 B2

Who to contact: Racecourse Rd (Bruce Hwy), Cluden (07) 4778 2412

544 Mission Beach Caravan Park

This caravan park with laundry facilities is on Porters Promenade in Mission Beach, about a 2 hr drive from Cairns or a 3 hr drive from Townsville. Known for its 14 km stretch of sandy beaches, the town is a jumping-off point to reach Dunk Island or Bedarra Island and it's just a 1 hr boat trip to the Great Barrier Reef. **Map refs:** 163 G4, 175 G4

Who to contact: Tully Visitor Information Centre (07) 4068 2288

545 Pelorus Island camping area (boat-based camping)

No permits or bookings are required for this free camping ground, known as a great jumping-off point to fantastic snorkelling around the coral reefs of Pelorus Island's west coast. The island is in the Great Barrier Reef Marine Park. If you're snorkelling, take note that there could be fast currents. The island is reached by private boat or commercial operator from Taylor's Beach. Wood fires are permitted, but campers must be self-sufficient, bringing all supplies, including drinking water. **Map refs:** 161 F3, 172 B1, 175 G5

Who to contact: Tyto Wetlands Visitor Information Centre (07) 4776 5211

546 Platypus Bush Camp

Hot showers with rainforest views and a superb, open-air camp kitchen are some of the excellent facilities at this popular campground. The camping area has plenty of space for groups, or you can stay in the tree-house huts nestled in the rainforest. Finch Hatton Gorge is 40 km east of Eungella. From the picnic area, a 2 km rainforest walk leads through the gorge to Araluen Falls. **Map refs:** 158 B4, 170 B1, 173 E5

How to book: Gorge Rd, Finch Hatton (07) 4958 3204 www.bushcamp.net

547 St Helens Beach camping area

This basic campground is in the township of St Helens Beach, 68 km north of Mackay, and is accessed via Murrays Rd. Firewood is supplied and camping attendants visit the site daily to collect fees. Mackay is on the Bruce Hwy about 125 km south of Proserpine, offering more than 30 sandy beaches and access to several tropical

Dawn at Mission Beach, near Mission Beach Caravan Park (p. 118)

islands in the Great Barrier Reef World Heritage Area. **Map refs:** 158 C4, 173 E5

Who to contact: Mackay Regional Council 1300 622 529; or Mackay Visitor Information Centre 1300 130 001

548 Seaforth camping area

This campground is 45 km north of Mackay along the Seaforth–Yakapari Rd. It has coin-operated showers. Camping attendants visit the site daily to collect fees. Mackay is on the Bruce Hwy about 125 km south of Proserpine, with more than 30 sandy beaches and access to several tropical islands in the Great Barrier Reef World Heritage Area. **Map refs:** 158 D4, 173 F5

Who to contact: (07) 4966 4359, 0427 373 358

Whitsunday Ngaro Sea Trail

The Whitsunday Ngaro Sea Trail is the most unusual of Qld's Great Walks for one simple reason – there's more sailing than walking involved. Keen sailors and sea kayakers who follow this trail between island campsites will discover gorgeous beaches, brilliant azure seas and challenging mountain climbs, as well as gaining insight into the Ngaro people's traditional way of life. Advance bookings are required for all camping.

Please note that campsites are listed in alphabetical order. Refer to the map on p. 158 for further information.

How to book: NPRSR 13 7468 www.nprsr.qld.gov.au
Permits: camping permit required

520 Chance Bay camping area (boat-based camping)

See p. 114.

522 Curlew Beach camping area (boat-based camping)

See p. 115.

523 Dugong Beach camping area (boat-based camping)

See p. 115.

527 Northern Spit camping area (boat-based camping)

See p. 115.

496 Paddle Bay camping area (boat-based camping)

See p. 109.

528 Peter Bay camping area (boat-based camping)

See p. 115.

499 Sandy Bay, South Molle Island camping area (boat-based camping)

See p. 110.

530 Whitehaven Beach camping area (boat-based camping)

See p. 116.

THE FAR NORTH

Stretching from Cairns to the Torres Strait islands off the tip of Cape York, Far North Qld's unique remoteness and stunning natural beauty is a boon for adventurous campers. Rugged 4WD tracks lead you through densely forested national parks to isolated waterholes and lagoons, tiny villages, outback roadhouses, riverside camping areas and beautiful unspoiled coastlines.

Watersports fanatics can make their way to Lake Tinaroo, south-west of Cairns, for sensational boating, fishing, canoeing, waterskiing and windsurfing. Visitors stay at the popular Lake Tinaroo Holiday Park or head for the peaceful lakeside camping areas in Danbulla State Forest, where you can take short walks to impressive crater lakes and enormous strangler fig trees.

North of Cairns near Cooktown, Rinyirru (Lakefield) National Park (CYPAL) is Qld's second largest national park, covering the area from the town of Laura to Princess Charlotte Bay. Anglers can set up camp at one of the many waterholes and fish for barramundi or catfish in the lakes and creeks – but beware of crocs! The park is also a significant traditional land for Indigenous people, a place for ceremonies and stories of ancestral spirits.

Famous hospitable roadhouses such as those at Hann River, Musgrave, Archer River and Bramwell Junction provide spacious campgrounds, tasty meals, fuel and supplies for those heading through Cape York, past Weipa to Australia's most northerly point on the mainland. Close to the tip is Jardine River National Park, known for its magnificent waterfalls, lookouts, rainforests and amazing wildlife.

At Northern Cape York, relaxing campgrounds such as Seisia Holiday Park and Punsand Bay Camping Resort – both with excellent facilities – are the perfect reward for making the trek all the way to the top. Offshore, campers can discover the wonders of the Great Barrier Reef and stay on Flinders, Lizard, Snapper, the Turtle Group and other island-based national parks.

Note: alcohol restrictions apply in certain areas of Cape York Peninsula, and it is illegal to bring alcohol into dry communities, even if you are only travelling through. Ensure that you have up-to-date information about alcohol restrictions before travelling by calling 13 7468.

CAMPSITES LOCATED IN PARKS AND RESERVES

BARNARD ISLAND GROUP NATIONAL PARK

The Barnard Island Group National Park is around 15 km offshore from Kurrimine Beach and about 90 km south of Cairns. The islands include Bresnahan, Hutchinson, Jessie, Kent and Lindquist (North Barnard group) and Sisters and Stephens (South Barnard group). Mainland access is from Mourilyan Harbour or Kurrimine Beach. Advance bookings are required to camp on Stephens Island.

How to book: NPRSR 13 7468 www.nprsr.qld.gov.au *Permits:* camping permit required *Camping fees:* fees can be paid and permits acquired for Kent Island at NPRSR Cairns business centre

549 Kent Island camping area (boat-based camping)

Self-sufficient camping is found on the west coast of Kent Island, part of the North Barnard group. This site is ideal for anglers and wildlife-watchers. There are 3 sites with a maximum of 5 people per site; bring all necessaries, including a gas/fuel stove. Be aware of marine stingers when swimming, particularly during Oct–May.
Map refs: 163 G4, 175 G4

550 Stephens Island camping area (boat-based camping)

This campground for self-sufficient campers is on the western side of Stephens Island, part of the

Mossman Gorge, Daintree
National Park (p. 124)

South Barnard group. There are 3 separate sites, each with a maximum of 4 people. Open fires and generators are not permitted; bring a gas/fuel stove. Access to some sections of the island is prohibited Sept–Mar to protect nesting seabirds. **Map refs:** 163 G4, 175 G4

CAPE MELVILLE NATIONAL PARK

Some gruelling 4WD tracks lead to this national park on Cape York Peninsula. At journey's end is a wild and rugged coastline of rocky headlands and sandy beaches bordered by wetlands and eucalypt woodlands stretching inland to the Melville and Altanmoui ranges. This is the land of the Daarba, Junjuu, Muli, Bagaarrmugu, Wurri, Manyamarr, Yiirrku and Gambiilmugu people. The ruins of homesteads, testament to early European pastoral settlement, are scattered throughout the region. Travel here from the west via Rinyirru (Lakefield) National Park (280 km, 6 hr) or from the south from Cooktown and Starcke Homestead along Coast Rd (250 km, 12 hr). Note: this park is closed for the wet season, Dec–Jul each year; access is 4WD only. Advance bookings are required for camping.

How to book: NPRSR 13 7468 www.nprsr.qld.gov.au
Permits: camping permit required

551 Crocodile camping area
(bush camping)

This camping area covers a 2 km stretch of beach on Bathurst Bay, between the Muck River estuary and the Nookai day-use area. There are no facilities, so bring all self-sufficient camping gear, including drinking water and rubbish bags. Open fires are permitted (bring your own firewood), but a gas/fuel stove is preferred. **Map refs:** 165 E1, 177 F3

552 Granite camping area (bush camping)

This camping site on the beach at Bathurst Bay stretches across the 4 km span between Oystercatcher camping area and the northernmost point of Cape Melville. Accessing the site requires

4 creek crossings, including a difficult and dangerous tidal creek crossing at the boundary between Oystercatcher and Granite camping areas – bring vehicle recovery equipment. There are no facilities, so bring all self-sufficient camping gear, including drinking water and rubbish bags. Open fires are permitted (bring your own firewood), but a gas/fuel stove is preferred. **Map refs:** 165 E1, 177 G3

553 Ninian Bay camping area
(bush camping)

This camping area lies on the east coast of Cape Melville National Park, 88 km from the camping areas at Bathurst Bay. A 1 km stretch of beach, it contains no facilities, so bring all self-sufficient camping gear, including drinking water and rubbish bags. The road into Ninian Bay is difficult and should be attempted only by experienced 4WD operators. Open fires are permitted (bring your own firewood), but a gas/fuel stove is preferred. **Map refs:** 165 E1, 177 G3

554 Oystercatcher camping area
(bush camping)

This camping area covers a 2 km stretch of beach on Bathurst Bay, between the Wongai and Granite camping areas. There are no facilities, so bring all self-sufficient camping gear, including drinking water and rubbish bags. Open fires are permitted (bring your own firewood), but a gas/fuel stove is preferred. **Map refs:** 165 E1, 177 F3

555 Wongai camping area
(bush camping)

This camping area covers a 2 km stretch of beach on Bathurst Bay, between the Nookai day-use area and Oystercatcher camping area. There are no facilities, so bring all self-sufficient camping gear, including drinking water and rubbish bags. Open fires are permitted (bring your own firewood), but a gas/fuel stove is preferred. **Map refs:** 157 G4, 165 E1, 169 G4, 177 F3

DAINTREE NATIONAL PARK

With its stunning scenery of rainforest-clad mountains sweeping down to long sandy beaches, Daintree National Park is one of the most revered parks in Australia. Its Cape Tribulation section, 100 km north of Cairns, is the only place on earth where 2 World Heritage areas exist side by side, as the Wet Tropics area meets the Great Barrier Reef. Advance bookings are required for camping.

How to book: NPRSR 13 7468 www.nprsr.qld.gov.au
Permits: camping permit required

556 Noah Beach camping area

Noah Beach campground is in a secluded spot just 50 m from the beach, about 8 km south of Cape Tribulation village. Throughout the Cape Tribulation section visitors will find facilities such as picnic areas, boardwalks to scenic sites, and viewing platforms. Conventional-vehicle access is via Cape Tribulation Rd after crossing the Daintree River via ferry. Note: open fires and generators are not permitted at this campsite. Bring all self-sufficient supplies; the tap water must be boiled or treated before drinking. **Map refs:** 175 F2

DANBULLA STATE FOREST

Less than 2 hrs' drive from Cairns, wildlife-rich Danbulla State Forest is on the north-east side of Lake Tinaroo on the Atherton Tablelands. Visitors can take the scenic Danbulla Forest Dr, have a picnic at one of 4 day-use areas, or go bushwalking on one of 5 tracks with varying degrees of difficulty. To get here, take the Danbulla Forest Dr north-east of Tinaroo Dam. Advance bookings are required for camping.

How to book: NPRSR 13 7468 www.nprsr.qld.gov.au
Permits: camping permit required

557 Curri Curri camping areas (boat-based camping)

Bush camping is available on the shores of Lake Tinaroo, to the east of the public boat ramp in Tinaroo township. There are 5 numbered campsites, each equipped with a fire ring (bring your own firewood). There are no other facilities, so bring all self-sufficient gear, including drinking water and rubbish bags. Gas/fuel stoves are preferred. **Map refs:** 163 E2, 175 F3

558 Downfall Creek camping area

This campground is 7 km from the western entrance and 21 km from the eastern entrance

Cape Tribulation, Daintree National Park

of the Danbulla Forest Dr. Campers can take the 2.4 km walk through the forest to Kauri Creek. Bring all self-sufficient supplies, including firewood; open fires are permitted in fire rings. **Map refs:** 163 E2, 175 F3

559 Fong-On Bay camping area

A favourite with waterskiers, this campground is divided into 2 sections with good water access: Bulmba and Gungul. To get here, turn off Danbulla Forest Dr 16.5 km from the western entrance, or 11.5 km from the eastern entrance, and continue 4.7 km to the camping area. Open fires are permitted in fire rings; no generators are allowed. Bring all self-sufficient supplies, including firewood. **Map refs:** 163 E2, 175 F3

560 Kauri Creek camping area

A great spot for swimming and canoeing, Kauri Creek is 9 km from the western entrance and 19 km from the eastern entrance of Danbulla Forest Dr. Open fires are allowed in fire rings; generators are not permitted. Visitors are advised to bring insect repellent, firewood and drinking water. A shower room is provided for campers who want to bring their own bush showers. **Map refs:** 163 E2, 175 F3

561 Platypus camping area

Platypus campground, 4 km from the western entrance, has 18 numbered sites for small tents, large tents and vans. Open fires are allowed here in the provided fire rings and BBQs (except when fire bans apply); bring your own firewood as well as all other self-sufficent supplies. **Map refs:** 163 E2, 175 F3

562 School Point camping area

School Point can be reached by 2WD or boat. It has has 8 numbered campsites with a gravel surface. To get here, turn off Danbulla Forest Dr 16 km from the western entrance, or 12 km from the eastern entrance, and follow the road 1 km to the campground. Bring all self-sufficient supplies, including firewood. **Map refs:** 163 E2, 175 F3

DAVIES CREEK NATIONAL PARK

The rugged boulder-lined Davies Creek is a popular region for scenic hikes, picnics and wildlife-watching. The access road to the national park is 21 km from Kuranda; follow it for another 7 km to reach the campground. The Davies Creek Falls circuit is an easy 1.1 km (20 min) track worth checking out; platypus are often spotted in the area.

Who to contact: NPRSR 13 7468 www.nprsr. qld.gov.au *Permits:* camping permit required *Camping fees:* fees can be paid and permits acquired at the self-registration station

563 Davies Creek camping area

Camp beside the creek at this clearing 6 km from the Kennedy Hwy, accessible by conventional vehicles. There are 8 sites with space for 10 campers per site. Bring firewood for the allocated fireplaces, and all self-sufficient supplies. Note: Davies Creek Rd is sometimes closed due to flooding. **Map refs:** 163 E1, 175 F3

DINDEN NATIONAL PARK

About 20 km south-west of Cairns, Dinden National Park is on the Atherton Tableland, just south of Davies Creek National Park. The park's eucalypt forests are threaded with excellent walking trails, including the Kahlpahlim Rock trail (12 km return, 6–7 hr) and Turtle Rock trail (8 km, 3–4 hr). Drive 22 km south of the Kennedy Hwy to the sites, preferably in a 4WD. Advance bookings are required for camping.

How to book: NPRSR 13 7468 www.nprsr.qld.gov.au *Permits:* camping permit required

564 Dinden camping area (bush camping)

A 4WD is advisable for accessing these 6 bush campsites, 5 km along Davies Creek Rd from Davies Creek National Park. It is preferable to visit in the dry season (Apr–Oct). Bring your own water, rubbish bags, and a gas/fuel stove. The Kahlpahlim Rock walking trail follows a former logging trail through rainforest and leads to views over the Davies Creek catchment. **Map refs:** 163 E1, 175 F3

FLINDERS GROUP NATIONAL PARK

Located 340 km north of Cairns, the remote islands of the Flinders Group National Park are part of the sea country of the Yiithuwarra 'saltwater people', and have important Indigenous sites. The group is east of the Cape York Peninsula between Cape Melville and Princess Charlotte Bay, accessible by private boat. Advance bookings are required for camping.

How to book: NPRSR 13 7468 www.nprsr.qld.gov.au
Permits: camping permit required

565 Flinders Island camping area (boat-based camping)

This is the only island in the group that permits camping. Bring all self-sufficient supplies; the water available here needs to be boiled or treated before use. The site is on the northern side of Flinders Island at Fredrick Point, accessible by private boat only. Respect cultural sites. **Map refs:** 164 D1, 177 F3

FRANKLAND GROUP NATIONAL PARK

About 45 km south of Cairns, this island group is known for its fringing reefs, rocky outcrops and varied wildlife. Access to the islands is by private boat from the Mulgrave and Russell rivers. Beware of the sandbar at the mouth of the Mulgrave River at Russell Heads. Advance bookings are required for camping.

How to book: NPRSR 13 7468 www.nprsr.qld.gov.au
Permits: camping permit required *Camping fees:* for

Russell Island, fees can be paid and permits acquired at NPRSR Cairns business centre

566 High Island camping area (boat-based camping)

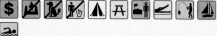

This campground on the north-west side of High Island has space for 14 self-sufficient campers. Open fires and generators are not permitted, so bring a gas/fuel stove. **Map refs:** 163 G2, 175 G3

567 Russell Island camping area (boat-based camping)

This sandy campground is on the north-east side of Russell Island, accessible by private boat. There are 6 numbered sites; open fires and generators are not permitted and you need to be self-sufficient. There are a few small walking tracks around the campground, but to protect nesting seabirds some areas have restricted access. **Map refs:** 163 G2, 175 G3

HEATHLANDS RESOURCES RESERVE

This large reserve, directly south of Jardine River National Park, protects a diverse array of wildlife, including Torresian crows and red-winged parrots. It is also the home of several stunning waterfalls, including Fruit Bat Falls, Eliot Falls and Twin Falls. Access is 4WD only via Telegraph Rd or Southern Bypass Rd. Advance bookings are required for camping.

Who to contact: Heathlands Ranger Station (07) 4060 3421 for the Telegraph Track *How to book:* NPRSR 13 7468 www.nprsr.qld.gov.au
Permits: camping permit required

568 Bertie Creek camping area (bush camping)

Bush camping is permitted at this site on the 4WD Telegraph Track, 1.4 km north of Dulhunty River camping area and 14.1 km south of Gunshot Creek. There are no facilities; bring all self-sufficient gear. **Map refs:** 178 D4

569 Captain Billy Landing camping area

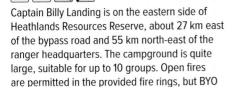

Captain Billy Landing is on the eastern side of Heathlands Resources Reserve, about 27 km east of the bypass road and 55 km north-east of the ranger headquarters. The campground is quite large, suitable for up to 10 groups. Open fires are permitted in the provided fire rings, but BYO firewood. **Map refs:** 179 E3

570 Cockatoo Creek camping area (bush camping)

Bush camping is permitted at this site on the 4WD Telegraph Track, 9.5 km north of Gunshot Creek camping area and 12 km south of the Eliot Falls turn-off. There are no facilities; bring all self-sufficient gear. **Map refs:** 178 D3

571 Dulhunty River camping area (bush camping)

On the 4WD Telegraph Track, bush camping is permitted at 2 sites either side of the Dulhunty River, 11.2 km north of North Alice Creek camping area and 1.4 km south of Bertie Creek. There are no facilities; bring all self-sufficient gear. **Map refs:** 178 D4

572 Eliot Falls camping area

This campground is known for its 3 short but scenic walking tracks that lead through the forest along creeks to Twin Falls and Eliot Falls. All tracks are suitable for inexperienced bushwalkers. The campground, with 31 numbered sites, is between Canal and Eliot creeks, close to the northern boundary of Heathlands Resources Reserve. Open fires are permitted (bring firewood) but gas/fuel stoves are preferred. **Map refs:** 178 D3

573 Gunshot Creek camping area (bush camping)

Bush camping is permitted at this site on the 4WD Telegraph Track, 14.1 km north of Bertie Creek

camping area and 9.5 km south of Cockatoo Creek. There are no facilities; bring all self-sufficient gear. **Map refs:** 178 D3

HERBERTON RANGE STATE FOREST

Directly west of Atherton, on the Atherton Tableland, Herberton Range State Forest protects some of the little remaining cloud forest in Qld. Cloud forests harvest water directly from clouds (in the form of fog, mist and rain), and their abundance of mosses and ferns makes them unique. The high elevation of Herberton Range yields great views over Atherton and the surrounding areas. Advance bookings are required for camping.

How to book: NPRSR 13 7468 www.nprsr.qld.gov.au
Permits: camping permit required

574 Bush camping areas

Self-sufficient campers can bush camp in most areas of Herberton Range State Forest, excluding the Herberton Range Ridge Rd. Vehicle-based campers (4WD only) are required to select sites adjacent to established roads. There are no facilities and fires are banned, so bring all self-sufficient camping gear, including drinking water, rubbish bags and a gas/fuel stove. **Map refs:** 163 E2, 175 F3

HOPE ISLANDS NATIONAL PARK

The traditional sea country of the Kuku Yalanji Indigenous people, East Hope Island is a sand cay 37 km south-east of Cooktown. Access is by boat only and it can be reached within a day's sailing from Cairns. Wildlife-watchers can view several species of sea and woodland birds on the islands, and there are good fishing opportunities. Advance bookings are required for camping.

How to book: NPRSR 13 7468 www.nprsr.qld.gov.au
Permits: camping permit required

575 East Hope Island camping area (boat-based camping)

This small sandy campground is on the western side of East Hope Island, accessible by private or commercially operated boat. Each of the 3 separate sites holds up to 4 people. There are no walking tracks on the island, but visitors can walk around the beach perimeter. Bring all self-sufficient supplies, including drinking water and a gas/fuel stove. **Map refs: 175 F1, 177 H5**

 **576** West Point camping area (boat-based camping)

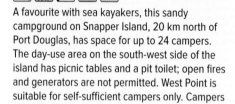

A favourite with sea kayakers, this sandy campground on Snapper Island, 20 km north of Port Douglas, has space for up to 24 campers. The day-use area on the south-west side of the island has picnic tables and a pit toilet; open fires and generators are not permitted. West Point is suitable for self-sufficient campers only. Campers should be aware that estuarine crocodiles are in the waters around the island. **Map refs: 175 F2**

JARDINE RIVER NATIONAL PARK

Inhabited for thousands of years by Indigenous 'sandbeach people', Jardine River National Park sprawls across 237 000 ha between Telegraph Rd and Cape York Peninsula's northern tip. The park includes the state's largest perennial waterway, the Jardine River, and provides a habitat for numerous bird species, such as the palm cockatoo and yellow-billed kingfisher. Access is by 4WD vehicles only. Advance bookings are required for camping.

Who to contact: Heathlands Ranger Station (07) 4060 3421 for the Telegraph Track *How to book:* NPRSR 13 7468 www.nprsr.qld.gov.au *Permits:* camping permit required

 **577** Bridge Creek camping area (bush camping)

Bush camping is permitted at this site, 19 km north of Sam Creek camping area at the far north end of the 4WD Telegraph Track. There are no facilities; bring all self-sufficient gear. **Map refs: 178 D3**

 **578** North Jardine River camping area (bush camping)

The Jardine River separates 2 camping areas, each within sight of each other. (The nearest crossing is the Jardine River ferry.) The camp on the northern side has 6 sites and is accessible via Telegraph Rd, south of the junction between Bamaga and Northern Bypass rds. Bring all self-sufficient supplies, including firewood or a gas/fuel stove. **Map refs: 178 D2**

 **579** Sam Creek camping area (bush camping)

Bush camping is permitted at this site on the 4WD Telegraph Track, 4.1 km north of the Eliot Falls turn-off and 19 km south of Bridge Creek. There are no facilities; bring all self-sufficient gear. **Map refs: 178 D3**

 **580** South Jardine River camping area (bush camping)

This campsite, on the southern side of the Jardine River facing the North Jardine River camping area, is accessible via Telegraph Rd. No facilities are provided, so bring all self-sufficient camping gear, including drinking water, rubbish bags firewood and a gas/fuel stove. **Map refs: 178 D2**

JARDINE RIVER RESOURCES RESERVE

Jardine River Resources Reserve is a large reserve to the north-east of Jardine River National Park. Several species of frogs, including the iconic white-lipped tree frog, can be spotted here. Access is 4WD only, via an infrequently maintained track off Bamaga Rd. Advance bookings are required for camping.

How to book: NPRSR 13 7468 www.nprsr.qld.gov.au *Permits:* camping permit required

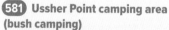 **581** Ussher Point camping area (bush camping)

This remote camping area, on the eastern boundary of the Jardine River Resources Reserve, offers a true sense of isolation and

remoteness – an authentic Cape York experience. No facilities are provided, so bring all self-sufficient gear, including firewood, water and rubbish bags. Quiet generators (less than 65 dBA at 7 m) are permitted. **Map refs: 178 D2**

KOOMBOOLOOMBA CONSERVATION PARK

Located on the shores of Koombooloomba Dam, 29 km south-east of Ravenshoe, Koombooloomba Conservation Park is surrounded on all sides by Koombooloomba National Park. The general region is part of the World Heritage–listed Wet Tropics Area, and is home to the endangered Lumholtz's tree-kangaroo. Access to the conservation park is via Koombooloomba National Park. Advance bookings are required for camping.

How to book: NPRSR 13 7468 www.nprsr.qld.gov.au
Permits: camping permit required

582 Koombooloomba Conservation Park camping area

This campsite, on the cricket oval of the former town of Koombooloomba, offers enviable access to the attractions of Koombooloomba Dam (including fishing, boating and waterskiing). There are 9 separate numbered sites, each with capacity for up to 6 campers. Bring drinking water, rubbish bags and firewood. **Map refs: 163 E4, 175 F4**

KOOMBOOLOOMBA NATIONAL PARK

Koombooloomba National Park, 27 km south-east of Ravenshoe and 53 km south-west of Innisfail, is part of the Wet Tropics World Heritage Area. The traditional land of the Jirrbal people, the land is rich with a diverse array of wildlife, including the rare golden bowerbird and the yellow-bellied glider. To get here, travel south from Raveshoe on Tully Falls Rd, through Tully Falls National Park. Advance bookings are required for camping.

How to book: NPRSR 13 7468 www.nprsr.qld.gov.au
Permits: camping permit required

583 Koombooloomba National Park camping area (bush camping)

This area adjacent to Koombooloomba Dam offers no facilities, but it has excellent access to the water and its attractions via the Koombooloomba Conservation Park. Bring all self-sufficient camping gear, including drinking water, rubbish bags and firewood or a gas/fuel stove. To get here, follow the sign marked 'bush camping' before reaching the former Koombooloomba town site. **Map refs: 163 E4, 175 F4**

584 Nitchaga Creek Road camping area (bush camping)

Bush camping is permitted in the areas adjacent to Nitchaga Creek Rd, west of the bush camping area by Koombooloomba Dam. No facilities are provided and fires are prohibited, so bring all self-sufficient camping gear, including drinking water, rubbish bags and a gas/fuel stove. **Map refs: 163 E4, 175 F4**

585 Wall Creek Road camping area (bush camping)

Bush camping is permitted in the areas adjacent to Wall Creek Rd, south of the bush camping area by Koombooloomba Dam. No facilities are provided and fires are prohibited, so bring all self-sufficient camping gear, including drinking water, rubbish bags and a gas/fuel stove. **Map refs: 163 E4, 175 F4**

KUTINI–PAYAMU (IRON RANGE) NATIONAL PARK (CYPAL)

Protecting a range of magnificent wildlife, including the palm cockatoo and green python, Kutini–Payamu (Iron Range) National Park (CYPAL) is a stunning natural reserve on the east coast of Cape York Peninsula. William Bligh landed here in 1792, goldminers came through in the 1930s and American troops were sent here during World War II. Access to the national park is by 4WD only. Advance bookings are required for camping.

How to book: NPRSR 13 7468 www.nprsr.qld.gov.au
Permits: camping permit required

586 Chilli Beach camping area

Chilli Beach is near the north-east boundary of the park, reached by 4WD off Portland Roads Rd. From this campsite for self-sufficient campers you can take the 5 km walk to the mouth of Chilli Creek at the southern end of the beach. Chilli Beach is 32 km north of the ranger headquarters and 24 km east of the Gordon Creek camping area.
Map refs: 179 F5

587 Cooks Hut camping area

Cooks Hut is near the Rainforest camping area on the banks of the Claudie River, near the junction of Portland Roads and Lockhart River rds. The campsite surface is a combination of dirt and grass and there are 4 defined campsites within the space. There is a hybrid toilet but the site is for self-sufficient campers only. A recommended activity is the 10 km return bushwalking track from the Rainforest camping area through open woodland. **Map refs:** 177 E1, 179 E5

588 Gordon Creek camping area (bush camping)

This campground is on the banks of Gordon Creek at the Portland Roads Rd, about 8 km north of the ranger HQ and less than a kilometre west of the Cooks Hut camping area. There are no facilities so you need to bring self-sufficient supplies, including water and a gas/fuel stove.
Map refs: 177 E1, 179 E5

589 Rainforest camping area (bush camping)

Accessible by 4WD only, the Rainforest campsite is set in riverine rainforest on the banks of the Claudie River. The campsite surface is a combination of dirt and grass and there are 4 defined campsites available within the space. There are no facilities; bring all self-sufficient supplies, including drinking water and a gas/fuel stove. **Map refs:** 177 E1, 179 E5

LIZARD ISLAND NATIONAL PARK

Situated 93 km north-east of Cooktown, Lizard Island National Park comprises 6 islands in the Great Barrier Reef World Heritage Area. The islands contain sacred sites of the Dingaal Aboriginal people and are known for being covered with thick grasslands. There are regular flights to Lizard Island from Cairns, and commercial charter vessels depart from Cairns, Port Douglas and Cooktown. Advance bookings are required for camping.

How to book: NPRSR 13 7468 www.nprsr.qld.gov.au
Permits: camping permit required

590 Watsons Bay camping area

This campground is just over 1 km from the airstrip at the northern end of Watsons Bay on Lizard Island, and is a great spot for snorkelling and swimming. The camping area is next to the day-use area and close to several walking tracks. Bring all self-sufficient supplies, including pots and pans – the gas BBQ in the campground is an open-flame burner without a hotplate. Water is available from a pump but must be boiled or treated before use. **Map refs:** 165 H2, 177 H4

NGALBA BULAL NATIONAL PARK

About 40 km south of Cooktown, Ngalba Bulal National Park attracts visitors with its beautiful sandy beaches. Getting to its Mangkalba (Cedar Bay) section is a little more challenging than most national parks; you can reach it by boat or along 2 difficult walking tracks. The Home Rule track (16 km one-way, 6–8 hrs) begins at Home Rule Rainforest Lodge, a private property 3 km off Cooktown–Bloomfield Rd from Rossville. The Gap Creek track (6 km one-way, 4–6 hrs) begins further south on the eastern side of Cooktown–Bloomfield Rd. Note: access to Rattlesnake Point is restricted to members of the Eastern Kuku Yalanji people.

Who to contact: QPWS Mossman 13 7468 *Permits:* camping permit required *Camping fees:* fees can be paid and permits acquired at QPWS Mossman; or NPRSR Atherton and Cairns business centres

 **Cedar Bay camping area (bush camping)**

This campground is just east of Centre Garden at the southern end of the beach. Access is via the Home Rule or Gap Creek walking tracks, or by boat. Generators are not permitted and gas/fuel stoves are preferred. Bring all self-sufficient supplies. Wildlife-watchers can look out for Bennett's tree-kangaroo, the endangered southern cassowary and beach stone-curlew. **Map refs:** 175 E1, 177 H5

OYALA THUMOTANG NATIONAL PARK (CYPAL)

An enormous wilderness park in central Cape York Peninsula, Oyala Thumotang National Park (CYPAL) covers 381 000 ha between the Coen and Archer rivers. The region is the home of the Wik Mungkan, Southern Kaanju and Ayapathu Indigenous peoples. 4WD access is from the Peninsula Developmental Rd, 24 km north of Coen; the ranger headquarters is 72 km west of the Peninsula Developmental Rd. Note: the park is closed Dec–Apr each year for the wet season. Advance bookings are required for camping.

How to book: NPRSR 13 7468 www.nprsr.qld.gov.au
Permits: camping permit required

 10 Mile Junction 7 camping area (bush camping)

A maximum of 6 self-sufficient campers are permitted to stay at this sandy site by the Archer River in the Langi section of the park. No facilities are provided, so bring all self-sufficient camping gear, including drinking water, rubbish bags and firewood or a gas/fuel stove. **Map refs:** 176 D2

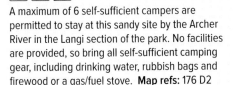 **10 Mile Junction 8 camping area (bush camping)**

A maximum of 6 self-sufficient campers are permitted to stay at this sandy site by the Archer River in the Langi section of the park. No facilities are provided, so bring all self-sufficient camping

gear, including drinking water, rubbish bags and firewood or a gas/fuel stove. **Map refs:** 176 D2

 Chong Swamp camping area (bush camping)

A maximum of 6 self-sufficient campers are permitted to stay at this clearing by the Chong Swamp in the Coen River section of the park. No facilities are provided, so bring all self-sufficient camping gear, including drinking water, rubbish bags and firewood or a gas/fuel stove. **Map refs:** 176 C2

 **First Coen River camping area (bush camping)**

A maximum of 8 self-sufficient campers are permitted to stay at this shady clearing by the Coen River in the Coen River section of the park. No facilities are provided, so bring all self-sufficient camping gear, including drinking water, rubbish bags and firewood or a gas/fuel stove. **Map refs:** 176 C2

 Governors Waterhole camping area (bush camping)

A maximum of 12 self-sufficient campers are permitted to stay in open woodland by Governors Waterhole in the Archer Bend section of the park. No facilities are provided, so bring all self-sufficient camping gear, including drinking water, rubbish bags and firewood or a gas/fuel stove. **Map refs:** 176 C2

 Horsetailer Waterhole camping area (bush camping)

A maximum of 10 self-sufficient campers are permitted to stay by the bank of the Archer River in the Archer Bend section of the park. No facilities are provided, so bring all self-sufficient camping gear, including drinking water, rubbish bags and firewood or a gas/fuel stove. **Map refs: 176 C2**

598 **Jerry Lagoon camping area (bush camping)**

A maximum of 6 self-sufficient campers are permitted to stay in the open woodland beside Jerry Lagoon in the Langi section of the park. No facilities are provided, so bring all self-sufficient camping gear, including drinking water, rubbish bags and firewood or a gas/fuel stove. **Map refs: 176 D2**

599 **Langi Lagoon camping area (bush camping)**

A maximum of 8 self-sufficient campers are permitted to stay in the open woodland beside Langi Lagoon in the Langi section of the park. No facilities are provided, so bring all self-sufficient camping gear, including drinking water, rubbish bags and firewood or a gas/fuel stove. **Map refs: 176 D2**

600 **Mango Lagoon 9 camping area (bush camping)**

A maximum of 8 self-sufficient campers are permitted to stay in this open woodland campsite beside Mango Lagoon in the Coen River section of the park. No facilities are provided, so bring all self-sufficient camping gear, including drinking water, rubbish bags and firewood or a gas/fuel stove. **Map refs: 176 C2**

601 **Mango Lagoon 10 camping area (bush camping)**

A maximum of 8 self-sufficient campers are permitted to stay in this open woodland campsite

beside Mango Lagoon in the Coen River section of the park. No facilities are provided, so bring all self-sufficient camping gear, including drinking water, rubbish bags and firewood or a gas/fuel stove. **Map refs: 176 C2**

602 **Mango Lagoon 11 camping area (bush camping)**

A maximum of 8 self-sufficient campers are permitted to stay in this open woodland campsite beside Mango Lagoon in the Coen River section of the park. No facilities are provided, so bring all self-sufficient camping gear, including drinking water, rubbish bags and firewood or a gas/fuel stove. **Map refs: 176 C2**

603 **Night Paddock Lagoon camping area (bush camping)**

A maximum of 6 self-sufficient campers are permitted to stay in the open woodland beside Night Paddock Lagoon in the Langi section of the park. No facilities are provided, so bring all self-sufficient camping gear, including drinking water, rubbish bags and firewood or a gas/fuel stove. **Map refs: 176 D2**

604 **Old Archer Crossing camping area (bush camping)**

A maximum of 8 self-sufficient campers are permitted to stay in this shady campsite on the banks of the Archer River in the Langi section of the park. No facilities are provided, so bring all self-sufficient camping gear, including drinking water, rubbish bags and firewood or a gas/fuel stove. **Map refs: 176 D2**

QUEENSLAND | THE FAR NORTH

605 Second Coen River 14 camping area (bush camping)

A maximum of 8 self-sufficient campers are permitted to stay in this clearing by the Coen River in the Coen River section of the park. No facilities are provided, so bring all self-sufficient camping gear including drinking water, rubbish bags and firewood or a gas/fuel stove. **Map refs:** 176 C2

606 Second Coen River 15 camping area (bush camping)

A maximum of 8 self-sufficient campers are permitted to stay in this clearing by the Coen River in the Coen River section of the park. No facilities are provided, so bring all self-sufficient camping gear, including drinking water, rubbish bags and firewood or a gas/fuel stove. **Map refs:** 176 C2

607 Twin Lagoons 5 camping area (bush camping)

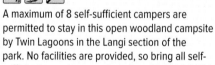

A maximum of 8 self-sufficient campers are permitted to stay in this open woodland campsite by Twin Lagoons in the Langi section of the park. No facilities are provided, so bring all self-sufficient camping gear, including drinking water, rubbish bags and firewood or a gas/fuel stove. **Map refs:** 176 D2

608 Twin Lagoons 6 camping area (bush camping)

A maximum of 8 self-sufficient campers are permitted to stay in this open woodland campsite by Twin Lagoons in the Langi section of the park. No facilities are provided, so bring all self-sufficient camping gear, including drinking water, rubbish bags and firewood or a gas/fuel stove. **Map refs:** 176 D2

609 Vardons Lagoon camping area (bush camping)

A maximum of 6 self-sufficient campers are permitted to stay in this cleared area by Vardons Lagoon in the Coen River section of the park. No facilities are provided, so bring all self-sufficient camping gear, including drinking water, rubbish bags and firewood or a gas/fuel stove. **Map refs:** 176 C2

PALMER GOLDFIELD RESOURCES RESERVE

About 280 km north-west of Cairns, Palmer Goldfield Resources Reserve was the site of a major gold rush from 1873. The goldfields have been inactive since the 1880s, but today visitors can view the old sites and reminders of the gold rush. Take the Whites Creek turn-off to Granite and Cannibal creeks from the Peninsula Developmental Rd, then turn north to Dog Leg Creek Junction south-east of Maytown.

Who to contact: NPRSR 13 7468 www.nprsr. qld.gov.au *Permits:* camping permit required *Camping fees:* fees can be paid and permits acquired at NPRSR Cairns business centre

610 Dog Leg Crossing camping area (bush camping)

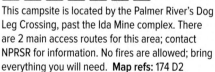

This campsite is located by the Palmer River's Dog Leg Crossing, past the Ida Mine complex. There are 2 main access routes for this area; contact NPRSR for information. No fires are allowed; bring everything you will need. **Map refs:** 174 D2

611 Palmer River camping area (bush camping)

This campground beside the North Palmer River is accessible by 4WD and suits self-sufficient campers only. As with Dog Leg Crossing camping area, there are 2 main access routes for the campground; contact NPRSR for information. **Map refs:** 174 D1

RINYIRRU (LAKEFIELD) NATIONAL PARK (CYPAL)

Rinyirru (Lakefield) National Park (CYPAL) on the Cape York Peninsula is Qld's second largest park. Stretching from the small outback town of Laura in the south to Princess Charlotte Bay in the north, it is renowned for its vast river systems and spectacular wetlands. Gallery rainforest grows along parts of the Normanby and Kennedy rivers, and monsoonal scrub is found on sections of the park's sandstone escarpments. Rinyirru is a favourite fishing destination of the Cape York Peninsula: anglers can target barramundi, tarpon, catfish and archerfish in the freshwater regions; and mangrove jack, fingermark, cod, trevally, queenfish and salmon in the saltwater areas. Note: the park is closed during the wet season, usually from Dec–Apr, and camping areas north of the Lakefield ranger base are closed until the end of May. Advance bookings are required for camping.

How to book: NPRSR 13 7468 www.nprsr.qld.gov.au
Permits: camping permit required

612 Annie River camping area (bush camping)

The 4WD access track to Annie River, the park's most northerly campground, is off Marina Plains Rd, about 14 km north of Lakefield Rd. Bring drinking water, firewood and a gas/fuel stove. Never swim, canoe, clean fish or prepare food at the water's edge, or camp close to deep waterholes, as estuarine crocodiles live in these waters. **Map refs:** 164 B2, 177 E3

613 Basin Hole camping area (bush camping)

This basic campsite for self-sufficient campers only is on Jam Tin Creek, 28 km north of Lakefield ranger base and 9 km north-east of Hann Crossing. Bring all self-sufficient gear, including drinking water, rubbish bags and firewood or a gas/fuel stove. **Map refs:** 164 C2, 177 F4

614 Bizant River camping area (bush camping)

This bush camp is located on a flat patch adjacent to the Bizant River boat ramp – an unformed boat launch that offers access to the tidal Bizant River and Princess Charlotte Bay. It is 25 km north-north-east of Hann Crossing by road. Bring all self-sufficient gear, including drinking water, rubbish bags and firewood or a gas/fuel stove. **Map refs:** 164 C2, 177 F4

615 Bottom Whiphandle Waterhole camping area (bush camping)

Just a few kilometres north of Top Whiphandle, Bottom Whiphandle Waterhole is about 29 km north-east of Hann Crossing, reached from Bizant Outstation. Recreational fishing is permitted at all camping areas. Check with a ranger for current fishing restrictions and regulations. Note: canoeing is not recommended due to the presence of crocodiles. **Map refs:** 164 D2, 177 F4

616 Brown Creek camping area (bush camping)

This campsite, close to the Bizant River boat ramp and camping area, lies at the junction of Brown Creek and Bizant River, 26 km north-north-east of Hann Crossing by road. Bring all self-sufficient gear, including drinking water, rubbish bags and firewood or a gas/fuel stove. **Map refs:** 164 C2, 177 F4

617 Dingo Waterhole camping area (bush camping)

Dingo Waterhole is 33 km north of New Laura Ranger Station and a further 9 km from the Lakefield Rd turn-off. Open fires are allowed but generators are not permitted. **Map refs:** 164 D4, 177 F4

618 Five Mile Creek camping area (bush camping)

This small site is about 5 km south-west of Annie River camping area, and suits self-sufficient campers only. Use the existing fire sites, and preferably bring a gas/fuel stove. **Map refs:** 164 B2, 177 E3

619 Hann Crossing camping area

Most campers visiting Rinyirru stay at either Kalpowar or this campground at Hann Crossing on Lakefield Rd, 29 km north of Lakefield Ranger Station. Accessible by 4WD only, there are 17 numbered sites for general use and 2 for commercial operators. Bring drinking water, firewood, rubbish bags and a gas/fuel stove. William Hann made a crossing of the North Kennedy River here during his expedition to Cape York in 1872. He also discovered gold on the Palmer River, initiating the rush of 1873, which resulted in the tracks through the southern end of the park. **Map refs:** 164 C3, 177 F4

620 Hanush's Waterhole camping area (bush camping)

To reach Hanush's Waterhole, take the access track signposted about 7 km north of Lakefield Ranger Station, then travel a further 7.5 km to the camping area. This site suits self-sufficient campers only; use existing fire sites (a gas/fuel stove is preferred). **Map refs:** 164 D3, 177 F4

621 Horseshoe Lagoon camping area (bush camping)

To reach this campground for self-sufficient campers, head for Old Laura Homestead then turn onto Battle Camp Rd and travel 29 km east of Old Laura to the turn-off. Check with a ranger

for current fishing restrictions and regulations. Canoeing is not recommended in some areas of the park due to the presence of crocodiles. **Map refs:** 165 E5, 177 G5

622 Kalpowar Crossing Campground

Rinyirru's most popular camping ground, with the best facilities, Kalpowar is 3 km east of the Lakefield Ranger Station, next to an 8 km stretch of permanent fresh waterholes on the Normanby River. Accessible by 4WD only, there are 14 numbered sites for general use and 4 numbered sites set aside for commercial operators. Wildlife-watchers can explore the 4 km walking track and boaties can launch their craft from the causeway. Water provided here must be boiled or treated before use. Bring your own firewood. Generators are not permitted. **Map refs:** 164 D3, 177 F4

623 Kennedy Bend Waterhole camping area (bush camping)

Kennedy Bend Waterhole is on Lakefield Rd, 8 km north of New Laura Ranger Station. Rinyirru (Lakefield) National Park (CYPAL) protects a number of threatened species, including the golden-shouldered parrot, star finch, red goshawk, Lakeland Downs mouse and spectacled hare-wallaby. A variety of fish inhabit the rivers, including barramundi. Campers need to use the existing fire sites and preferably bring a gas/fuel stove. **Map refs:** 164 D4, 177 F4

624 Melaleuca Waterhole camping area (bush camping)

This waterhole's access track is signposted about 7 km north-west of Lakefield Ranger Station; approximately 19 km further on you'll find the camping area with 4 sites. Rinyirru has an extensive river system comprising the Normanby, Morehead and North Kennedy rivers and their tributaries. During the wet season, these waterways join to flood vast areas, eventually draining into Princess Charlotte Bay. Bring all self-sufficient supplies. **Map refs: 164 D3, 177 F4**

625 Mick Fienn Waterhole camping area (bush camping)

Mick Fienn Waterhole is 33 km north of New Laura Ranger Station and a further 9 km from the Lakefield Rd turn-off, just north of Dingo Waterhole. There are 5 numbered sites; campsites 1, 2 and 5 provide good shade and access to permanent deep holes in the river. During the dry season, the rivers and creeks in the region shrink, leaving large permanent waterholes, lakes and lagoons interspersed with flood plains, ridges and riverbeds. Bring all self-sufficient supplies. **Map refs: 164 D3, 177 F4**

626 Midway Waterhole camping area (bush camping)

The access track to Midway Waterhole is signposted about 6 km north-west of Lakefield Ranger Station; then it's a further 3.7 km to the camping area. This site suits self-sufficient campers only; use existing fire sites (gas/fuel stove preferred). For wildlife-watchers, in the open woodland and grassland areas of Rinyirru (Lakefield) National Park (CYPAL), agile wallabies are abundant; the northern nailtail wallaby and Australian bustard are harder to find. **Map refs: 164 D3, 177 F4**

627 Old Faithful Waterhole camping area (bush camping)

Turn off about 23 km north of New Laura Ranger Station to reach this campground, about 6 km east of Lakefield Rd. There are 3 numbered campsites next to the waterhole on the Normanby River, an ideal spot for fishing. Open fires and generators are allowed; a gas/fuel stove is preferred. **Map refs: 164 D4, 177 F4**

628 Old Laura Homestead camping area (bush camping)

This campsite is next to the historical Old Laura Homestead, a cattle homestead recently restored from years of decay and vandalism and now protected by the Queensland Heritage Register. There are no facilities, so bring all self-sufficient gear, including drinking water, rubbish bags and firewood or a gas/fuel stove. **Map refs: 165 E5, 177 F5**

629 Orange Plain Waterhole camping area (bush camping)

This waterhole is about 18 km north-east of Hann Crossing via Bizant Outstation. Campers must be totally self-sufficient; bring drinking water, firewood and preferably a gas/fuel stove. During the dry season, the rivers and creeks shrink, leaving large permanent waterholes, lakes and lagoons interspersed with flood plains, ridges and riverbeds. **Map refs: 164 D3, 177 F4**

630 Saltwater Crossing camping area (bush camping)

This campground is on Lakefield Rd, about 32 km north-west of Hann Crossing and about 8 km east of Marina Plains Rd. There are 2 areas – on the east and west side of the causeway – both with 2 campsites for self-sufficient campers only. **Map refs: 164 C2, 177 F4**

631 Six Mile Waterhole camping area (bush camping)

Six Mile Waterhole is about 15 km south of the New Laura Ranger Station, 3 km east of Lakefield Rd. The park's wetlands attract a diversity of animals, particularly waterbirds. Look for brolgas, sarus cranes, black-necked storks, comb-crested jacanas, magpie geese and ducks. It is for self-sufficient campers only; use the existing fire sites. **Map refs:** 165 E4, 177 F5

 Sweetwater Lake camping area (bush camping)

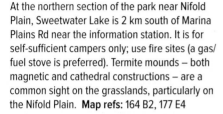

At the northern section of the park near Nifold Plain, Sweetwater Lake is 2 km south of Marina Plains Rd near the information station. It is for self-sufficient campers only; use fire sites (a gas/fuel stove is preferred). Termite mounds – both magnetic and cathedral constructions – are a common sight on the grasslands, particularly on the Nifold Plain. **Map refs:** 164 B2, 177 E4

 Top Whiphandle Waterhole camping area (bush camping)

Top Whiphandle Waterhole is about 20 km north-east of Hann Crossing via Bizant Outstation. Campers must be totally self-sufficient, and preferably bring a gas/fuel stove; use existing fire sites. **Map refs:** 164 D2, 177 F4

 Twelve Mile Lagoon camping area (bush camping)

Twelve Mile Lagoon is near the Normanby River about 12 km east of Lakefield Rd; take the turn-off opposite New Laura Ranger Station. There are 9 numbered sites; open fires are allowed in the provided rings and generators are permitted. Bring all self-sufficient supplies. Rinyirru (Lakefield) has an extensive river system comprising the Normanby, Morehead and North Kennedy rivers and their tributaries. During the wet season, these waterways join to flood vast areas, eventually draining into Princess Charlotte Bay. **Map refs:** 165 E4, 177 F4

 **Welcome Waterhole camping area (bush camping)**

The Welcome Waterhole is about 7 km from Horseshoe Lagoon and about 6 km north of Battle Camp Rd. The turn-off from Battle Camp Rd is about 30 km east of Old Laura Homestead. Bring all self-sufficient supplies. **Map refs:** 165 E4, 177 G5

RUSSELL RIVER NATIONAL PARK

Situated about 83 km south-east of Cairns, Russell River National Park is a small coastal park within the Wet Tropics World Heritage Area. The park occupies a section of the Graham Range between the Russell River and the coastal mangroves. There is a high incidence of estuarine crocodiles in the region.

Who to contact: NPRSR 13 7468 www.nprsr. qld.gov.au *Permits:* camping permit required *Camping fees:* fees can be paid and permits acquired at the self-registration station

 **Graham Range camping area (bush camping)**

This sandy campground with 5 separate sites is next to the beach and accessible only by 4WD. To get here, turn off the Bruce Hwy at Miriwinni, 65 km south of Cairns, and follow the road for 17 km to Bramston Beach. At Bramston Beach, turn left onto Sassafras St and follow the track for 5.5 km to Bluemetal Creek. From the mouth of Bluemetal Creek, follow the unsealed road 1.5 km to the self-registration stand. This camping area is suitable for self-sufficient campers only; fires are permitted (bring firewood) but a gas/fuel stove is preferred. **Map refs:** 163 G2, 175 G3

SPEEWAH CONSERVATION PARK

Speewah Conservation Park is a small (15.2 ha) park on the western border of Barron Gorge National Park, 42 km north-west of Cairns. It provides excellent access to Barron Gorge's tropical wonderland of rainforests, butterflies and waterfalls. The Skyrail and scenic train provide picturesque jaunts through the area, reached from Kuranda on the Kennedy Hwy. *Who to contact:* NPRSR 13 7468 www.nprsr. qld.gov.au *Permits:* camping permit required *Camping fees:* fees can be paid and permits acquired at the self-registration station

637 Speewah Campground

This campground is in the conservation park adjacent to Barron Gorge National Park's western boundary. It is reached from the Kennedy Hwy, 10 km west of Kuranda, then a further 6 km east to the site. You can also get here from Stoney Creek Rd, off Speewah Rd. Fires are prohibited, so bring a gas/fuel stove along with all other self-sufficient supplies (water is provided). Take the 570 m bush boardwalk to the falls, or check out Wrights Lookout, a 1 km (30 min) walk from the Barron Falls carpark. **Map refs:** 163 E1, 175 F3

THREE ISLANDS GROUP NATIONAL PARK

An archipelago stretching 44–72 km north-east of Cooktown, Three Islands Group National Park is one of the most remote and unspoiled national parks in Qld. These islands are particularly significant as breeding sites for seabirds, including the wedge-tailed shearwater. Access is by private boat or accredited tour company only. Advance bookings are required for camping.

How to book: NPRSR 13 7468 www.nprsr.qld.gov.au *Permits:* camping permit required

638 Two Islands camping area (boat-based camping)

Bush camping is permitted on Two Islands A, the larger western island in the Two Islands group, between Apr and Aug each year. Camping outside these times is prohibited, to protect nesting seabirds. There are no facilities and open fires are not permitted; bring all self-sufficient camping gear, including drinking water, rubbish bags and a gas/fuel stove. **Map refs:** 165 H4, 177 H4

TULLY FALLS NATIONAL PARK

Bring an umbrella or raincoat with you when you visit Tully Falls National Park – part of the Wet Tropics World Heritage Area, it is one of the wettest places in Australia, receiving approximately 400 cm of rain per annum. Tully Falls protects a dazzling variety of wildlife, including species found only in the Wet Tropics, such as Lumholtz's tree-kangaroo and the golden bowerbird. Camping in the park is prohibited except for hikers taking the Misty Mountains Wilderness Walking Tracks. Advance bookings are required for camping.

How to book: NPRSR 13 7468 www.nprsr.qld.gov.au *Permits:* camping permit required

639 Cannabullen Creek camping area (walk-in camping)

This campsite on the Cardwell Range track is 11 km from Hinson Creek trailhead, 10 km from Hinson Creek camping area and 9.5 km from Cardwell Range trailhead. There are no facilities provided; bring all self-sufficient camping gear, including drinking water, rubbish bags and a gas/fuel stove. **Map refs:** 163 E4, 175 F4

640 Carter Creek camping area (walk-in camping)

This campsite on the Cannabullen Creek track is 8 km from the Hinson Creek trailhead, 6.5 km from Hinson Creek camping area, and 6.5 km from Cochable Creek camping area (Tully Gorge National Park). There are no facilities provided; bring all self-sufficient camping gear, including drinking water, rubbish bags and a gas/fuel stove. **Map refs:** 163 E4, 175 F4

641 Hinson Creek camping area (walk-in camping)

This campsite near the intersection of the Cannabullen Creek and Cardwell Range tracks is 19 km from Cardwell Range trailhead, 10 km from Cannabullen Creek camping area, 6.5 km from Carter Creek camping area and 1 km from Hinson Creek trailhead. There are no facilities provided; bring all self-sufficient camping gear, including drinking water, rubbish bags and a gas/fuel stove. **Map refs:** 163 E4, 175 F4

 **642 Koolmoon Creek Headwaters camping area (walk-in camping)**

This campsite on the Koolmoon Creek track is 1.3 km from Koolmoon Creek Headwaters trailhead and 12.3 km from Walters Waterhole camping area. There are no facilities provided; bring all self-sufficient camping gear, including drinking water, rubbish bags and a gas/fuel stove. **Map refs:** 163 E4, 175 F4

643 Walters Waterhole camping area (walk-in camping)

This campsite on the Koolmoon Creek track is 3.4 km from Djilgarrin trailhead, 12.3 km from Koolmoon Creek Headwaters and 12 km from Cochable Creek camping area (Tully Gorge National Park). There are no facilities provided; bring all self-sufficient camping gear, including drinking water, rubbish bags and a gas/fuel stove. **Map refs:** 163 E4, 175 F4

TULLY GORGE NATIONAL PARK

Famous for the whitewater rafting on the Tully River, Tully Gorge National Park is 35 km north-west of the town of Tully. Home to the Jirrbal Indigenous people, the park offers bushwalking, swimming and panoramic lookouts. The park can be accessed by conventional vehicle along Cardstone and Gulnay rds. The Misty Mountains Wilderness Walking Tracks pass through Tully Gorge; the campsite at Cochable Creek is for hikers only. Advance bookings are required for camping.

How to book: NPRSR 13 7468 www.nprsr.qld.gov.au
Permits: camping permit required

644 Cochable Creek camping area

This campsite at the intersection of the Koolmoon Creek and Cannabullen Creek tracks is 15.4 km from Djilgarrin trailhead, 14.5 km from Hinson Creek trailhead and 12 km from Walters Waterhole (Tully Falls National Park). It is one of the few camping areas on the Misty Mountains tracks

that can be accessed by car. Basic facilities are provided; bring all self-sufficient camping gear, including drinking water, rubbish bags and a gas/fuel stove. **Map refs:** 163 E4, 175 F4

 645 Tully Gorge camping area

Accessible by 2WD via a bitumen road, this grassy site is the only campground in the national park available to non-hikers. A 375 m return, wheelchair-accessible rainforest walk starts from the picnic and camping area. Watch the whitewater rafters from Flip Wilson Lookout, 2 km beyond the campground. Note: open fires are prohibited; bring all self-sufficient supplies. **Map refs:** 163 E4, 175 F4

TURTLE GROUP NATIONAL PARK

Turtle Group National Park protects 4 very small islands in the Great Barrier Reef Marine Park, about 30 km west of Lizard Island. Access is by private boat only. Visitors should be aware that estuarine crocodiles live in the surrounding waters and that marine stingers are present Oct–May. Advance bookings are required for camping.

How to book: NPRSR 13 7468 www.nprsr.qld.gov.au
Permits: camping permit required

 646 Nymph Island camping area (boat-based camping)

Camping is permitted on the northern edge of Nymph Island, 35 km east of Murdoch Point. There are no facilities on site; bring all self-sufficient supplies. Note: fishing is prohibited in the waters of the Turtle Group. **Map refs:** 165 H2, 177 H4

647 Turtle Group A camping area (boat-based camping)

Camping is permitted anywhere on Turtle Group A, the second largest islet in the Turtle Group, west of Turtle Group B. There are no facilities on site; bring all self-sufficient supplies. Note: fishing is prohibited in the waters surrounding the Turtle Group. **Map refs:** 165 G3, 177 H4

Josephine Falls, Wooroonooran National Park

648 Turtle Group B camping area
(boat-based camping)

Camping is permitted anywhere on Turtle Group B, the largest and southernmost islet in the Turtle Group. There are no facilities on site; bring all self-sufficient supplies. Note: fishing is prohibited in the waters surrounding the Turtle Group. **Map refs:** 165 G3, 177 H4

649 Turtle Group F camping area
(boat-based camping)

Camping is permitted anywhere on Turtle Group F, the second most northerly islet in the Turtle Group. There are no facilities on site; bring all self-sufficient supplies. Note: fishing is prohibited in the waters surrounding the Turtle Group. **Map refs:** 165 G3, 177 H4

WOOROONOORAN NATIONAL PARK

Part of the Wet Tropics World Heritage Area, Wooroonooran National Park boasts the 2 highest mountains in Qld, including Mt Bartle Frere, along with wild rivers, spectacular waterfalls and lush rainforests, which blanket the landscape from foothills to summits. Widely regarded as one of the most scenic areas of the Wet Tropics, yet receiving few visitors, Wooroonooran is one of Qld's best-kept secrets.

The Misty Mountains Wilderness Walking Tracks pass through Wooroonooran; the campsite at Downey Creek is for hikers only. A small number of self-registration sites are available at Goldsborough Valley, but advance bookings are required for all other areas.

How to book: NPRSR 13 7468 www.nprsr.qld.gov.au *Permits:* camping permit required *Camping fees:* fees can be paid and permits acquired for Goldsborough Valley at the self-registration station

Bartle Frere Trail

Please note that campsites are listed in alphabetical order, not track order. Refer to the map on p. 163 for further information.

650 Big Rock camping area
(walk-in camping)

The Big Rock camp clearing is a 3 km walk north-west of the Josephine Falls parking area, and is suitable for self-sufficient campers only. For experienced walkers, Josephine Falls is the starting point for the difficult Mt Bartle Frere Trail (15 km one-way, 2 days), which leads to the summit and back. Broken Nose Track (10 km return, 8 hr) offers a shorter but equally steep alternative. The summit can also be approached from the Atherton Tableland, again a challenging 2-day walk. **Map refs:** 163 F3, 175 F4

651 Eastern Summit camping area (walk-in camping)

This campground for self-sufficient campers has excellent views over Innisfail and the undulating Atherton Tableland. The site is 4 km north-west of Big Rock camping area and 7 km from the Josephine Falls parking area. Make sure you check weather conditions with the ranger before undertaking the Bartle Frere Trail, as clouds can move in quickly on the upper reaches of the mountain and rainstorms are common all year. The dry season, May–Oct, is the best time to walk the trail. **Map refs:** 163 F3, 175 F4

652 Junction camping area (bush camping)

At the western end of the Mt Bartle Frere Trail, campers can walk in or access the site via road (unsuitable for conventional vehicles when wet). Go birdwatching during the day and search for possums by spotlight at night. The many beautiful waterfalls along the national park's walking tracks are a photographer's delight. There are no facilities on site; campers must be self-sufficient. **Map refs:** 163 F3, 175 F4

653 Western Summit camping area (walk-in camping)

Accessible only on foot, this campground is an 8 km walk from the Junction camping area at the Atherton Tableland (west) end of the walking trail. The Bartle Frere summit is just 750 m from this camp. There are no facilities. The Mt Bartle Frere area is the spiritual home of the Noongyanbudda Ngadjon people, and the place their spirits return to when they die. **Map refs:** 163 F3, 175 F4

654 Downey Creek camping area (walk-in camping)

This campsite on the Gorrell track, one of the Misty Mountains Wilderness Walking Tracks, is 15.5 km from eastern Gorrell trailhead and 10.3 km from western Gorrell trailhead. There are no facilities provided; bring all self-sufficient camping gear, including drinking water, rubbish bags an. gas/fuel stove. **Map refs:** 163 F4, 175 F4

655 Goldsborough Valley camping area

This grassy, shady site for self-sufficient campers is on the banks of the Mulgrave River, 25 km south-west of Gordonvale. There are 4 numbered sites for e-permit holders, each with its own alcove. Open fires are permitted in the existing fire rings. Check out the Goldfield trail, a 19 km one-way (7–9 hr) track following the footsteps of the gold prospectors from the camping area along the Mulgrave River. Bring firewood and drinking water. **Map refs:** 163 F2, 175 F3

656 Henrietta Creek camping area

Accessible by 2WD, this grassy camping area is signposted off the Palmerston Hwy, 38 km from Innisfail. There are 3 numbered and 20 unnumbered sites. The park's Wet Tropics' endemics include the tiny musky rat-kangaroo, double-eyed fig-parrot and chowchilla. At Henrietta Creek there are also platypus and freshwater turtles. Golden bowerbirds, which only live at elevations above 900 m between Paluma and Cooktown, can be seen Nov–Jan in this section of the park. Bring drinking water. **Map refs:** 163 F3, 175 F4

657 South Johnstone camping area

This small spot on the banks of the South Johnstone River offers room for about 5 tents (camper trailers are accommodated in the nearby carpark). The main activities here are swimming and short walks, and it connects with the Misty Mountains Wilderness Walking Tracks. It is 12.3 km from Palmerston Hwy on K-Tree Rd, or 2.4 km from the western Gorrell track trailhead. Fires are prohibited: bring water and a gas/fuel stove. **Map refs:** 163 F3, 175 F4

ND NATIONAL PARK (CYPAL)

orth of Lockhart River, Wuthara
ark (CYPAL) comprises 3 islands
...the Wuthara Group. These steep, high
continental islands are covered in melaleuca
scrub and dramatic headlands. Access is by
private boat from Lockhart River or accredited
tour company only. Advance bookings are
required for camping.

How to book: NPRSR 13 7468 www.nprsr.qld.gov.au
Permits: camping permit required

658 Wuthara Island camping area (boat-based camping)

Bush camping is permitted above the high-water
mark on the main beach on the north-west of
the main Wuthara Island. There are no facilities
and open fires are not permitted; bring all
self-sufficient camping gear, including drinking
water, rubbish bags and a gas/fuel stove.
Map refs: 179 F4

CAMPSITES LOCATED IN OTHER AREAS

659 Archer River Roadhouse

Archer River Roadhouse is open Apr–Dec and
closed at other times due to the wet season. The
licensed roadhouse offers meals, fuel and basic
mechanical repairs. In addition to the camping
facilities, 10 single air-conditioned rooms and
4 twin rooms are also available on site. The
roadhouse is on the Peninsula Developmental Rd,
64 km north of Coen. **Map refs:** 176 D2

How to book: Peninsula Developmental Rd,
Archer River (07) 4060 3266

660 Armbrust & Co camping area

Across the road from the Exchange Hotel on
Regent St in the centre of the town of Coen, this

campground has 14 campsites and space for
2 vehicles per site; bring your own firewood.
Due to the summer wet season and impassable
roads, the campground is open Apr–Dec. Coen is
about 100 km north of the Musgrave Roadhouse
and 65 km south of the Archer River Roadhouse.
Map refs: 176 D3

How to book: Regent St, Coen (07) 4060 1134

661 Babinda Creek camping area

This campground beside the creek is a great spot
for camping with kids. It's east of the Bruce Hwy
on Howard Kennedy Dr in Babinda, 24 km north
of Innisfail. There is a maximum stay of 72 hr.
Map refs: 163 F3, 175 F3

Who to contact: Babinda Information Centre
(07) 4067 1008

662 The Bend camping area

This small campground has space for 6 caravans
or camper trailers, so make it an overnight
stop only. It is set beside the Coen River on the
Peninsula Developmental Rd, 3 km north of
Coen. In the centre of the Cape York Peninsula,
Coen is part of the large Cook Shire Council.
Note: there are no showers at the toilet block.
Map refs: 176 D2

Who to contact: Cooktown Tourist Information
Centre (07) 4069 6004

663 BIG4 Port Douglas Glengarry Holiday Park

This holiday park offers campers a quiet getaway
tucked in the undisturbed Mowbray River Valley,
6 km from Port Douglas. It offers a variety of
creature comforts, including free wireless internet,
a laundry and a jumping pillow. It also offers
caravan and vehicle storage for those who wish to
explore the cape in a rented 4WD. Bookings are
recommended. **Map refs:** 175 F2

How to book: Mowbray River Rd, Craiglie
(07) 4098 5922, 1800 888 134
www.glengarrypark.com.au

 664 The Boulders camping area

This campground beside a creek is 6 km west of
Babinda on Boulders Rd, with signposted access
off the Bruce Hwy. There are 5 sites with no more
than 5 people per site. There is a maximum stay
of 48 hr. **Map refs:** 163 F3, 175 F3

Who to contact: Babinda Information Centre
(07) 4067 1008

 665 Bramston Beach Campground

This campground in a small village with just a
general store provides a quiet, relaxing stopover
or weekend getaway. Bramston Beach is on
the coast, 10 km north-east of Miriwinni on
the Bruce Hwy, with excellent coastal scenery.

The campground is on Evans Rd. There are no
powered sites, but a washing machine is available
for use. There is a boat ramp 1.5 km down the
road. Bookings are required at peak periods.
Map refs: 163 G3, 175 G3

How to book: Evans Rd, Bramston Beach
(07) 4067 4121

 666 Bramwell Junction camping area

Refuel with hamburgers and beverages at the
roadhouse, then set up camp at this site at the
junction of the Telegraph Track and Bypass Rd,
about 40 km north of Cape York's Old Moreton
Telegraph Station. Fireplaces are provided
but you will need to bring your own firewood.
Map refs: 178 D4

Who to contact: cnr Telegraph Track and
Bypass Rd (07) 4060 3230

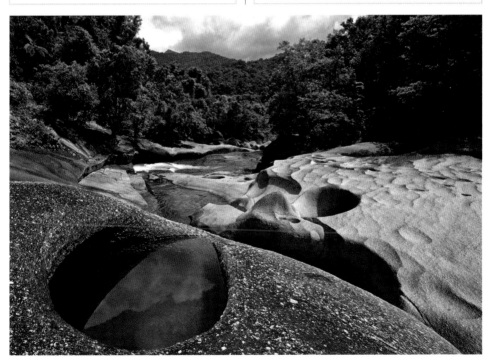

Babinda Creek, near Babinda Creek camping area (p. 142)

143

'l Station Tourist Park

The most northerly cattle station in Australia, Bramwell Station is east of Cape York's Peninsula Developmental Rd, signposted 12 km south of Bramwell Junction. The campground is grassy and shady, with several mango and frangipani trees. Bring your own firewood. The station has a licensed bar and serves meals. Unit accommodation is also available on site. **Map refs:** 178 D4

Who to contact: Bramwell Station (07) 4060 3300 www.bramwellstationtouristpark.com.au

668 Bull Crossing camping area

This campground is east of the Kowanyama Aboriginal community, a traditional land open for camping and barramundi fishing June–Sept. There is a boat launch suitable for small boats. Due to limited space, permission from the Kowanyama Land Office is essential for camping here; advance bookings are recommended. Bring all self-sufficient supplies. Note: alcohol is prohibited on Kowanyama lands; heavy fines apply. **Map refs:** 176 B5, 189 G1

How to book: Kowanyama Land Office (07) 4060 5187 *Permits:* camping permit required

669 Cairns Coconut Holiday Resort

This holiday park, located just outside the hustle and bustle of Cairns, offers excellent facilities and enviable access to the region's attractions. Facilities include a water park for the kids, an 18-hole minigolf course and outdoor movies under the stars. Advance bookings are recommended. **Map refs:** 163 F1, 175 F3

How to book: 23–51 Anderson Rd, Woree (07) 4054 6644 www.coconut.com.au

670 Cape York camping areas (bush camping)

It isn't an easy route, with river crossings to navigate and unstable road conditions, but driving to the tip of Cape York is one of Australia's most sensationally scenic 4WD trips. You'll find a number of bush campsites throughout the Cape, north from the Dulhunty River on Injinoo Community Council land. The best time to visit is June–Sept. Note: alcohol restrictions apply in the far north cape; check limits and zoned areas before embarking. **Map refs:** 178 C2

Who to contact: Northern Peninsula Area Regional Council (07) 4069 3252 *Camping fees:* included in the Jardine River Ferry fee

671 Chapman River camping area

This camping area at the mouth of the river near the airstrip is a great spot for fishing. The Pormpuraaw Aboriginal Community is on the western coast of Cape York on the Gulf of Carpentaria, about 200 km west of Musgrave. The access road is open from late May, depending on the wet season; a 4WD is recommended. Note: alcohol is strictly prohibited in Pormpuraaw; heavy penalties apply. **Map refs:** 176 B4

How to book: Pormpuraaw Shire Council (07) 4060 4600 www.pormpuraaw.qld.gov.au *Permits:* camping and vehicle permits required in advance

672 Chuulangun Aboriginal Corporation Campgrounds

A great spot for birdwatching and enjoying the natural surrounds, Chuulangun Aboriginal Corporation Campgrounds are about 5 km from the upper Wenlock crossing on Portland Roads Rd. There are no facilities besides the amenities block. No alcohol is permitted on site and you need to bring your own drinking water. **Map refs:** 176 D1

Who to contact: Kaanju Chuulangun Aboriginal Corporation (07) 4060 3240 www.kaanjungaachi. com.au *Permits:* a permit may be required for activities other than camping; contact Kaanju Chuulangun Aboriginal Corporation to discuss your proposed itinerary *Camping fees:* fees can be paid at the self-registration station or to the ranger

673 Cullen Point camping area

Self-sufficient campers can stay at Cullen Point, 10 km north of Mapoon and 95 km north of Weipa, with access via Mapoon Rd. Note: alcohol restrictions are enforced in Mapoon Shire and heavy penalties apply; check current limits before embarking. This campsite is closed during the wet season. **Map refs:** 178 C4

Who to contact: Weipa Camping Ground (07) 4069 7871 *Permits:* camping and vehicle access permits required *Camping fees:* fees can be paid and permits acquired at Weipa Camping Ground

674 Discovery Holiday Parks – Lake Tinaroo

Just 150 m from Lake Tinaroo, this caravan park has an excellent range of facilities for a comfortable stay after a day of boating or waterskiing on the lake. Other activities include fishing for barramundi or sooty grunter, or driving through Danbulla State Forest nearby. The caravan park is on Tinaroo Falls Dam Rd, about 16 km north-east of Atherton. There's a general store on site, laundry facilities, a swimming pool and the option of staying in villas or cabins. Bookings are recommended at peak periods. **Map refs:** 163 E2, 175 F3

How to book: 4–28 Tinaroo Falls Dam Rd, Tinarooo (07) 4095 8232, 1300 727 044 www.discoveryholidayparks.com.au/qld/atherton_tableland/lake_tinaroo

675 Ducie Creek camping area (bush camping)

Bush camping is permitted at this site on the 4WD Telegraph Track, 2.6 km north of Palm Creek camping area and 12.5 km south of North Alice Creek. There are no facilities; bring all self-sufficient gear. **Map refs:** 178 D4

Who to contact: Bramwell Junction (07) 4060 3230; or Northern Peninsula Regional Council (07) 4069 6800

676 False Pera Head camping area

This campground for self-sufficient campers is north of the Aurukun Community, reached from Aurukun Rd, off the Peninsula Developmental Rd. Camping and vehicle permits are required and you need to bring all self-sufficient camping gear. Note: alcohol is prohibited; heavy fines apply. **Map refs:** 176 B1

How to book: Aurukun Land and Sea Management (07) 4060 6831 *Permits:* camping and access permit required *Camping fees:* acquire permits and pay fees in advance through Aurukun Land and Sea Management

677 Granite Gorge Nature Park

Formed millions of years ago by ancient volcanoes, the boulders at Granite Gorge are a natural wonder well worth checking out. Some, allegedly, are shaped like animals. The tent sites are shady; safari tent accommodation is also available and there's a kiosk serving light lunches. Laundry facilities are also available. Take a walk beside the creek, go fishing or feed the wallabies. Granite Gorge Nature Park is 12 km west of Mareeba on Chewko Rd. **Map refs:** 162 D1, 175 F3

How to book: Chewko Rd, Chewko (07) 4093 2259 www.granitegorge.com.au

678 Hann River Roadhouse

This riverside camping ground is a great spot for watching wildlife such as birds and wallabies. It is next to the roadhouse on Peninsula Developmental Rd, 74 km north-west of Laura and 62 km south of Musgrave. The roadhouse serves food daily and stocks basic food supplies. **Map refs:** 164 C4, 177 F4

Who to contact: (07) 4060 3242

679 Home Rule Rainforest Lodge

Camp on the riverbank at this site on the Cooktown–Bloomfield Rd in Rossville. From Cape Tribulation, drive 50 km to Bloomfield (across the Bloomfield River) and along the edge of Cedar Bay National Park to reach Rossville. On-site facilities include a coin-operated washing machine and dryer, licensed bar, canoe hire and budget meals. **Map refs:** 175 E1, 177 H5

How to book: Home Rule Rd, Rossville (07) 4060 3925 www.home-rule.com.au

680 Jardine River Ferry camping area

This basic campsite is located near the Jardine River ferry crossing at the Northern Bypass Rd, 290 km north of the Archer River Roadhouse. Bring your own drinking water or treat or boil the river water before using. **Map refs:** 178 D2

Who to contact: Jardine River Ferry (07) 4069 1369

681 Kurrimine Beach Caravan Park

This very basic council campground is on Robert Johnson Pde in Kurrimine Beach, about 9 km east of the Bruce Hwy, accessed from Silkwood. The closest major town is Innisfail, about 30 km north of Kurrimine. The nearby Kurrimine Conservation Park features a 600 m walking track through a vine

forest that's great for wildlife-watching. There are laundry facilities on site, and you need to bring a gas/fuel stove. **Map refs:** 163 G4, 175 G4

Who to contact: Tully Visitor Information Centre (07) 4068 2288

682 Lakeland Caravan Park

Lakeland Caravan Park is at the junction of the Mulligan Hwy and Peninsula Development Rd in the town of Lakeland, between the Laura and Normanby rivers. On site you'll find a small internet cafe with 3 coin-operated computers, and a shop for groceries and fuel. Backpacker rooms are also available. **Map refs:** 175 E1, 177 G5

How to book: 1 Sesame St, Lakeland (07) 4060 2033 www.lakelandcaravanpark.com.au

683 Lions Den Hotel

One of Cape York's iconic pubs, the Lions Den offers excellent riverside camping on its spacious property with plenty of shade and natural surrounds. Powered campsites have access to an amenities block and drinkable water, as well as washing machines and dryers. Unpowered sites are near cool swimming holes and semi-rainforest settings. The Lions Den is at Helenvale, 32 km south of Cooktown on the Bloomfield Track. Safari lodges and air-conditioned 'donga' demountable accommodation are also available. Bookings are essential June–Oct. **Map refs:** 175 E1, 177 H5

How to book: 398 Shiptons Flat Rd, Helenvale (07) 4060 3911 www.lionsdenhotel.com.au

684 Loyalty Beach Campground and Fishing Lodge

Loyalty Beach is a 500 m strip of beachfront campsites just 45 min from Australia's most northerly point. The region is a popular place for fishing, 4WD tours and scenic flights over the

islands. The campground has laundry facilities and a kiosk with gas and ice, and pets are permitted under supervision. Other accommodation options include the air-conditioned fishing lodge and 2-storey, open-air guesthouse. It is 3 km north of Seisia Wharf, signposted from Seisia. Note: this campsite is a designated 'wet' area, but alcohol restrictions apply in the surrounding areas; check current restrictions before embarking. **Map refs:** 178 D2

How to book: 1 Loyalty Beach Rd, New Mapoon (07) 4069 3372 www.loyaltybeach.com.au

Misty Mountains Wilderness Walking Tracks

This 130 km network of walking tracks takes hikers through high-altitude tropical rainforests with crystal-clear creeks and stunning views. There are 4 main walking tracks (Koolmoon Creek, Cannabullen Creek, Cardwell Range and Gorrell) which wind their way through several national parks (Millstream Falls, Tully Falls, Tully Gorge and Wooroonooran) in a region roughly bounded by Tully, Innisfail, Mena Creek, Millaa Millaa and Ravenshoe. Advance bookings are required for camping.

Please note that campsites are listed in alphabetical order, not track order. Refer to the map on p. 163 for further information.

How to book: NPRSR 13 7468 www.nprsr.qld.gov.au
Permits: camping permit required

639 **Cannabullen Creek camping area (walk-in camping)**
See p. 138.

640 **Carter Creek camping area (walk-in camping)**
See p. 138.

644 **Cochable Creek camping area**
See p. 139.

654 **Downey Creek camping area (walk-in camping)**
See p. 141.

641 **Hinson Creek camping area (walk-in camping)**
See p. 138.

642 **Koolmoon Creek Headwaters camping area (walk-in camping)**
See p. 139.

657 **South Johnstone camping area**
See p. 141.

643 **Walters Waterhole camping area (walk-in camping)**
See p. 139.

685 **Moreton Telegraph Station**

Moreton Telegraph Station is an ideal stopover if you're travelling to the tip of Cape York. It is just under 300 km south of the tip, about 130 km from the nearest town of Weipa. The 6 ha grounds are spacious and shady for comfortable camping, and there are on-site safari tents with beds, towels and linen provided. A kiosk has basic supplies and souvenirs; firewood is not supplied. Road conditions can vary throughout the year; call ahead for up-to-date access information. **Map refs:** 178 D4

How to book: Telegraph Rd, Wenlock (07) 4060 3360 www.moretonstation.com.au

686 **Mungkun River camping area**

This camping area for self-sufficient campers is 7.5 km north of the Pormpuraaw Aboriginal Community of approximately 600 people, on the western coast of Cape York – the Gulf of Carpentaria – about 200 km west of Musgrave. The access road is open from late May, depending on the wet season. Access by 4WD is recommended. There is a boat launch on site. Note: alcohol is strictly prohibited in Pormpuraaw; heavy penalties apply. **Map refs:** 176 B4

How to book: Pormpuraaw Shire Council (07) 4060 4600 www.pormpuraaw.qld.gov.au
Permits: camping and vehicle permits required in advance

687 Musgrave Roadhouse

Owned and operated by the same local family for generations, this popular old roadhouse – formerly a telegraph station, dating back to 1887 – serves up food and fuel daily. The camping area is spacious and grassy and there is plenty of shade. The licensed kiosk provides basic food supplies, ice, fuel and souvenirs. Musgrave Roadhouse is 136 km north of Laura on the Peninsula Developmental Rd. The roads from Lakefield, Kowanyama and Pormpuraaw all meet at Musgrave. **Map refs:** 164 A3, 177 E4

How to book: Peninsula Developmental Rd, Musgrave (07) 4060 3229 www.musgraveroadhouse.com.au

688 North Alice Creek camping area (bush camping)

Bush camping is permitted at this site on the 4WD Telegraph Track, 12.5 km north of Ducie Creek camping area and 11.2 km south of Dulhunty River. There are no facilities; bring all self-sufficient gear. **Map refs:** 178 D4

Who to contact: Bramwell Junction (07) 4060 3230; or Northern Peninsula Regional Council (07) 4069 6800

689 Palm Creek camping area (bush camping)

Bush camping is permitted at this site on the 4WD Telegraph Track, 3.4 km north of Bramwell Junction at the southern end of the Telegraph Track, and 2.6 km south of Palm Creek. There are no facilities; bring all self-sufficient gear. **Map refs:** 178 D4

Who to contact: Bramwell Junction (07) 4060 3230; or Northern Peninsula Regional Council (07) 4069 6800

690 Palmer River Roadhouse

This scenic campground on an old 1870s goldmining site is on the Mulligan Hwy (Peninsula Developmental Rd), about 150 km north-west of Mareeba and 30 km south of Lakeland. Up to 17 000 diggers lived in the area in the mid 1870s – check out the artefacts at the pub. Mainly unsealed, the Peninsula Developmental Rd heads north from Mareeba for 750 km to Weipa, and is the main Cape York road. **Map refs:** 175 E2

How to book: Mulligan Hwy, Palmer River (07) 4060 2020 http://palmerriverroadhouse.com.au

691 Paronella Park Caravan Park

This basic caravan park is located beside the fascinating Paronella Park, a slowly decaying castle and grounds created by José Paronella, Catalonian emigrant canecutter, in the 1930s. Guided tours through the site are recommended. You can get here via the Old Bruce Hwy south of Innisfail. Bookings are recommended for peak periods. **Map refs:** 163 F4, 175 F4

How to book: Japoonvale Rd (Old Bruce Hwy), Mena Creek (07) 4065 3225 www.paronellapark. com.au

692 Pennefather River camping area

This basic campground for self-sufficient campers is 71 km north of Weipa, signposted off Mapoon Rd. Camping and vehicle permits can be obtained from the Weipa Camping Ground. This campsite is closed during the wet season. Note: alcohol restrictions are enforced in Mapoon Shire and heavy penalties apply; check current limits before embarking. **Map refs:** 178 C4

Who to contact: Weipa Camping Ground (07) 4069 7871 *Permits:* camping and vehicle access permits required *Camping fees:* fees can be paid and permits acquired at Weipa Camping Ground

693 Punsand Bay Camping Resort

Punsand Bay provides beachfront camping a short distance from popular ocean and river fishing locations. The campground has powered and unpowered sites, cabins with air-conditioning, on site tents (with or without ensuite) and a laundry. There's a swimming pool, licensed bar and restaurant, kiosk and internet facility. The campground is on the esplanade, 30 km north of Bamaga. A ferry to Thursday Island operates May–Oct. Note: alcohol restrictions apply in the areas around Punsand Bay; check current limits before embarking. Bookings are recommended for June–Dec. **Map refs: 178 D2**

How to book: Lot 11, Punsand Bay (07) 4069 1722 www.punsand.com.au

694 Quinkan Hotel

Camping is permitted on the grounds of this hotel in the remote township of Laura, about 140 km west of Cooktown. Hotel accommodation with air-conditioning and laundry facilities is also available on site. Meals are available at the pub, open daily to midnight. The region's biggest annual drawcard is the Laura Aboriginal Dance Festival, one of the nation's largest Indigenous cultural events. The festival is staged in June and features dance, song, workshops and films. **Map refs: 165 E5, 174 D1, 177 F5**

How to book: Terminus St, Laura (07) 4060 3393

695 Seisia Holiday Park

This holiday park in the Torres Strait Islander community of Seisia has powered and unpowered sites in beachfront and garden settings, suitable for everything from a swag to a luxury caravan. Other accommodation options on site include self-contained A-frame villas and cottages with

air-conditioning. There is a kiosk and restaurant on site. Access is via the Development Rd or the Telegraph Track; both require a 4WD and both have varying road conditions – vehicle damage is common. Several airlines and ferries regularly go to Seisia or nearby. Note: the holiday park is a designated 'wet' area but alcohol restrictions apply in the surrounding areas; check current limits before embarking. **Map refs: 178 D2**

How to book: Koraba Rd, Seisia (07) 4069 3243 www.seisiaholidaypark.com

696 Shelso camping area

This campground is on Kowanyama–Pormpuraaw Rd, north-east of the Kowanyama Indigenous community, a traditional land open for camping and barramundi fishing Aug–Sept. Due to limited space, permission from the Kowanyama Land Office is essential for camping. There is a boat launch suitable for small boats. Bring all self-sufficient supplies. Advance bookings are recommended. Note: alcohol is prohibited on Kowanyama lands; heavy penalties apply. **Map refs: 176 B5, 189 G1**

How to book: Kowanyama Land Office (07) 4060 5187 *Permits:* camping permit required

697 Stoneys Crossing camping area (bush camping)

This basic campground for self-sufficient campers is 30 km east of Mapoon Rd and 58 km north-east of Weipa. Camping and vehicle permits can be obtained from the Weipa Camping Ground. This campsite is closed during the wet season. Note: alcohol restrictions are enforced in Mapoon Shire and heavy penalties apply; check current limits before embarking. **Map refs: 178 C4**

Who to contact: Weipa Camping Ground (07) 4069 7871 *Permits:* camping and vehicle access permits required *Camping fees:* fees can be paid and permits acquired at Weipa Camping Ground

Telegraph Track

The Telegraph Track is an icon of wild Cape York. The track, which follows a nearly straight line from Bramwell Junction to Punsand Bay, used to be a service route for maintaining the telegraph line that connected Cape York to the rest of the world. The telegraph itself has been retired, but its service route lives on as this notorious 4WD challenge. The tradition is to take the Telegraph Track on the way north and return via the easier bypass roads. Owing to the difficulty of several creek crossings, the Telegraph Track should only be attempted during the dry season (May–Nov) by seasoned 4WD operators with vehicle recovery equipment and spare parts. Off-road caravans and camper trailers can be towed as far north as Eliot Falls, but are not recommended beyond this point.

Please note that campsites are listed in alphabetical order, not track order. Refer to the map on p. 178 for further information.

Who to contact: Bramwell Junction (07) 4060 3230; or Northern Peninsula Regional Council (07) 4069 6800; or Heathlands Ranger Station (07) 4060 3421

568 **Bertie Creek camping area**
(bush camping)
See p. 126.

577 **Bridge Creek camping area**
(bush camping)
See p. 128.

570 **Cockatoo Creek camping area**
(bush camping)
See p. 127.

675 **Ducie Creek camping area**
(bush camping)
See p. 145.

571 **Dulhunty River camping area**
(bush camping)
See p. 127.

573 **Gunshot Creek camping area**
(bush camping)
See p. 127.

688 **North Alice Creek camping area**
(bush camping)
See p. 148.

689 **Palm Creek camping area**
(bush camping)
See p. 148.

579 **Sam Creek camping area**
(bush camping)
See p. 128.

698 **Topsy Creek camping area**

Hundreds of anglers make the annual trip to Kowanyama every year during barramundi season to experience some of the best fishing the Far North has to offer. Topsy Creek, about 45 km west of the Kowanyama Aboriginal community, is open June–Sept. There is a boat launch for small boats. Bring all self-sufficient supplies. Note: due to limited space, permission to camp is essential on this traditional land and advance bookings are recommended; alcohol is prohibited on Kowanyama lands; heavy penalties apply.
Map refs: 176 B5, 189 G1

How to book: Kowanyama Land Office (07) 4060 5187 *Permits:* camping permit required

699 **Umagico Camping Ground**

This beachfront campground is on Umagico Beach, 4 km south-west of Bamaga. Visitors should be aware that the roads through the Cape York region can be difficult and challenging, with numerous river crossings and changing conditions. The dry season, June–Sept, is the peak period and preferred time to visit. Laundry facilities are available at the campground.
Map refs: 178 D2

Who to contact: Northern Peninsula Area Regional Council (07) 4069 3266

700 Undara Experience

Next to Undara Volcanic National Park and its lava-tube cave system, the Undara Experience has a spacious caravan park and campground with laundry, swimming pool, bar and restaurant. Other accommodation options on site include restored railway carriages, swag tents, a wilderness lodge and safari shelter. Activities include evening wildlife-spotlighting walks, campfires and bushwalking, while qualified Savannah guides conduct tours of the lava tubes. The Undara Experience is 275 km south-west of Cairns. Advance bookings are recommended. **Map refs:** 174 D5, 187 F1

How to book: Savannah Way, Undara Volcanic National Park (07) 4097 1900, 1800 990 992 www.undara.com.au

701 Weipa Camping Ground

A 5.5 ha beachfront camping ground on Kerr Point Rd, this site has a pool, general supplies kiosk and laundry facilities. If upgrading, an accommodation block on site has 12 air-conditioned units. Weipa is at the northern end of the unsealed Peninsula Developmental Rd, about 200 km north-west of the Archer River Roadhouse. Ask about fishing and mining tours. Note: alcohol restrictions apply in the areas surrounding Weipa; check current limits before embarking. **Map refs:** 176 B1, 178 C5

How to book: Kerr Point Rd, Weipa (07) 4069 7871 www.campweipa.com

702 Wonya camping area (bush camping)

This campground is north-east of the Kowanyama Aboriginal community, a traditional land open for camping and barramundi fishing June–Sept. Due to limited space, permission from the Kowanyama Land Office is essential for camping here and advance bookings are recommended. There is a boat launch for small boats. Bring all self-sufficient supplies. Note: alcohol is prohibited on Kowanyama lands; heavy penalties apply. **Map refs:** 176 B5, 189 G1

How to book: Kowanyama Land Office (07) 4060 5187 *Permits:* camping permit required Larapinta Trail

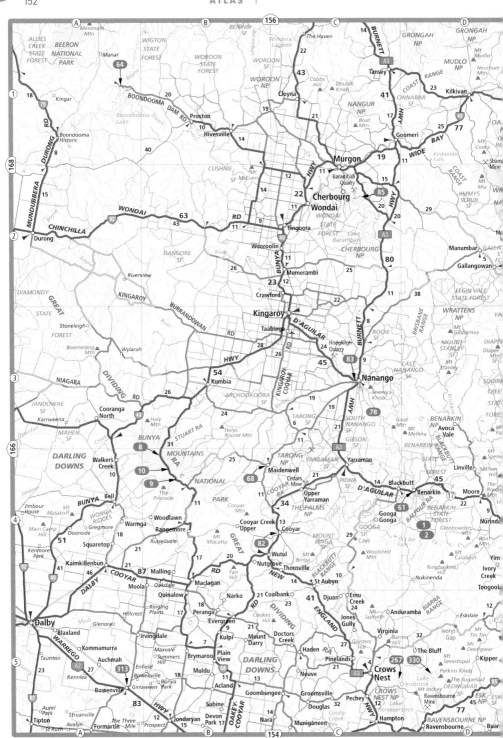

0   5   10 km

N

CORAL

SEA

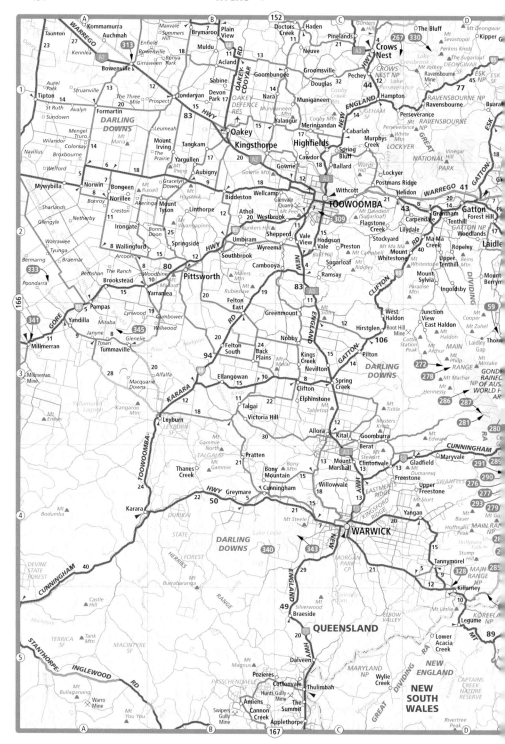

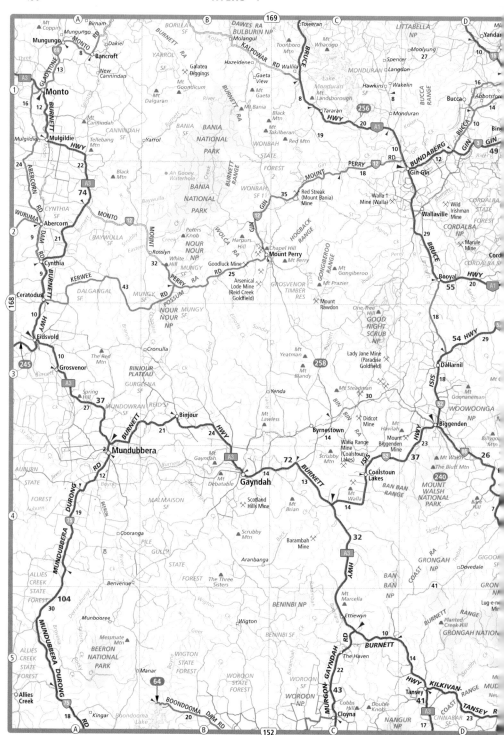

0   5   10 km

169

CORAL

SEA

N

Porpoise
Shoal

SANDY
CAPE CP   97

Sandy Cape
Lighthouse

Moore
Park

BARUBBRA
ISLAND CP
Bundaberg Harbour

Burnett   South Head
Heads

MON REPOS CP

Bargara

21

15   13

6

BUNDABERG

nato
ls

7   7
5   5   20

Clayton

Innes Park
Quarry

Barolin
Quarries

Elliott Heads
Elliott
Heads

Coonarr

Ferguson
Spit

Rooney
Point

Manoolcoong
Lakes

Station Hill

Calarga
Lagoon

Bare
Hill

146   Lake
Yeenan

Moondoora
Lagoon
Nth Ngkala
Rocks

109

Lake
Minker   142

107

Mananah Beach

ERA

GOODWOOD
RD

31

55

Goodwood   19

BURRUM
COAST
NATIONAL
PARK

192   Woodgate

Hervey

Bay

FRASER
ISLAND
WORLD
HERITAGE
AREA

Platypus
Bay

Wathumba
Swamp

152

130

Towoi
Swamp

GREAT
SANDY

NATIONAL

Marloo
Bay   149

Orchid
Beach

Waddy
Point

Indian
Head

96

19

Gregory   Ck

Walkers
Point   191

North Shore Pt
Burrum Head

2

PARK
Lake Gnarann

White Lake   155

Corroboree
Beach

110

19

Buxton

BURRUM

COAST NP

Coongul Pt

FRASER

ISLAND

Lake
Bowarrady   126

156

Bowarrah

Beach

ers
9

Junction
Mtn

26

BRUCE

57

Howard

Dundee Mine

Port of
Maryborough

Toogoom

Point
Vernon

VERNON
SF

21

Pialba
Scarness
Torquay
Urangan   HERVEY BAY

Sandy Pt

Pine
Hill

112   98

150

Mile

RD

Lake
Lenthall

171

22

RESERVE

Torbanlea
Two Mile
Mine

Churchill
Mine

Torbanlea
Mine

VERNON
CP

15

MARYBOROUGH
HERVEY BAY

57

23

38

20

Datum Pt

Woody
Island

Duck
Is

Mangrove
Point

River
Heads

178

128

Burrgum
Hill

111

116

Mahero
Beach

129

125

Happy
Valley
Rainbow Gorge

3

Musket
Flat Mtn

Mt
oongul

WONGI
NP

41

RD

Whitestone
Mine

MARYBOROUGH
BIGGENDEN

56

THINOOMBA
STATE FOREST

Mungar   179

MARYBOROUGH   POONA

Kangaroo
Island

Lake McKenzie
(Boorangoora)

GREAT SANDY
CONSERVATION
PARK
Turkey Is

117

148   Lake
Birrabeen

99

118   143

Leading
Hill

Nulwar
Hill

119

145   153

121

105

114   Eurong

154

5

HWY

Cabbage
Tree Mtn

Grout
Mtn

20

Garden
Is

Maaroom

Dream
Is

115

Boomanjin
Hill

Lake Boomanjin

COO
P

ST MARY
STATE
FOREST

Maryborough
Quarries

Owanyilla

25

Stewart
Is

Boonooroo
Point

Tuan

124   106

Sheep
Station
Lagoons

4

CORAL

SEA

GLENBAR

32

STATE

Tiaro

TIARO
STATE
FOREST

TUAN   Tuan

122

GREAT

SANDY

NATIONAL

108

131

Jabiru
Swamp

FOREST

Penny
Mtn

87

MOUNT
BAUPLE NP
Mt Bauple

14

Bauple

BAUPLE
STATE

COOLOOLA

40

FOREST

Cowra
Pt

169

Tin
Can
Bay   104

123   North
Spit

Hook Point
Inskip Point

159

NBAR
NP

Sugar
Loaf
Mtn

Gundiah

GLENBAR
SF

MIVA
SF

Miva

GUNDYAH

19

Gragy
Mtn

NEERDIE
STATE

168

WIDE BAY
TRAINING
AREA

158

160

162

161

DOUBLE ISLAND
POINT CP

Double
Island
Point

5

BAUPLE

WOOLOOGA
RD

BRUCE

Gunalda   15

Mt
Kanigan

Mt Eaton

FOREST

Neerdie

Eudlo
Pt

Tin Can
Bay

Mt
Herman

Mt
Thomas

9

Rainbow
Beach

Poona
Lake

103

120

DE

BAY

31

WOOLOOGA
99

Woologa

Devils
Mtn

Mt
Scatchy

16

HWY

Black
Knob

Butlers
Knob

CURRA
STATE
FOREST

Erins
Knob

GYMPIE
NP

13

144

TIN   CAN

BAY

RD

RAINBOW

GREAT

SANDY

16

BEACH
RD

Mount
Bilewilam
Quarry

Sinkholes

132

Noosa

102

River

NP

153

ATLAS

157

Sandy Cape

H

1

173

170

172

B

C

D

Gloucester Head
Middle Is
OUCESTER ISLAND NP
Gloucester Is
Rattray Is
Eshelby Is ★
469
470
468
Saddleback Is
GLOUCESTER ISLAND NP
Edgecumbe Bay
DRYANDER NP
467
Armit Is
Grassy Is
Earlando

GREAT BARRIER REEF MARINE PARK

CORAL SEA

GREAT BARRIER REEF WORLD HERITAGE AREA

Hayman Is
Hayman Island
525
529
521
Pinnacle Peak
Hook Peak ★
Rocky Hill
Hook Is
WHITSUNDAY
Deloraine Is
Border Is
ISLANDS
Petrel Isf

Double Cone Is

66

Mt Cavana
Mt Danger
Mt Lee
A1
Mt Challenger
The Knobblers
PROSERPINE SF
Mt Dryander
Collingvale
DRYANDER NATIONAL PARK
454

Airlie Beach
Cannonvale
532
446
533
Shute Harbour
447
448
449
500
536
Sugarloaf
59
36
Mt Marlow
High Mtn
527

496
494
499
497
526
495
524
MOLLE ISLANDS NP
Long Is
498
NATIONAL

522
523
528
Whitsunday Is
NP
Mt Robinson
Whitsunday Peak
530
Haslewood Is
520
Hamilton Island
Hamilton Is

Black and White Hill
Roma Peak
PROSERPINE SF
Mt McGuire
Mt Pluto
Proserpine
26
Proserpine
Lake Proserpine
Pretty Bend
PROSERPINE STATE FOREST
Mt Quandong
Breadalbane
CAMPBELLS PLAIN
22
CONWAY RD
Mt Proserpine
Little Conway Mtn
Conway Beach
PARK
Cedar Falls
CONWAY
Cowrie Is
491
Pentecost Is
LIND
Cole Is
Maher Is
ISL.
Mt Oldfield
492
NAT
P.
Lindeman Is
LINDEMAN GROUP
Shaw Is
Mansel
Shaw Peak
Genesta Bay
Mt Arthur Keyser Is

2

26

Mt Roundhill
Mt Roundback
Mt Mamelon
ANDROMACHE SF
Mt Flat Top
Mt Hector
Mount Hector
Mt Pine Mtn
Cattle Vale
Amelia Vale
New Beach
Covering Beach
Repulse Bay
Cape Conway
Thomas Is
East Repulse Is
REPULSE ISLANDS
South Repulse Is
REPULSE ISLANDS NP
512
Bennett Rock
Silversmith Is
ANCHOR ISLANDS
Blacksmith Is
Hammer Is
Ladysmith Is
515
SIR SMIT
SMITH ISLANDS NATIONAL PARK
Goldsmith Is
Ingo Islets

CLARKE
NORMANBY RANGE
Mt Bullock
Dingo Mtn
13
16
Midge Point
Midge Is
Ten Mile Beach
Tonga Mtn
Mentmore Beach
Rocky Mtn
HILLSBOROUGH
CHANNEL

3

Emu
East
Mt Marion
Mt Campbell
Mt Crompton
MACARTNEY
KANGAROO CREEK TABLELAND SF
Gorge Waterfall
190
Mt Millar
Elaroo
442
CATHU STATE FOREST
Rocky Mtn
Yalboroo
CLARKE RANGE
Mt Macartney
Mt Catherine
23
Poison Mtn
Skull Knob
547
St Helens Bay
Rabbit Is
502
503
501
NEWRY ISLANDS NP
Seaforth
548
531
437
436
CAPE HILLSBOROUGH
Andrews Pt
Ball Bay
Sand Bay
Williamsons Beach
Gree

4

BROKEN RIVER RANGE
Exmoor
Mt Cauley
Urannah
EUNGELLA
DICKS TABLELAND
NATIONAL
Mt Margaret
Mt Consuelo
Mt Pelion
MOUNT OSSA NP
Mt Roy
Mt Jukes
Crazy Cat Mtn
St Helens
Mt Omega
Mount Charlton
Mt Dalrymple
PELION SF
The Pinnacle
Mt Martin
Mount Ossa
16
MIRANI
A1
HWY
Mt Sweetland
Kuttabul
Mt Gabrovo
13
5
The Sister
21
Miltons Lookout
The Bl Mtn
Sho
Bue
3
12 S

Blenheim
Redcliffe Vale
Mt Dingo
Dingo SF
Mt Conical
Mt Blenheim
Turrawalla
CREDITON SF
537
Lake Eungella
455
452
450
Eungella
MACKAY
Finch Hatton
31
Mt Pinnacle
64
Gargett
78
14
LONELY VALLEY
PINNACLE RD
MIRANI-
Mt Turney
Mirani
Lake Kinchant
Marian
Walkerston
15
12
A1
BRUCE
HWY
RD
24
7
9
Su Sugarloa
Farleigh
22
M

5

Limestone Hill
Exevale
HOMEVALE NP
Bon Hill
Mt Cona
451
CREDITON STATE FOREST
DENHAM RANGE
The Stalk
Teemburra Creek Dam
493
MIA MIA
Mt Mia Mia
Mt Jimmy Jacky SF
24
Blue Mtn
MIRANI-
ETON RD
PEAK
Mt McBryde
BEN MOHR SF
Mt Bridgman
70
Dals Lookout
15
Eton
Homebush
Scrubby Mtn
Baker Creek
22
HW

Glenden
Mount Hilalong
Suttor
A
B
C
D

BRUCE
A1
BODES
Mt
Greta
Billy
Don
HWY
CONWAY
BRUCE
TONGA RANGE
MOUNT OSSA
DOWNS

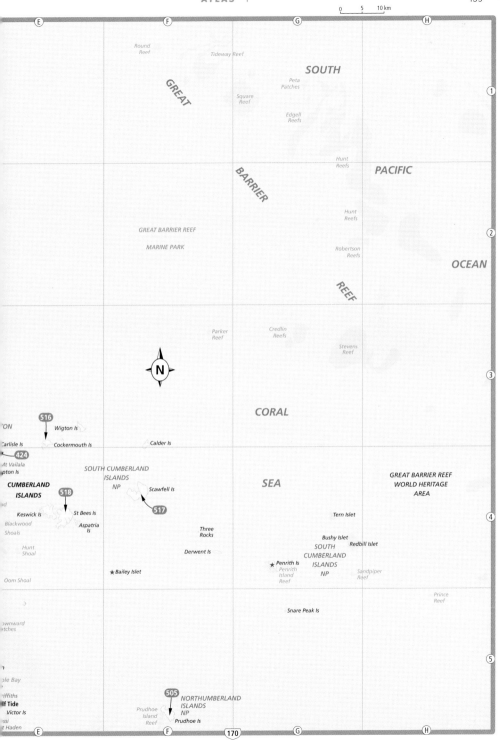

0   5   10 km

E   F   G   H

Round
Reef

Tideway Reef

SOUTH

GREAT

Peta
Patches

Square
Reef

Edgell
Reefs

1

Hunt
Reefs

PACIFIC

BARRIER

Hunt
Reefs

GREAT BARRIER REEF

MARINE PARK

Robertson
Reefs

2

OCEAN

REEF

Parker
Reef

Credlin
Reefs

Stevens
Reef

N

3

CORAL

516

'ON

Wigton Is

Carlisle Is   Cockermouth Is   Calder Is

424

Mt Vailala
pton Is

SOUTH CUMBERLAND
ISLANDS
NP

CUMBERLAND
ISLANDS

518

Scawfell Is

SEA

GREAT BARRIER REEF
WORLD HERITAGE
AREA

d

Keswick Is   St Bees Is

517

Tern Islet

4

Blackwood
Shoals

Aspatria
Is

Three
Rocks

Bushy Islet   Redbill Islet

SOUTH
CUMBERLAND
ISLANDS
NP

Hunt
Shoal

Derwent Is

★ Penrith Is
Penrith
Island
Reef

Sandpiper
Reef

Oom Shoal

★ Bailey Islet

Prince
Reef

Snare Peak Is

5

le Bay

riffiths

lf Tide
Victor Is

ssi
t Haden

505

Prudhoe
Island
Reef

NORTHUMBERLAND
ISLANDS
NP

Prudhoe Is

E   F   170   G   H

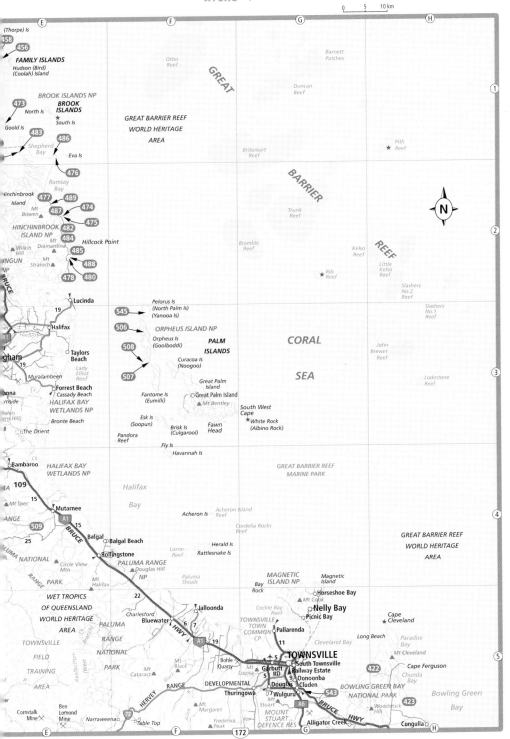

0   5   10 km

(Thorpe) Is
458
456
FAMILY ISLANDS
Hudson (Bird)
(Coolah) Island

Barnett
Patches

Duncan
Reef

BROOK ISLANDS NP
473
North Is
**BROOK
ISLANDS**
★ South Is
Goold Is
483
486
Shepherd
Bay
Eva Is
476

GREAT BARRIER REEF
WORLD HERITAGE
AREA

Britomart
Reef

Pith
★ Reef

Ramsay
Bay
Hinchinbrook
Island
477
489
Mt
Bowen
487
474
475
482
HINCHINBROOK
ISLAND NP
484
Mt
Diamantina
Hillcock Point
485
Wilkin
Hill
INGUN
Mt
Straloch
488
478
480

BARRIER

Trunk
Reef

Bramble
Reef

Kelso
Reef

Little
Kelso
Reef

REEF

Rib
★ Reef

Slashers
No.2
Reef

Slashers
No.1
Reef

BRUCE
Lucinda
19
Halifax
Herbert
gham
19
Taylors
Beach
Muralambeen
anna
rnside
Forrest Beach
Cassady Beach
**HALIFAX BAY
WETLANDS NP**
elen
ns Hill)
Bronte Beach
The Orient
ll

545
506
508
507

Pelorus Is
(North Palm Is)
(Yanooa Is)
ORPHEUS ISLAND NP
Orpheus Is
(Goolboddi)
**PALM
ISLANDS**
Curacoa Is
(Noogoo)
Lady
Elliot
Reef
Fantome Is
(Eumilli)
Great Palm
Island
Great Palm Island
Mt Bentley
Esk Is
(Soopun)
Brisk Is
(Culgarool)
Fawn
Head
Pandora
Reef
Fly Is
Havannah Is

South West
Cape
★White Rock
(Albino Rock)

CORAL

SEA

John
Brewer
Reef

Lodestone
Reef

Bambaroo
**HALIFAX BAY
WETLANDS NP**
MA 109
15
Mt Spec
Mutarnee
ANGE
A1
15
509
25
Balgal
Balgal Beach
Rollingstone
PALUMA RANGE
Douglas Hill
LUMA NATIONAL
Circle View
Mtn
NP
Mt
Halifax
PARK
RANGE

Halifax

Bay

Acheron Is

Acheron Island
Reef

Cordelia Rocks
Reef

Herald Is

Lorne
Reef
Rattlesnake Is

Paluma
Shoals

GREAT BARRIER REEF
MARINE PARK

GREAT BARRIER REEF
WORLD HERITAGE
AREA

**WET TROPICS
OF QUEENSLAND
WORLD HERITAGE
AREA**
TOWNSVILLE
FIELD
TRAINING
AREA

Charlesford
Bluewater
PALUMA
RANGE
NATIONAL
PARK
Mt
Cataract

22
Jalloonda
6
7
HWY
A1
19

Mt
Black
Bohle
Quarry
5
Douglas
5

MAGNETIC
ISLAND NP
Bay
Rock
Cockle Bay
Reef
TOWNSVILLE
TOWN
COMMON
CP
Pallarenda
11
5
TOWNSVILLE
Garbutt
RD
Railway Estate
9
Oonoonba
Cluden

Magnetic
Island

Horseshoe Bay
Mt Cook
Nelly Bay
Picnic Bay

Cape
★ Cleveland

Long Beach
Paradise
Bay

Cleveland Bay

Mt Cleveland

422

Cape Ferguson
Chunda
Bay

Cornstalk
Mine
Ben
Lomond
Mine
72
Narraweena
Table Top
DEVELOPMENTAL
Thuringowa
Mt
Louisa
Wulguru
Mt
Margaret
Frederick
Peak
**MOUNT
STUART
DEFENCE RES**
A6
Alligator Creek
BRUCE
HWY

BOWLING GREEN BAY
NATIONAL PARK
Woodstock
Hill
543
423

Cungulla

Bowling Green

Bay

Keelbottom
(West)
Black
HERVEY
RANGE
Alice

109
15
25
22
6
7
19
11
5
5
9

E   F   G   H
172

N

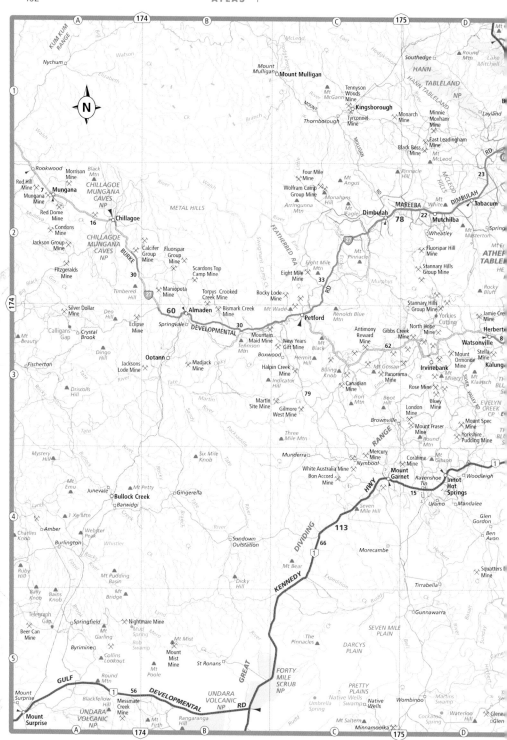

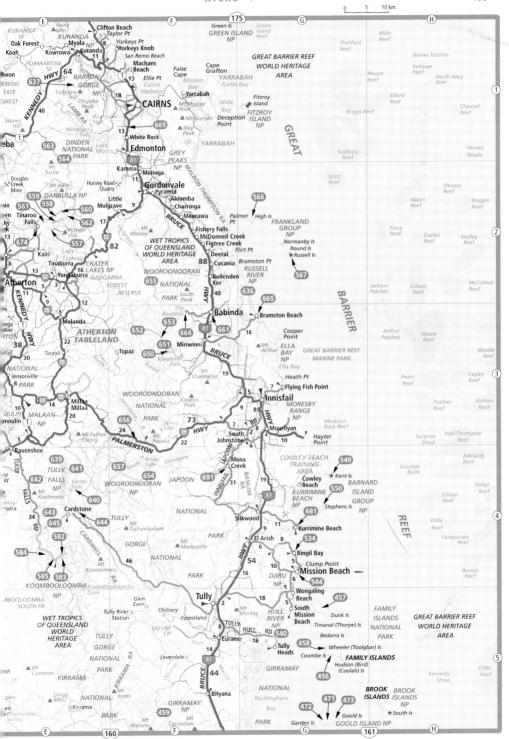

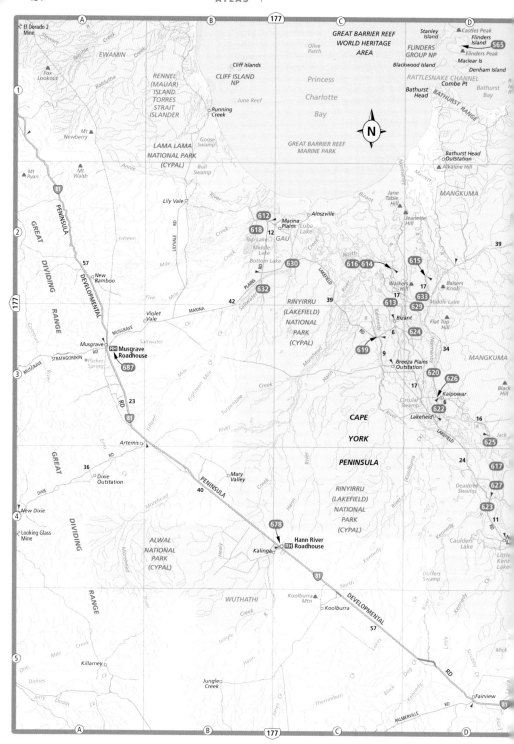

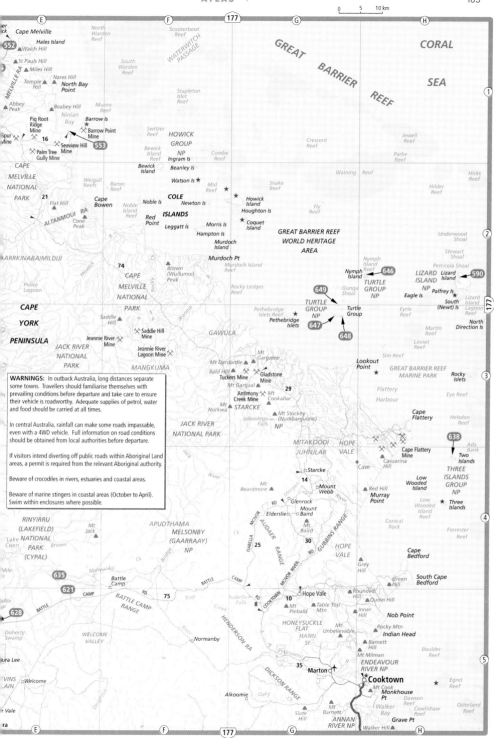

0   5   10 km

E   177   F   G   H

Cape Melville
North Warden Reef
Scooterboot Reef
WATERWITCH PASSAGE
GREAT
BARRIER
REEF
CORAL
SEA

552
Hales Island
Walch Hill
MELVILLE RA
St Pauls Hill
Miles Hill
South Warden Reef
1

Nares Hill
Temple Hill
North Bay Point
Stapleton Islet Reef

Abbey Peak
Beabey Hill
Munro Reef
Ninian Bay
Barrow Is

Pig Root Ridge Mine
16
Barrow Point Mine
Switzer Reef
HOWICK GROUP
Crescent Reef
Jewell Reef

Spur Mine
Palm Tree Gully Mine
Seaview Hill Mine
553
Bewick Island Reef
NP
Ingram Is
Combe Reef
Parke Reef

CAPE MELVILLE NATIONAL PARK
Bewick Island
Beanley Is
Waining Reef
Hicks Reef

Weigall Reefs
Baron Reef
Watson Is
Mid Reef
Snake Reef
Hilder Reef

21
Flat Hill
Cape Bowen
Noble Island Reef
Noble Is
COLE
Newton Is
Howick Island
Houghton Is
Fly Reef

ALTANMOUI RA
Cone Peak
Red Point
ISLANDS
Leggatt Is
Morris Is
Hampton Is
Coquet Island
GREAT BARRIER REEF
WORLD HERITAGE
AREA
Underwood Shoal
2

ARRKINABA/MILDIJI
74
Murdoch Island
Murdoch Pt
Nymph Island Reef
Stewart Shoal
Petricola Shoal

Brown (Wullumoi) Peak
Murdoch Island Reef
Nymph Island
646
LIZARD ISLAND
Lizard Island
590

CAPE MELVILLE NATIONAL PARK
649
Rocky Ledges
Gunga Shoal
TURTLE GROUP
NP
Eagle Is
Palfrey Is

Police Lagoon
Petehbridge Islets Reef
TURTLE GROUP NP
Turtle Group
Eyrie Reef
South (Newt) Is
Lizard Lagoon Reef
177

CAPE YORK PENINSULA
Saddle Hill
Petehbridge Islets
647
648
Martin Reef
North Direction Is

Jeannie River Mine
Saddle Hill Mine
GAWULA
Linnet Reef

JACK RIVER NATIONAL PARK
Jeannie River Lagoon Mine
Sim Reef

MANGKUMA
Mt Gargalee
Lookout Point
GREAT BARRIER REEF MARINE PARK
Rocky Islets
3

Mt Dardardie
Bald Hill
Tuckers Mine
Gladstone Mine
Flattery Harbour
Eye Reef

WARNINGS: In outback Australia, long distances separate some towns. Travellers should familiarise themselves with prevailing conditions before departure and take care to ensure their vehicle is roadworthy. Adequate supplies of petrol, water and food should be carried at all times.

In central Australia, rainfall can make some roads impassable, even with a 4WD vehicle. Full information on road conditions should be obtained from local authorities before departure.

If visitors intend diverting off public roads within Aboriginal Land areas, a permit is required from the relevant Aboriginal authority.

Beware of crocodiles in rivers, estuaries and coastal areas.

Beware of marine stingers in coastal areas (October to April). Swim within enclosures where possible.

Mt Gargaal
Antimony Creek Mine
Mt Cookabar
29
STARCKE
Mt Stockey (Numbarguline)
Cape Flattery
Helsdon Reef

Jahoolego Falls
NP
Mt Cook
MITAKOODI
JUHNJLAR
HOPE VALE
Cape Flattery Mine
638
Ada Bank

JACK RIVER NATIONAL PARK
Starcke
14
Mount Webb
Cave
Casuarina Hill
Two Islands
THREE ISLANDS GROUP NP

Mt Beardmore
Red Hill
Murray Point
Low Wooded Island
Low Wooded Island Reef
Three Islands

RINYIRRU (LAKEFIELD) NATIONAL PARK (CYPAL)
Mt Jack
APUDTHAMA MELSONBY (GAARRAAY) NP
Glenrock
Mount Baird
Elderslie
Mt Baird
Conical Rock
Forrester Reef
4

Lake Coen
Brown
25
30
HOPE VALE
Grey Hill
Cape Bedford

635
Battle Camp
75
Isabella Falls
Hope Vale
10
Green Hill
Rounded Hill
South Cape Bedford

621
CAMP
BATTLE CAMP RANGE
8
Mt Piebald
Table Top Mtn
Quoin Hill
Inner Hill
Nob Point

628
BATTLE
Normanby
HONEYSUCKLE FLAT
Mt Unbelievable
Rocky Mtn
Indian Head

Doherty Swamp
WELCOME VALLEY
HANN SF
Barnett Hill
Boulder Reef

ura Lee
35
Marton
Mt Milman
ENDEAVOUR RIVER NP
Egret Reef
5

VINS AIN
Welcome
Cooktown
Mt Cook
Monkhouse Pt
Dawson Reef

Vale
Alkoomie
Oaky
Mt Barnett
Slate Hill
ANNAN RIVER NP
Walker Bay
Walker Hill
Cowlishaw Reef
Osterland Reef

E   177   F   G   H

0 10 20 km

CORAL SEA

SOUTH PACIFIC OCEAN

Wooroolin
Memerambi
Crawford
Kingaroy
Taabinga
Nanango
Kumbia
Maidenwell
BUNYA MTNS NP
Rangemore
Cooyar
Wutul
Thornville
Emu Creek
Ivory Creek
Toogoolawah
Crows Nest
Hampton
Highfields
Gatton
Helidon
Grantham
TOOWOOMBA
Pittsworth
Southbrook
Ramsay
Greenmount
Laidley
Rosewood
IPSWICH
WARWICK
Killarney
Tannymorel
Legume
Stanthorpe
Amiens
Applethorpe
Liston
Tenterfield
Bluff Rock
Mole River
Bungulla
Torrington
Deepwater

Manambar Mine
Manumbar
Gallangowan
Imbil
Brooloo
Cooran
Tewantin
Noosa Heads
Sunshine Beach
Marcus Beach
Peregian Beach
Coolum Beach
Eumundi
Yandina
Bli Bli
Mudjimba
MAROOCHYDORE
MOOLOOLABA
NAMBOUR
BUDERIM
Mapleton
Montville
Maleny
Eudlo
Warana
CALOUNDRA
Landsborough
Beerwah
Glass House Mountains
BRIBIE ISLAND
BONGAREE
Cape Moreton
BRIBIE IS NP
Beachmere
Bulwer
Mt Tempest
CABOOLTURE
Burpengary
Deception Bay
MORETON ISLAND (GNOORGANBIN)
Narangba
Scarborough
Redcliffe
Tangalooma
MORETON ISLAND NP
Petrie
Brighton
Moreton Bay (Quandamooka)
Nudgee
Kooringal
Samford
BRISBANE
Wynnum
Amity Point
Point Lookout
Dunwich
NORTH STRADBROKE ISLAND (MINJERRIBA)
Indooroopilly
Cleveland
Victoria Point
Redland Bay
Sunnybank
Oxley
Inala
Slacks Creek
Logan
SOUTH STRADBROKE ISLAND
Beenleigh
Jimboomba
Tamborine
Coomera
Sanctuary Cove
Paradise Point
Labrador
Main Beach
Surfers Paradise
Broadbeach
Beaudesert
NERANG
Helensvale
Mudgeeraba
Burleigh Heads
Currumbin
Coolangatta
Tweed Heads
Springbrook
Banora Point
Chinderah
Kingscliff
Murwillumbah
Bogangar
Hastings Point
Pottsville
Crabbes Creek
Ocean Shores
Brunswick Heads
Mullumbimby
Byron Bay
Cape Byron
Suffolk Park
Bangalow
Newrybar
Knockrow
Lennox Head
LISMORE
Alstonville
BALLINA
Empire Vale
Coraki
Broadwater
Evans Head
Woodburn
New Italy
Tabbimoble
BUNDJALUNG NP
Ten Mile Beach
Whiporie
Lawrence
Chatsworth
Iluka
Yamba
Angourie
YURAYGIR NP
Maclean
Casino
Kyogle
Mummulgum
Tabulam
Drake
Alice
Rappville
Baryulgil

N

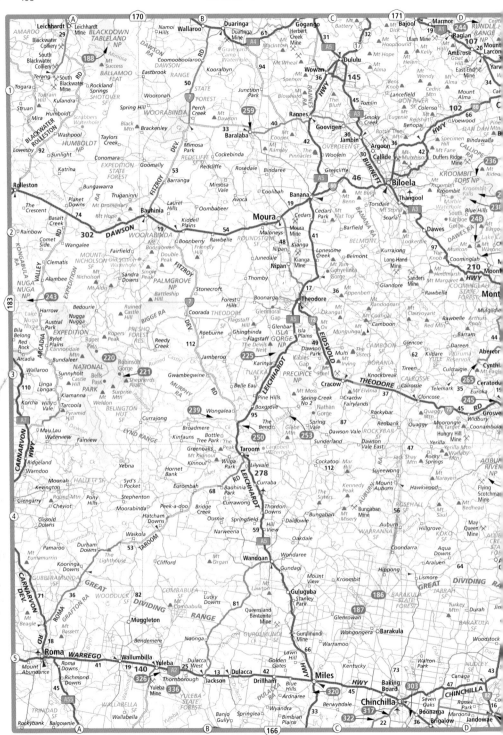

0 10 20 km

E 171 F G H

Rock Cod
Shoal
209
210
land
262
260
Facing Island
LADSTONE 257
Boyne Island
Tannum Sands
Benaraby 246
Turkey
Beach 217
219
Fitzroy
Reef
Llewellyn
Reef
Boult Reef
Hoskyn
Islands
Hoskyn
Islands
Reef
Fairfax Islands Fairfax Islands Reef
Lady
Musgrave
Island
193
GREAT BARRIER REEF
MARINE PARK
CAPRICORNIA
CAYS
NATIONAL
PARK
Lady Musgrave
Island Reef
GREAT BARRIER REEF
WORLD HERITAGE
AREA
1

RODDS PENINSULA
EURIMBULA NP
Rodds
Bay
EURIMBULA RESOURCES RES
Middle Island
Bustard
Bay
247
Seventeen Seventy
Agnes Water
264
Lady Elliot
Island
Lady Elliot
Island Reef
Herald Patches

CASTLE
TOWER
NP
64
Milton
Mining
Field
Miriam
Vale
Invarcoe
Briarwood
Kia Ora
Bororen
EURIMBULA
NP
218
216
Captain
Creek
Round
Hill
214
215
A1
Taronne
DEEPWATER NP

CORAL
SEA

BULBURIN
agoorin NP
Littlemere
Rockview
Bompa
219 61
Oreti
Builyan
Many
Peaks
226
BULBURIN
NP
Lovemead
Rosevale
Wandoona
Rules Beach
241
Glenview
Bauer
Mountain
View
LITTABELLA NP
Long
Shoal

N

190
Conella
WARRO
SF
Rosedale
25
Miara
Moore
Park
242
Porpoise
Shoal
Breaksea Spit
Sandy Cape Shoal
97
Sandy Cape
2

Towerang
Molangul
Gaeta
View
Wallila
Yandaran
Avondale
Flagstone
Creek
16
45
One Tree
Hill
Langdon
Wakelin
34
20
Barubbra
Island
Burnett Heads
Bargara
107
Rooney Point
Ferguson Spit
Manann Beach
Bare Hill
109
130

Gaeta
Monduran
Bucca
Bingera
256
12
Red Streak
(Mount Bania)
Mine
38
Gin
Gin
51
Clayton
53
Elliott Heads
Coonarr
BUNDABERG
BURRUM
COAST
NP
Hervey
Bay
Station Hill
146
Platypus Bay
142
Towoi Swamp
Orchid
Beach
Marloo Bay
Waddy Point
Indian Head
149
96 FRASER ISLAND
Corroboree Beach
3

HOGBACK RANGE
Walla 1
Mine
(Walla)
Wallaville
A1
29
Marule
Mine
192
37
Walkers
Point
Woodgate
Burrum Heads
Buxton
191
GREAT SANDY NP
Coongul
Point
110
155 FRASER ISLAND
WORLD HERITAGE
AREA

GOOD
NIGHT
SCRUB
NP
Mount
Perry
Mount
Rawdon
Cordalba
Apple Tree Creek
Childers
Booyal
27
29
17
82
HWY
35
Toogoom
Pialba
Scarness
Urangan
Port of
Maryborough
HERVEY
BAY
156
126
150
128
129
98
112
116
111 125

258
Dallarnil
18
WONGI
SF
57
Torbanlea
Lenthall
Jimchon
Mtn
33
178
Woody
Island
River
Heads
148
117
121
119
145
153
105 118

Binjour
47
Byrnestown
40
Biggenden
ISIS
Brooweena
Aramara
26
Mungar
55
24
MARYBOROUGH
POONA
Maroom
114
99
Eurong
143
154
Lake Boomanjin
124

Gayndah
15
13
Coalstoun
Lakes
MOUNT
WALSH
NP
240
Owanyilla
Tiaro
179
19
TUAN
STATE
FOREST
Tuan
169
168
104
122
106
108
131
123
SOUTH
PACIFIC
OCEAN
4

BENINBI NP
149
Ettiewyn
BURNETT
NP
GRONGAH
NP
MUDLO
NP
Dovedale
Gundiah
Bauple
A1
170
40
WIDE BAY
TRAINING
AREA
Hook Point
Inskip Point
158 159 160 161 162
Rainbow
Beach
Double Island
Point

Proston
64
Hivesville
Cloyna
Tansey
Kilkivan
Miva
Gunalda
Woolooga
Neerdie
89
33
144
103 120
GREAT SANDY NP

Murgon
19
Goomeri
85
COAST RA
WRATTENS
NP
Widgee
22
77
16
Noga
Mine
14
GYMPIE
132
102
140 141
101 127 133 134 135 136
137 138 139 147 151

Wondai
Cherbourg
WONDAI
SF
86
Amamoor
Cooran
Tewantin
113
100
Boreen
Point
Noosa Heads
Sunshine Beach
172
183
184
Teewah

Kingaroy
Memerambi
A3
Gallangowan
Imbil
Brooloo
165
Cooroy
Eumundi
Yandina
Bli
Bli
162
Marcus Beach
Peregian Beach
Coolum Beach
174
166 167

170
Kumbia
84
Nanango
JIMNA
157
163
93
Kenilworth
NAMBOUR
BUDERIM
182
MAROOCHYDORE
MOOLOOLABA
175 180
181
Mudjimba
Maleny
Eudlo
M1
Warana

BUNYA
MTNS NP
Avoca Vale
92 91 90
Jimna
164
Conondale
5

E F 167 G H

For more detail
see pages 152–3
& 156–7

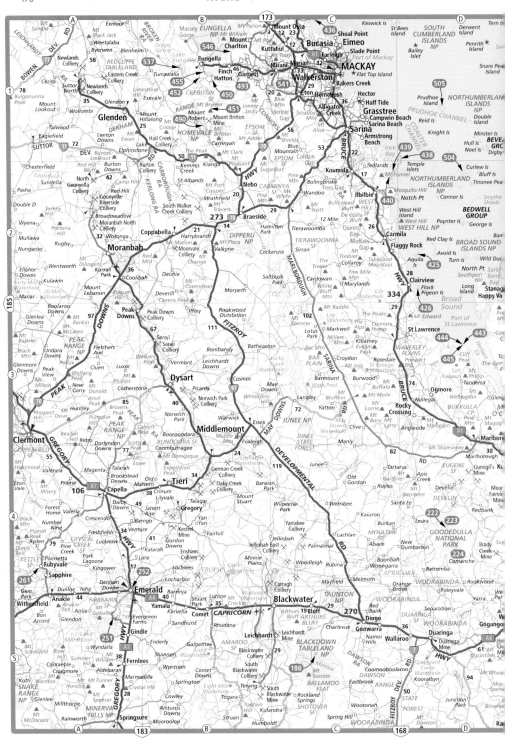

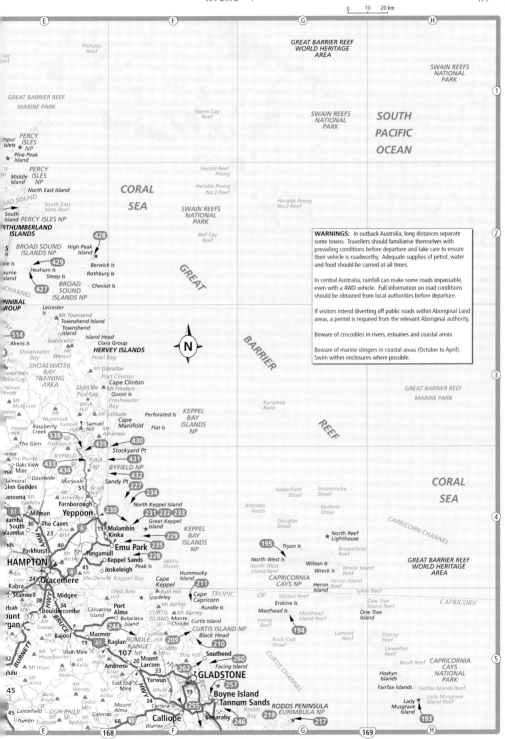

0 10 20 km

E **F** **G** **H**

GREAT BARRIER REEF
WORLD HERITAGE
AREA

SWAIN REEFS
NATIONAL
PARK

1

Pompey
Reef

GREAT BARRIER REEF
MARINE PARK

Storm Cay
Reef

SWAIN REEFS
NATIONAL
PARK

SOUTH

PACIFIC

OCEAN

spur
Islets

PERCY
ISLES
★ NP
Pine Peak
Island

PERCY ISLES
Middle
Island
NP

North East Island

Herald Reef
Prong

Heralds Prong
No.3 Reef

2

AD SOUND

South
Island
PERCY ISLES NP

South East
Islets Reef

CORAL

SEA

SWAIN REEFS
NATIONAL
PARK

Heralds Prong
No.2 Reef

RTHUMBERLAND
ISLANDS

BROAD SOUND
ISLANDS NP

High Peak
Island

428

Bell Cay
Reef

WARNINGS: In outback Australia, long distances separate
some towns. Travellers should familiarise themselves with
prevailing conditions before departure and take care to ensure
their vehicle is roadworthy. Adequate supplies of petrol, water
and food should be carried at all times.

In central Australia, rainfall can make some roads impassable,
even with a 4WD vehicle. Full information on road conditions
should be obtained from local authorities before departure.

If visitors intend diverting off public roads within Aboriginal Land
areas, a permit is required from the relevant Aboriginal authority.

Beware of crocodiles in rivers, estuaries and coastal areas.

Beware of marine stingers in coastal areas (October to April).
Swim within enclosures where possible.

le Is

urne
sland

429
Berwick Is

Hexham Is
Steep Is

Rothbury Is

BROAD
SOUND
ISLANDS NP

Cheviot Is

CHANNEL

427

NNIBAL
ROUP

Leicester
Is

Mt Townsend
Townshend Island
Townshend
Island
Island Head

GREAT

514
Akens Is

Notch Mtn
Clara Group

BARRIER

Karamea
Bank

GREAT BARRIER REEF
MARINE PARK

3

Fitz

Shoalwater
Bay

Mt
Westall

HERVEY ISLANDS
Pearl Bay

SHOALWATER
BAY
TRAINING
AREA

Seventeen
Mile Gap
Palmer
Knob

Mt Gibraltar

Port Clinton
Cape Clinton
Mt Flinders
Quoin Is
Freshwater
Bay

REEF

Mt
Mulgrave

Light Me
Pipd Gap

West
Hill

Mt Solitude

CORAL

SEA

pps

enor
The Pointer
Oaks View
al Mine

Hummock
Raspberry
Creek

Samuel
Hill

Samuel
Hill

Mt
Atherton

Perforated Is

KEPPEL
BAY
ISLANDS
NP

Flat Is

Cape
Manifold

Haberfield
Shoal

Innamincka
Shoal

4

Hower
Hill

The Glen

538
Patnassus

435

Stockyard Pt

431

Johnson
Patch

Guthrie
Shoal

CAPRICORN CHANNEL

BYFIELD

BYFIELD NP

Pistol
Gap

Douglas
Shoal

Balmoral
Glen Geddes

433
434

432

Doorside

Maryvale

Sandy Pt

Mt
Atherton

Grays
Hill

227

North Reef
Lighthouse

anoona

A1
Milman

51

234

North Keppel Island

Broomfield
Reef

GREAT BARRIER REEF
WORLD HERITAGE
AREA

aamba
South
aamba

The Caves

Farnborough

230
Yeppoon

231 **232** **233**

Great Keppel
Island

KEPPEL
BAY
ISLANDS
NP

195
Tryon Is

North West Is

Wilson Is

Wreck Island
Reef

nds
Parkhurst

30
23

19

Pine
Mtn

Mulambin
Kinka

229

North West
Island Reef

Wreck Is

Heron Island
Reef

CAPRICORN

HAMPTON

40

Mt
Archer

Tungamull
Emu Park **235**

228

Jabiru
Shoals

CAPRICORNIA
CAYS NP

Heron
Island

Sykes Reef

Lion
Kabra

24

Mt
Kelly

Keppel Sands
Joskeleigh

Peak Is

Hummocky
Island

211

One Tree
Island Reef

CAPRICORN

Stanwell

Midgee

MacDonald
Keppel Bay

Cape
Keppel

West Arm

Bald Hill
Spadeley

TROPIC
Cape
Capricorn

Masthead Is

Masthead
Island Reef

One Tree
Island

rbah
unt
gan

38
34

Boulcombe

17

Casuarina
Island

Port
Alma
Balaclava
Island

Mt Barker
CURTIS
ISLAND
Monte
Christo

Rundle Is

Irving
Reef

194

Gavial

Bajool
Marmor

Raglan

244

RUNDLE
RANGE

Curtis Island

CURTIS ISLAND NP
Black Head

Rock Cod
Shoal

Lamont
Reef

Fitzroy
Reef

Mt
Dick

Ulam Mine

19
A1

Central
RANGE
Scrubby
Hill

209

210

Llewellyn
Reef

CAPRICORNIA
CAYS
NATIONAL
PARK

ulu

Mt
Hoopbund

107 NP
20

Mount
Larcom

Ship Hill

Southend

260

Boult Reef

32

Mt Hope

Mt
Helen

Ambrose

33

262

GLADSTONE

257

Hoskyn
Reef

Fairfax Islands Reef

45
Lancefield

DON RIVER

Mt
Wendy

Mt
Kelly

Goat
Hill

East End
Mine

Yarwun

255

Boyne Island
Tannum Sands

Fairfax Islands

Lady
Musgrave
Island

Lady Musgrave
Island Reef

193

Tomlin

Eugenie

SF
Redshirt

Mount
Alma

White
Hill

Carrara

19

RODDS PENINSULA
EURIMBULA NP

217

45

Colenso

Calliope
66

60
Warree

Benaraby

219

246

Rodds
Bay

E **F** **G** **H**

168 **169**

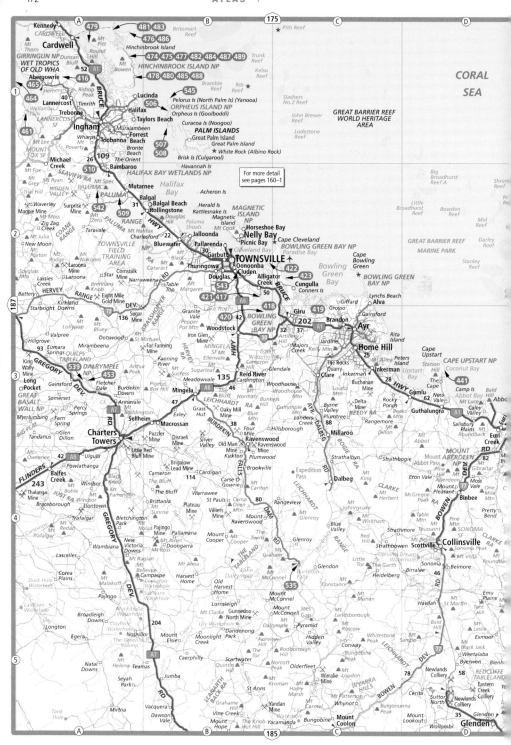

0   10   20 km

E   F   G   H

SOUTH   PACIFIC   OCEAN

1

WARNINGS: In outback Australia, long distances separate some towns. Travellers should familiarise themselves with prevailing conditions before departure and take care to ensure their vehicle is roadworthy. Adequate supplies of petrol, water and food should be carried at all times.

In central Australia, rainfall can make some roads impassable, even with a 4WD vehicle. Full information on road conditions should be obtained from local authorities before departure.

If visitors intend diverting off public roads within Aboriginal Land areas, a permit is required from the relevant Aboriginal authority.

Beware of crocodiles in rivers, estuaries and coastal areas.

Beware of marine stingers in coastal areas (October to April). Swim within enclosures where possible.

2

GREAT

BARRIER

ion
reef

Jaguar
Reef

Lynx Reef

ux Reef

go
F

Dingo
Reef F

go
f B

Tiger Reef

Reef A

Kangaroo Reef A

ith
ef

Hope
Reef

GREAT BARRIER REEF
MARINE PARK

REEF

GREAT BARRIER REEF
WORLD HERITAGE
AREA

3

CORAL
SEA

URNE
O NP
lbourne
and

UCESTER
SLAND
NP Gloucester
Island

470   467   499   497   496   495   494

Hayman
Island

525 529

WHITSUNDAY
ISLANDS NP

Round
Reef

Tideway
Reef

Peta
Patches

DRYANDER NP

nbe Earlando   Grassy Is

521

Hook Is   522   WHITSUNDAY
GROUP

Square
Reef

Edgell
Reefs

Hunt
Reefs

454   Mt Dryander

Airlie
Beach

Border Is

523 524 526 528

532   Sugarloaf   527

Whitsunday Island   Edward Is

Whitsunday
Peak

WHITSUNDAY ISLANDS NP

CE Cannonvale

36   Shute
Harbour

Mt
Marlow   High
Mtn

Hamilton Island   520 530
Hamilton Is

For more detail
see pages 158–9

Robertson
Reefs

4

oserpine
Breadalbane
int

A1   39

CONWAY
NP

498   491   492

LINDEMAN ISLANDS NP

26   Round
Head

uandong   Conway
Beach

Cape
Conway

Shaw Is   LINDEMAN
GROUP

Parker
Reef

Credlin
Reefs

447 446   Repulse Bay   REPULSE
ISLANDS

Thomas Is

449 448   Midge
Point

Silversmith Is

SMITH ISLANDS NP

533 500   190

REPULSE
ISLANDS
NP

512   Blacksmith Is   SIR JAMES SMITH
GROUP

Stevens
Reef

Gorg
Waterfa   Bloomsbury

Tonga   Mtn

Goldsmith Is   Linne Is

Tinsmith Is

SOUTH
CUMBERLAND
ISLANDS

CATHU   16   Elaroo

Rocky Mtn

547   503   501   515   424

Wigton Is   NP

GREAT BARRIER REEF

apton   Yalboroo

Mt
Macartney

548   Carlisle Is   Cockermouth
Island

Calder Is

MARINE PARK

ah   HWY   28

531   Brampton Is   CUMBERLAND
ISLANDS   518

Scawfell
Island

Tern
Islet

ssey EUNGELLA
NP

Calen   437   436   Keswick
Island

St Bees
Island

517

Redbill
Islet

Pompey
Reef

Seaforth   22   Ball
Bay   Sand Bay

Mt Pelion

ge   Mt William   12   Ossa   23

Shoal Point

Bailey
Islet

Derwent
Island

Penrith
Island

Sandpiper
Reef

546   Mount
Charlton   Kuttabul   12   Bucasia   Eimeo

Mt Toby

SOUTH
CUMBERLAND
ISLANDS
NP

Prince
Reef

5

Eungella   Farleigh   A1

Slade Point

Finch   46   Gargett   Mirani   Marian   22   Port of Mackay

Hatton   33   MACKAY

Snare Peak
Island

EDITON
RA   St

Walkerston   Flat Top Island

EY   450   Mt Bryden   541   20   Eton   Homebush   29   Bakers Creek

VALE   451   Jimmy
Jacky   Blue
Mtn   Spencer   70   Hector

Mt   Half Tide

NORTHUMBERLAND
ISLANDS NP

493   Scrubby
Mtn   36   Alligator Creek   505   Prudhoe
Island

E   Gap   Grasstree   F

170   G   H

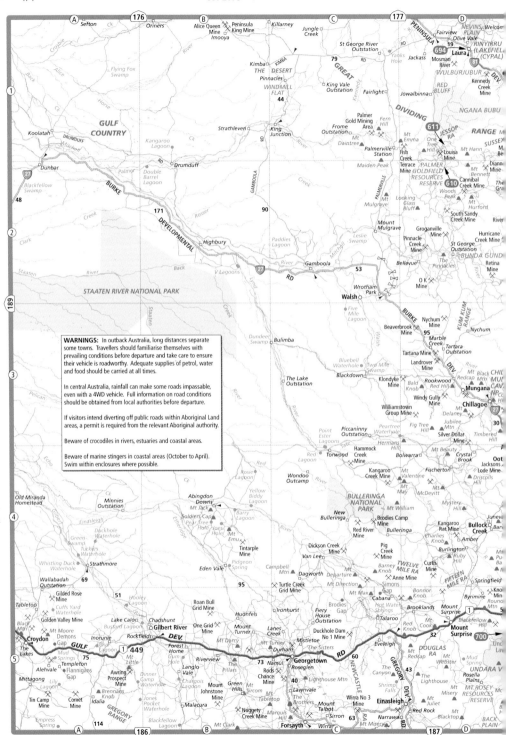

WARNINGS: In outback Australia, long distances separate some towns. Travellers should familiarise themselves with prevailing conditions before departure and take care to ensure their vehicle is roadworthy. Adequate supplies of petrol, water and food should be carried at all times.

In central Australia, rainfall can make some roads impassable, even with a 4WD vehicle. Full information on road conditions should be obtained from local authorities before departure.

If visitors intend diverting off public roads within Aboriginal Land areas, a permit is required from the relevant Aboriginal authority.

Beware of crocodiles in rivers, estuaries and coastal areas.

Beware of marine stingers in coastal areas (October to April). Swim within enclosures where possible.

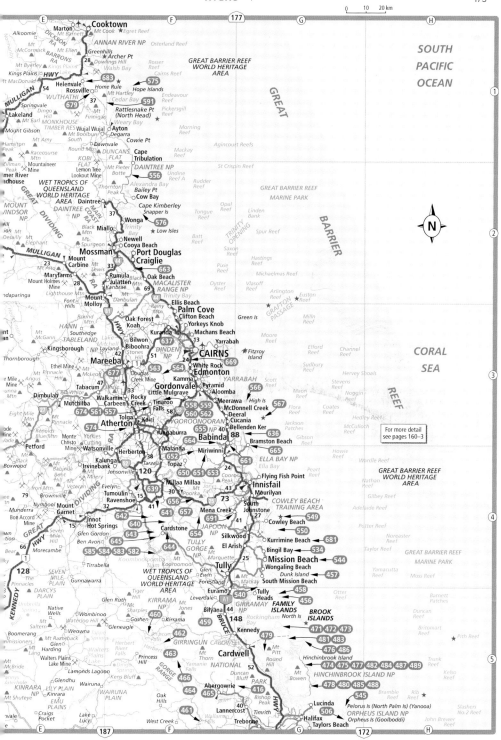

0 10 20 km

SOUTH
PACIFIC
OCEAN

GREAT BARRIER REEF
WORLD HERITAGE
AREA

CORAL
SEA

For more detail
see pages 160–3

GREAT BARRIER REEF
WORLD HERITAGE
AREA

GREAT BARRIER REEF
MARINE PARK

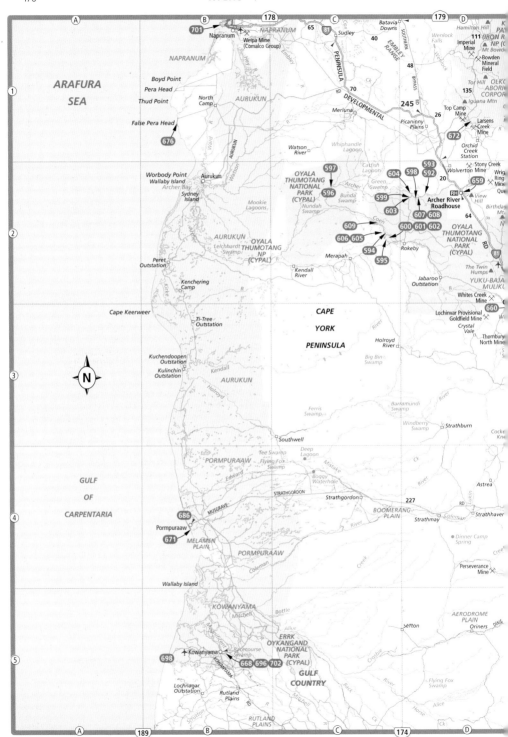

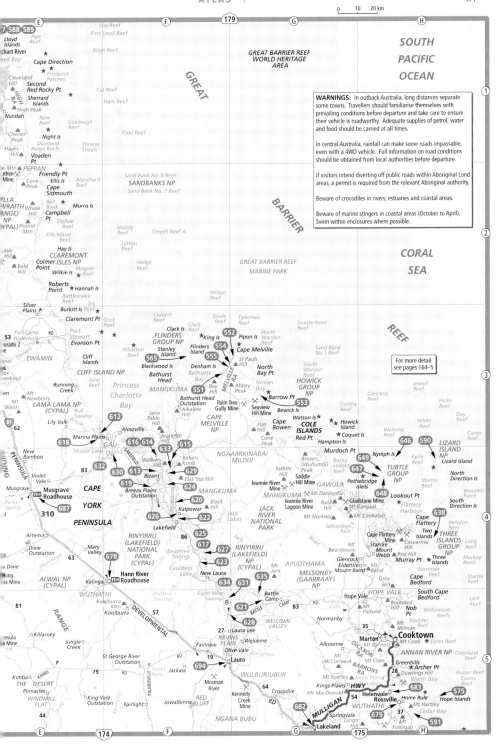

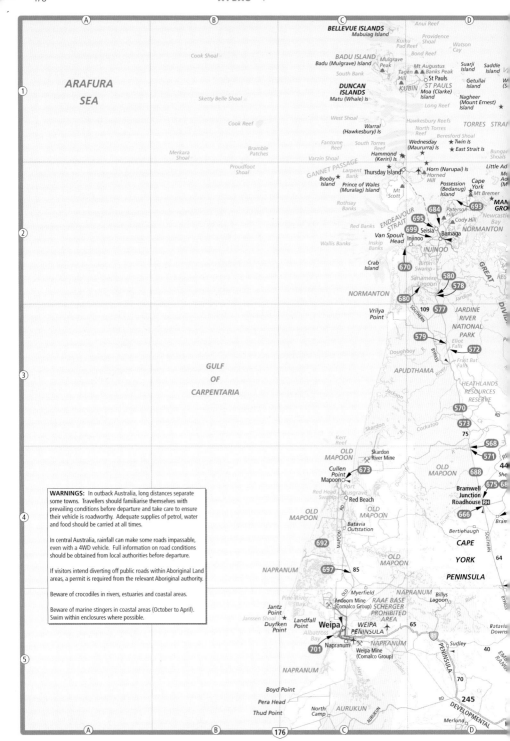

ARAFURA
SEA

BELLEVUE ISLANDS
Mabuiag Island

Anui Reef

Cook Shoal

BADU ISLAND
Badu (Mulgrave) Island
South Bank

DUNCAN ISLANDS
Matu (Whale) Is

Sketty Belle Shoal

Kuiku
Pad Reef
Providence
Shoal
Watson
Cay
Bond Reef

Mulgrave
Peak
Mt Augustus
Tagen ▲▲ Banks Peak
Hill
o St Pauls
ST PAULS
KUBIN Moa (Clarke)
Island
Long Reef

Suarji
Island
Saddle
Island

Getullai
Island
W
(S

Nagheer
(Mount Ernest)
Island

Cook Reef

West Shoal
Warral
(Hawkesbury) Is

Hawkesbury Reefs
North Torres
Reef
TORRES STRAI
Beresford Shoal

Merkara
Shoal
Bramble
Patches

Fantome
Reef
South Torres
Reef
Varzin Shoal
Hammond
(Keriri) Is
Wednesday
(Maururra) Is
★ Twin Is
★ East Strait Is
Bungar
Shoals

Proudfoot
Shoal
GANNET PASSAGE
Larpent
Bank
Thursday Island
Booby ★
Island
Prince of Wales
(Muralag) Island
Mt
Scott

Horn (Narupai) Is
Horned
Hill
Possession
(Bedanug)
Island
Cape
York
Mt Bremer

Little Adol
Mc
Ao
(M

Rothsay
Banks
**MAN
GRO**

Red Banks
ENDEAVOUR
STRAIT
684 Paterson
Hill
693
Newcastle
Bay
695 Cody Hill
699 Seisia
Van Spoult
Head Injinoo
680 Bamaga
NORMANTON

Wallis Banks
Inskip
Banks
INJINOO

Crab
Island
670 Biffin
Swamp
Sanamere
Lagoon
580
578

GREAT

NORMANTON
680
Jardine

Vrilya
Point
109 577
SOUTHERN
**JARDINE
RIVER
NATIONAL
PARK**
DIVI

579
Eliot
Falls
Doughboy
BYPASS
572
Fruit Bat
Falls

**GULF
OF
CARPENTARIA**

APUDTHAMA
Jackson
River

HEATHLANDS
RESOURCES
RESERVE
570
573
RD
75

Kerr
Reef
Skardon
R
Cockatoo
568
571
RI

OLD
MAPOON
Skardon
River Mine
Cullen
Point
Mapoon
673
OLD
MAPOON
688
She
44

Red Head
Swamp
Musgrave
Red Beach
Port
OLD
MAPOON
675 68
**Bramwell
Junction
Roadhouse** RH
666
Bram

OLD
MAPOON
Batavia
Outstation
Bertiehaugh
CAPE

WARNINGS: In outback Australia, long distances separate
some towns. Travellers should familiarise themselves with
prevailing conditions before departure and take care to ensure
their vehicle is roadworthy. Adequate supplies of petrol, water
and food should be carried at all times.

In central Australia, rainfall can make some roads impassable,
even with a 4WD vehicle. Full information on road conditions
should be obtained from local authorities before departure.

If visitors intend diverting off public roads within Aboriginal Land
areas, a permit is required from the relevant Aboriginal authority.

Beware of crocodiles in rivers, estuaries and coastal areas.

Beware of marine stingers in coastal areas (October to April).
Swim within enclosures where possible.

692
OLD
MAPOON

NAPRANUM
697
85

YORK

PENINSULA
64

SOUTHERN
BYPASS

Myerfield
NAPRANUM
Andoom Mine RAAF BASE
(Comalco Group)
Billys
Lagoon
Bivk
SCHERGER
PROHIBITED
AREA

Pine River
Bay
Jantz
Point
Janssen Shoal ★
Landfall
Point
Duyfken
Point
Albatross
Bay
Weipa
**WEIPA
PENINSULA**
65
Batavia
Downs

701
Napranum
Weipa Mine
(Comalco Group)
NAPRANUM
Sudley
40
PENINSULA
EMB
RANG

NAPRANUM
70

Boyd Point
Pera Head
Thud Point
North
Camp
AURUKUN
Hwy
245
DEVELOPMENTAL
Merluna

0   10   20 km

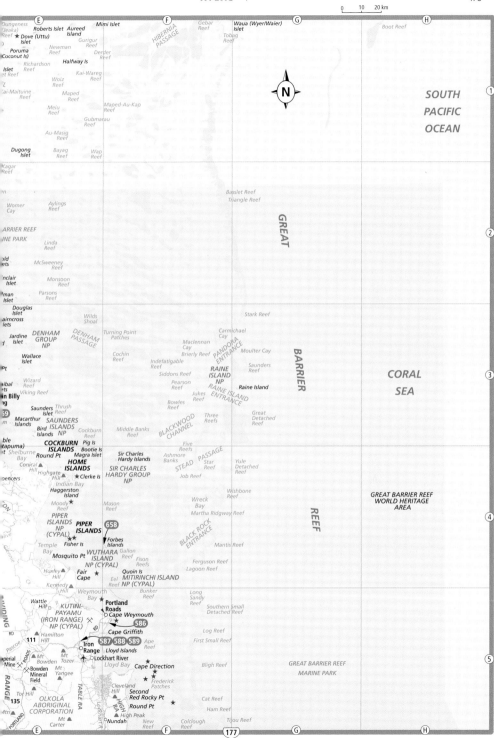

SOUTH
PACIFIC
OCEAN

GREAT

BARRIER

REEF

CORAL
SEA

GREAT BARRIER REEF
WORLD HERITAGE
AREA

GREAT BARRIER REEF
MARINE PARK

E — **F** — **G** — **H**
1 **2** **3** **4** **5**

Dungeness
(Jeaka)
Reef ★ Dove (Uttu)
Islet
Poruma
(Coconut Is)
Islet
t Reef
ai-Maituine
Reef
'Z

Kagar
Reef

en

Womer
Cay

ARRIER REEF
NE PARK

old
ets

nclair
Islet

man
Islet

Jardine
Islet
d

Pt

ibal
ts
n Billy
ng

39

m

ble
tapuma)
t Shelburne
Bay
Round Pt

encers

N

DI

alive

Glennie

ON

RANGE

NDING

RD

aperial
Mine

135

Roberts Islet Aureed
Island
Newman   Gurigur
Reef   Reef
Halfway Is
Richardson   Kai-Wareg
Reef   Reef
Woiz
Reef
Maped
Reef
Meiu   Maped-Au-Kap
Reef
Gubmarau
Reef
Au-Masig
Reef
Dugong   Bayag   Wap
Islet   Reef   Reef

Aylings
Reef

Linda
Reef

McSweeney
Reef

Monsoon
Reef

Parsons
Reef

Douglas
Islet
airncross
lets
DENHAM
GROUP
NP
Wallace
Islet

Wizard
Reef
Viking Reef

Saunders Thrush
Islet   Reef
Macarthur
Islands SAUNDERS
Bird   ISLANDS
Islands NP   Cockburn
Reef
COCKBURN Pig Is
ISLANDS Bootie Is
HOME   Magra Islet
Conical ▲ Highate ISLANDS
Hill   Hill ★ Clerke Is
Indian Bay
Haggerston
Island
Moody ★
PIPER
ISLANDS
Temple   Fisher Is
Bay
Mosquito Pt WUTHARA
Huxley ▲   ISLAND
Hill   Fair   NP (CYPAL)
Cape
Kennedy ▲
Hill
Wattle
Hill   KUTINI-
Hamilton PAYAMU
111 Hill (IRON RANGE)
Pascoe NP (CYPAL)
Mt Iron
Mt Bowden Tozer Range
Bowden Mt
Mineral Yangee
Field
Tor Hill High Peak
OLKOLA
ABORIGINAL Mt
CORPORATION Carter

Mimi Islet

Gebar   Waua (Wyer/Waier)
Reef   Islet
Tobag
Reef

Bootie Reef

Derder
Reef

Maped-Au-Kap

Basslet Reef
Triangle Reef

Stark Reef

Turning Point Carmichael
Patches Maclennan Cay
Cay
Cochin Brierly Reef Moulter Cay
Reef Indefatigable RAINE Saunders
Reef ISLAND Reef
Siddons Reef NP
Pearson Raine Island
Reef RAINE ISLAND
Jukes ENTRANCE
Bowles Reef
Reef Three Great
Middle Banks Reef Detached
Reef Reef
Five
Sir Charles Reefs
Hardy Islands Ashmore STEAD PASSAGE
Banks Star
SIR CHARLES Reef
HARDY GROUP Job Reef
NP
Wishbone
Reef
Mason Wreck
Reef Bay
Martha Ridgway Reef
BLACK ROCK
ENTRANCE
Mantis Reef
Gallon
Reef Fison
Reefs Ferguson Reef
Quoin Is Eel Lagoon Reef
MITIRINCHI ISLAND
Reef NP (CYPAL)
Weymouth Long
Bay Reef Sandy
Reef Southern Small
Portland Detached Reef
Roads
O Cape Weymouth
586
Cape Griffith Log Reef
587 588 589 Ape First Small Reef
Lloyd Islands Reef
Lockhart River
Lloyd Bay Cape Direction Bligh Reef
Cleveland Frederick
Hill Second Patches
Red Rocky Pt
Round Pt Cat Reef
Nundah Ham Reef
New Colclough Tijou Reef
Reef Reef

HIBERNIA
PASSAGE

DENHAM
PASSAGE

PANDORA
ENTRANCE

BLACKWOOD
CHANNEL

Yule
Detached
Reef

658

Forbes
Islands

111

135

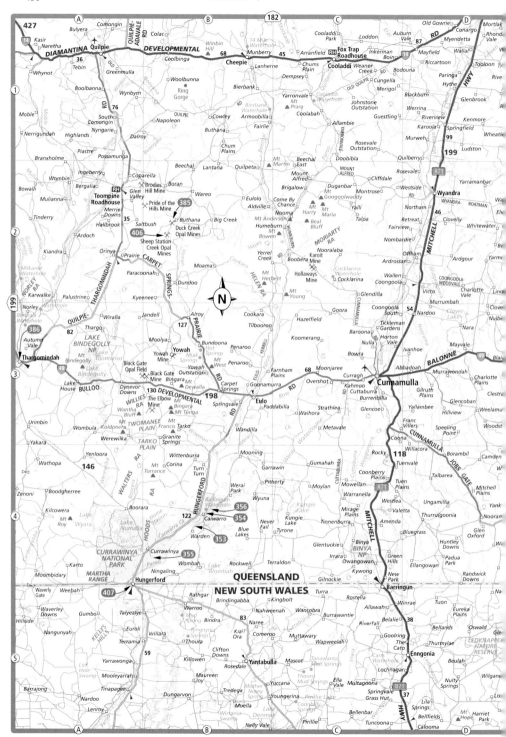

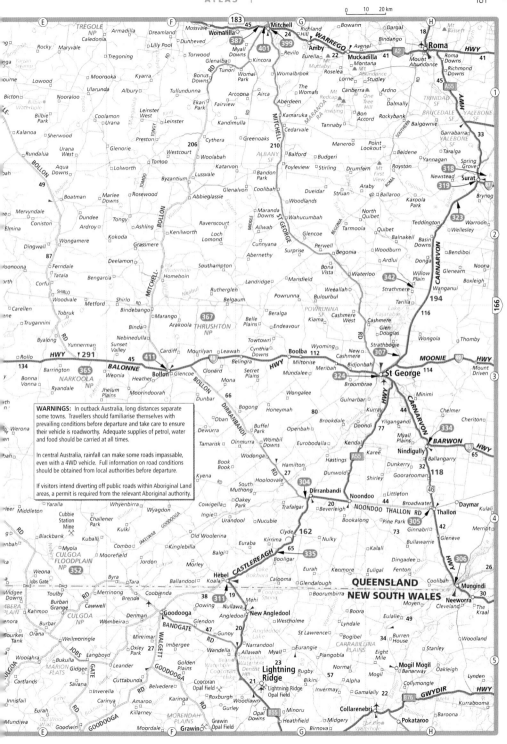

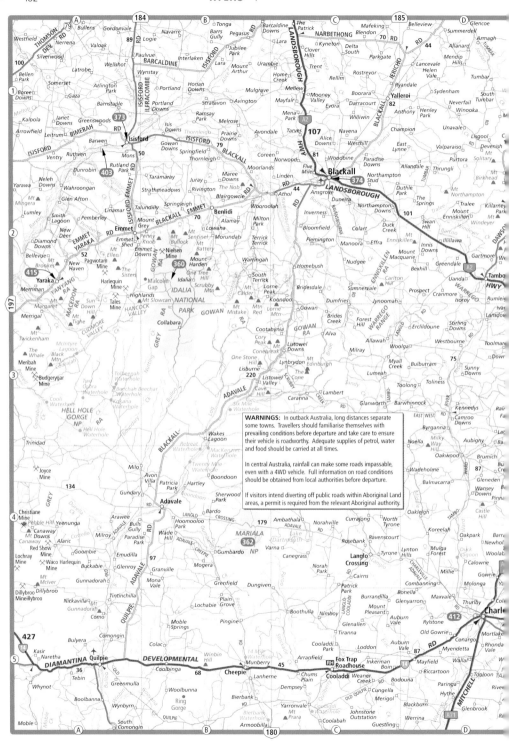

WARNINGS: In outback Australia, long distances separate some towns. Travellers should familiarise themselves with prevailing conditions before departure and take care to ensure their vehicle is roadworthy. Adequate supplies of petrol, water and food should be carried at all times.

In central Australia, rainfall can make some roads impassable, even with a 4WD vehicle. Full information on road conditions should be obtained from local authorities before departure.

If visitors intend diverting off public roads within Aboriginal Land areas, a permit is required from the relevant Aboriginal authority.

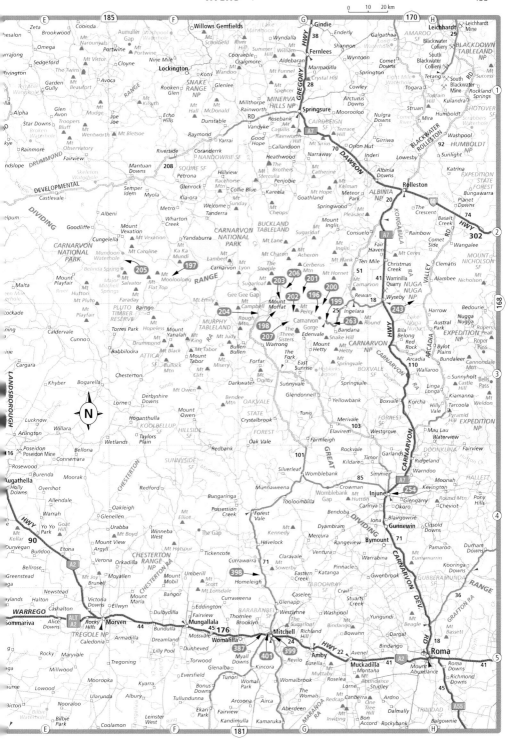

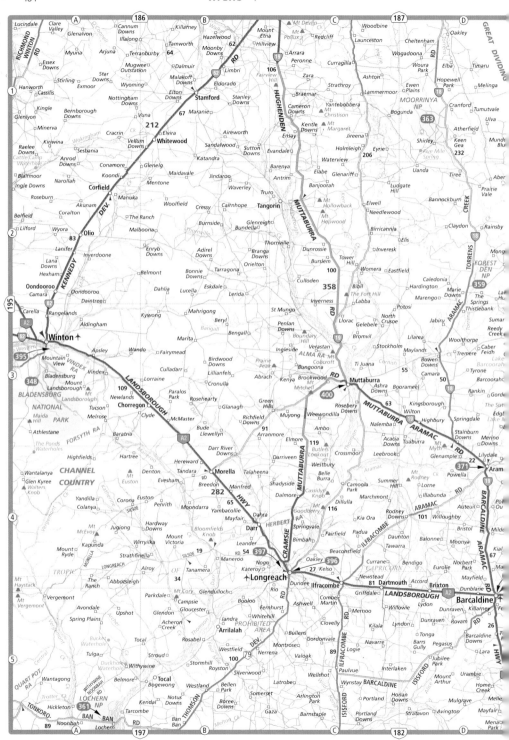

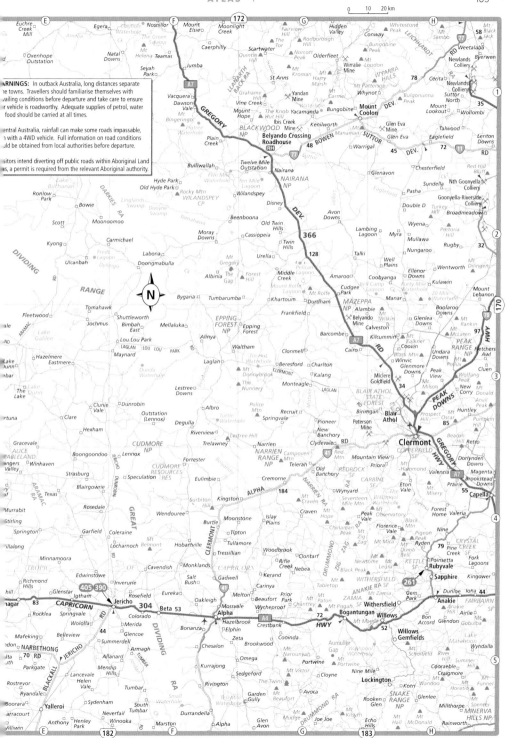

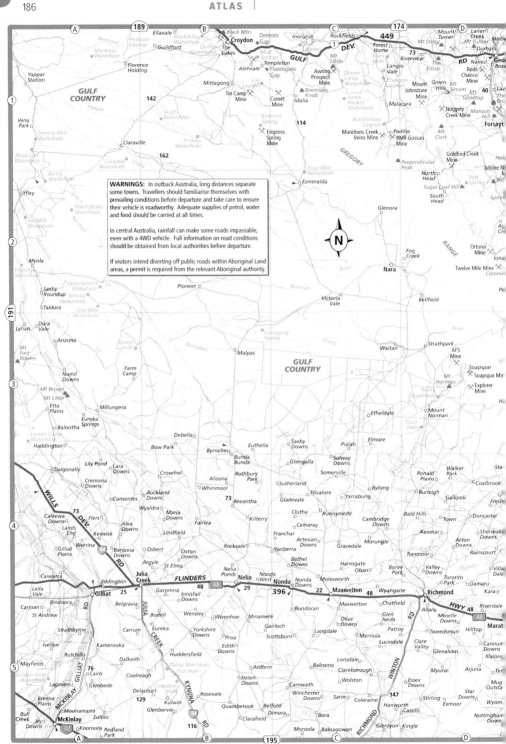

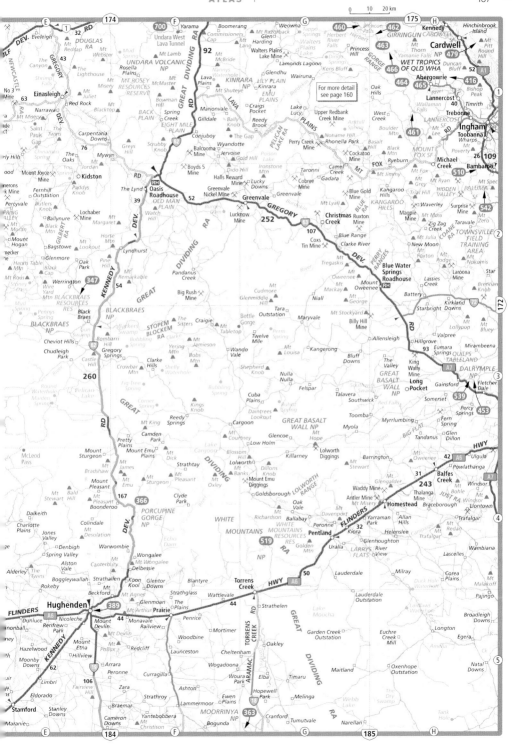

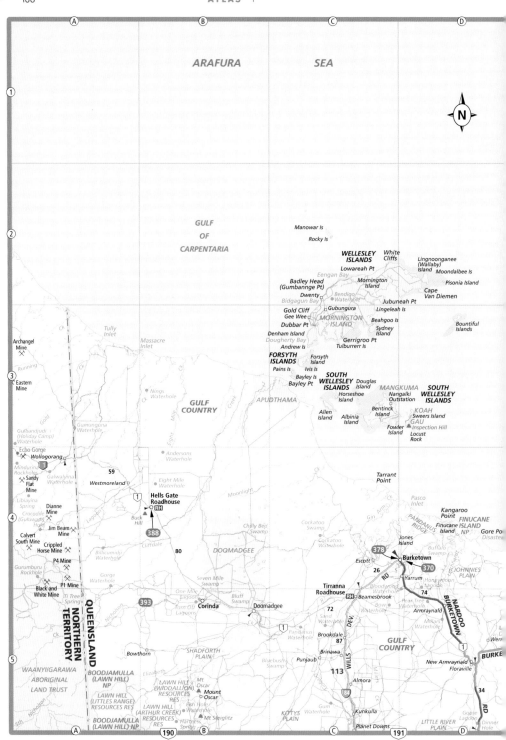

ARAFURA SEA

N

GULF
OF
CARPENTARIA

Manowar Is
Rocky Is

WELLESLEY
ISLANDS
Lowareah Pt

White
Cliffs

Lingnoonganee
(Wallaby)
Island   Moondalbee Is

Eengan Bay

Badley Head
(Gumbannge Pt)
Dwenty

Mornington
Island

Pisonia Island

Bendigo
Waterhole

Cape
Van Diemen

Bidgagun Bay

Jubuneah Pt   Lingeleah Is

Gold Cliff
Gee Wee
Dubbar Pt

Gubungura

MORNINGTON
ISLAND

Beahgoo Is
Sydney
Island

Bountiful
Islands

Tully
Inlet

Massacre
Inlet

Denham Island
Dougherty Bay
Andrew Is

Gerrigroo Pt
Tulburrerr Is

Archangel
Mine

FORSYTH
ISLANDS

Forsyth
Island

Running

Eastern
Mine

Pains Is   Ivis Is

Bayley Is
Bayley Pt

SOUTH
WELLESLEY
ISLANDS

Douglas
Island

MANGKUMA

SOUTH
WELLESLEY
ISLANDS

GULF
COUNTRY

APUDTHAMA

Horseshoe
Island

Nangalki
Outstation

KOAH

Nings
Waterhole

Gulbandjudi
(Holiday Camp)
Waterhole

Gumungina
Waterhole

Allen
Island

Albinia
Island

Bentinck
Island

GAU

Fowler
Island

Sweers Island
Inspection Hill
Locust
Rock

Echo Gorge
Woliogorang

Gold

Mindurinda
Rockholes
Sandy
Flat
Mine

Galwalyina
Waterhole

Andersons
Waterhole

Tarrant
Point

Pasco
Inlet

Libiayina
Spring
Crocodile
(Guluwan)
Hole

Dianne
Mine

59

Westmoreland

Eight Mile
Waterhole

Moonlight

Kangaroo
Point

FINUCANE

PANDANUS
RIDGE

Finucane
Island

FINUCANE ISLAND
NP

Gore Po
Disaster

Jim Beam
Mine

Hells Gate
Roadhouse
RH

Buck
Hill

Gin   Arm

Cockatoo
Swamp

Jones
Island

Calvert
South Mine
Crippled
Horse Mine

388

Cliffdale

80

DOOMADGEE

Chilly Beg
Swamp

Cockatoo
Waterhole

Escott

378

Burketown

370

Buffalo
Swamp

JOHNNIES
PLAIN

P4 Mine

Billicumidji
Waterhole

26

RD

Yarrum

Honeymoon
Lagoon

74

Gurumburu
Rockhole

P1 Mine

Gorge
Waterhole

Seven Mile
Swamp

Tirranna
Roadhouse
RH

Beamsbrook

Bow
Waterhole

NARDOO
BURKETOWN

Black and
White Mine

Ti Tree
Spring

393

One Mile
Lagoon

Bluff
Swamp

72

Sand
Waterhole

Armraynald

Milans
Waterhole

Turn Off
Lagoon

Corinda

Doomadgee

Pandanus
Waterhole

1

GULF
COUNTRY

WILLS
DEV

Bowthorn

SHADFORTH
PLAIN

Brookdale

87

Brinawa

1

BURKE

WAANYIIGARAWA
ABORIGINAL
LAND TRUST

BOODJAMULLA
(LAWN HILL)
NP

Elizabeth

Bluebush
Swamp

Punjaub

113

New Armraynald
Floraville

Werr

84

Almora

34

LAWN HILL
(WIDDALLION)
RESOURCES
RES

Mt
Oscar

Mount
Oscar

QUEENSLAND
NORTHERN
TERRITORY

LAWN HILL
(LITTLES RANGE)
RESOURCES RES

BOODJAMULLA
(LAWN HILL) NP

Sth Nicholson

LAWN HILL
(ARTHUR CREEK)
RESOURCES
RES

Redholes
Waterhole

Mt Steiglitz

Hartons
Spring

KOTTYS
PLAIN

Gum
Waterhole

Kunkulla

Planet Downs

LITTLE RIVER
PLAIN

RD

Goose
Lagoon

Dinner
Hole

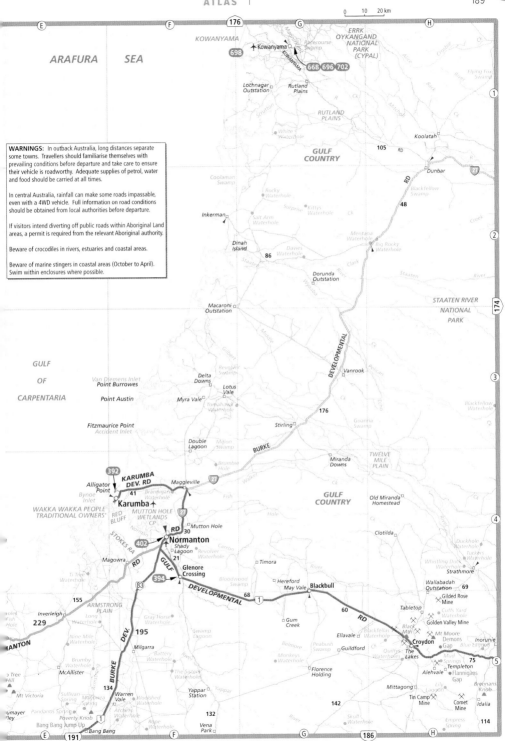

0   10   20 km

WARNINGS: In outback Australia, long distances separate some towns. Travellers should familiarise themselves with prevailing conditions before departure and take care to ensure their vehicle is roadworthy. Adequate supplies of petrol, water and food should be carried at all times.

In central Australia, rainfall can make some roads impassable, even with a 4WD vehicle. Full information on road conditions should be obtained from local authorities before departure.

If visitors intend diverting off public roads within Aboriginal Land areas, a permit is required from the relevant Aboriginal authority.

Beware of crocodiles in rivers, estuaries and coastal areas.

Beware of marine stingers in coastal areas (October to April). Swim within enclosures where possible.

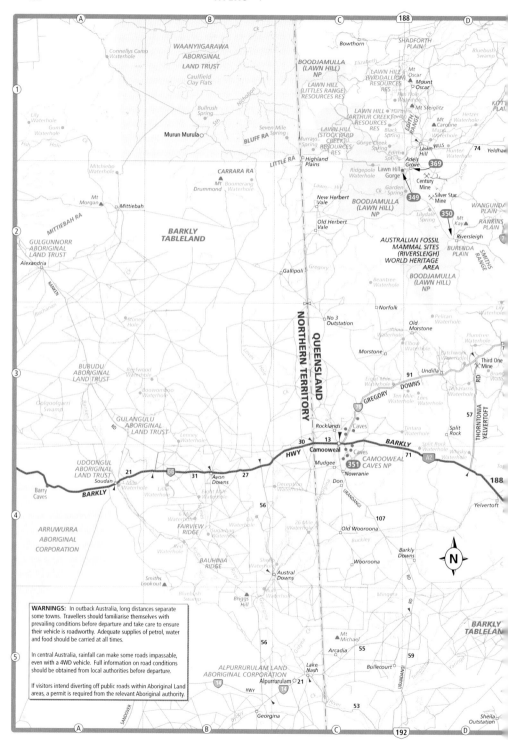

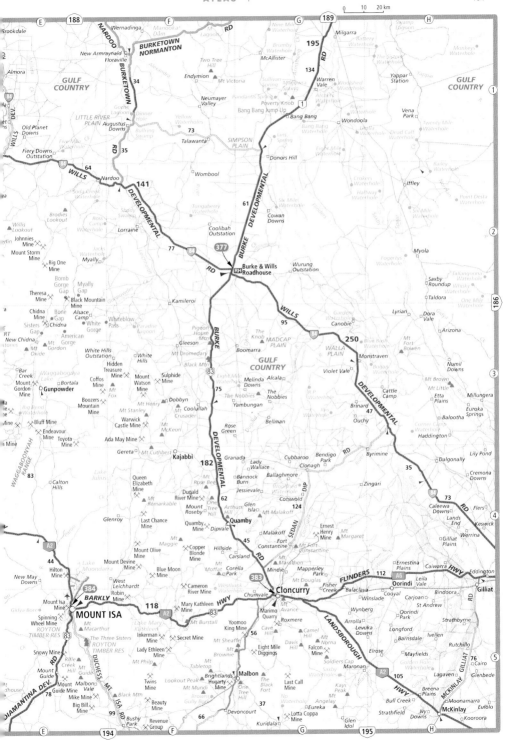

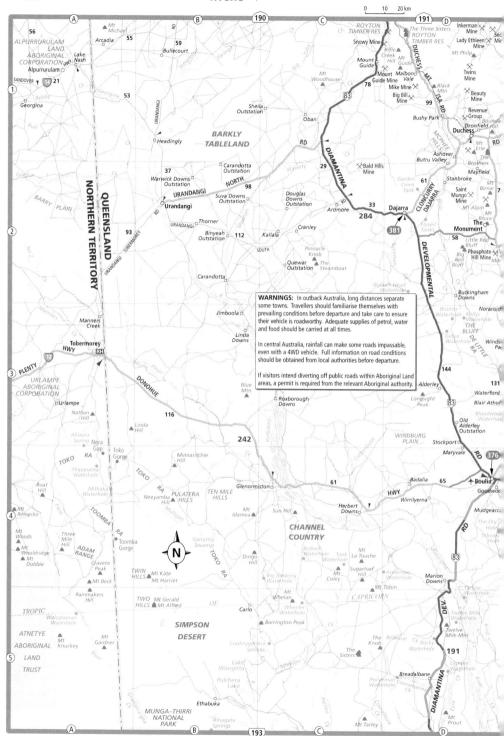

WARNINGS: In outback Australia, long distances separate some towns. Travellers should familiarise themselves with prevailing conditions before departure and take care to ensure their vehicle is roadworthy. Adequate supplies of petrol, water and food should be carried at all times.

In central Australia, rainfall can make some roads impassable, even with a 4WD vehicle. Full information on road conditions should be obtained from local authorities before departure.

If visitors intend diverting off public roads within Aboriginal Land areas, a permit is required from the relevant Aboriginal authority.

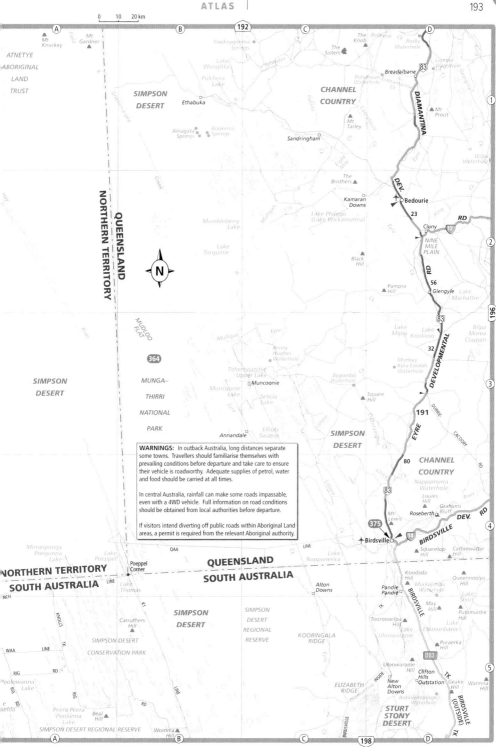

0 10 20 km

WARNINGS: In outback Australia, long distances separate some towns. Travellers should familiarise themselves with prevailing conditions before departure and take care to ensure their vehicle is roadworthy. Adequate supplies of petrol, water and food should be carried at all times.

In central Australia, rainfall can make some roads impassable, even with a 4WD vehicle. Full information on road conditions should be obtained from local authorities before departure.

If visitors intend diverting off public roads within Aboriginal Land areas, a permit is required from the relevant Aboriginal authority.

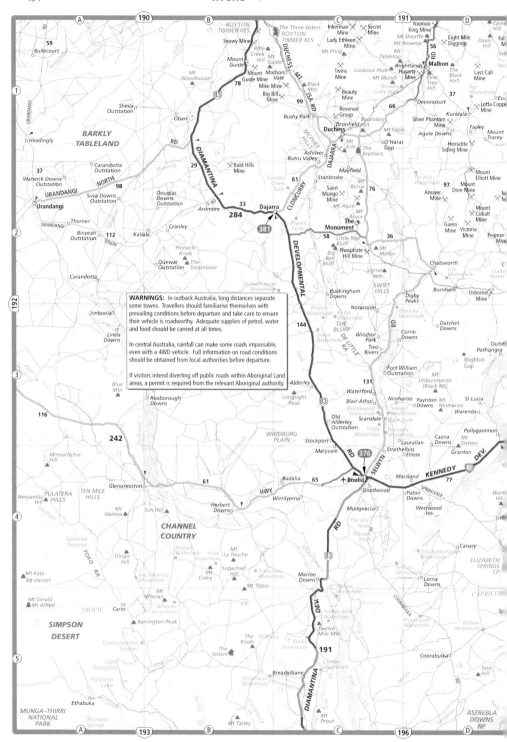

WARNINGS: In outback Australia, long distances separate some towns. Travellers should familiarise themselves with prevailing conditions before departure and take care to ensure their vehicle is roadworthy. Adequate supplies of petrol, water and food should be carried at all times.

In central Australia, rainfall can make some roads impassable, even with a 4WD vehicle. Full information on road conditions should be obtained from local authorities before departure.

If visitors intend diverting off public roads within Aboriginal Land areas, a permit is required from the relevant Aboriginal authority.

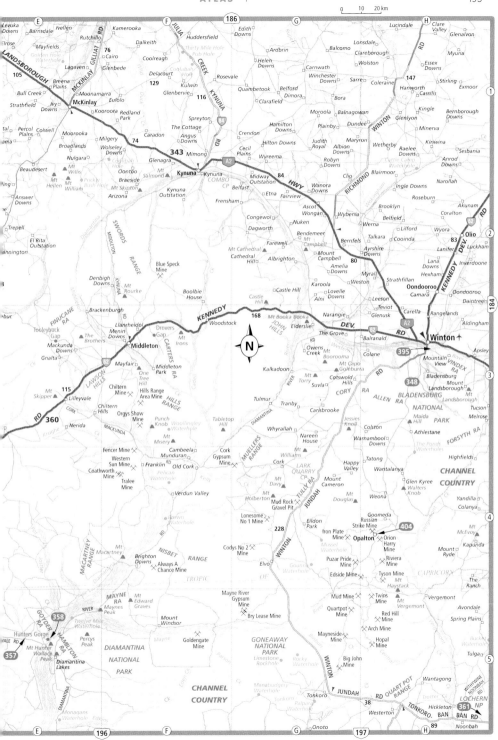

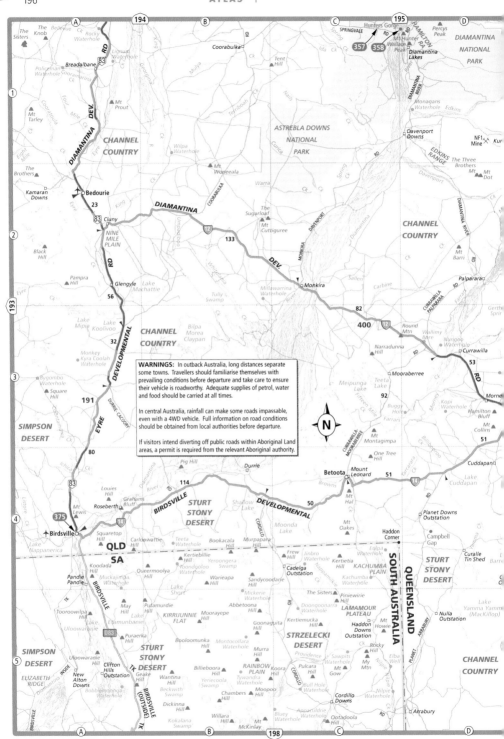

WARNINGS: In outback Australia, long distances separate some towns. Travellers should familiarise themselves with prevailing conditions before departure and take care to ensure their vehicle is roadworthy. Adequate supplies of petrol, water and food should be carried at all times.

In central Australia, rainfall can make some roads impassable, even with a 4WD vehicle. Full information on road conditions should be obtained from local authorities before departure.

If visitors intend diverting off public roads within Aboriginal Land areas, a permit is required from the relevant Aboriginal authority.

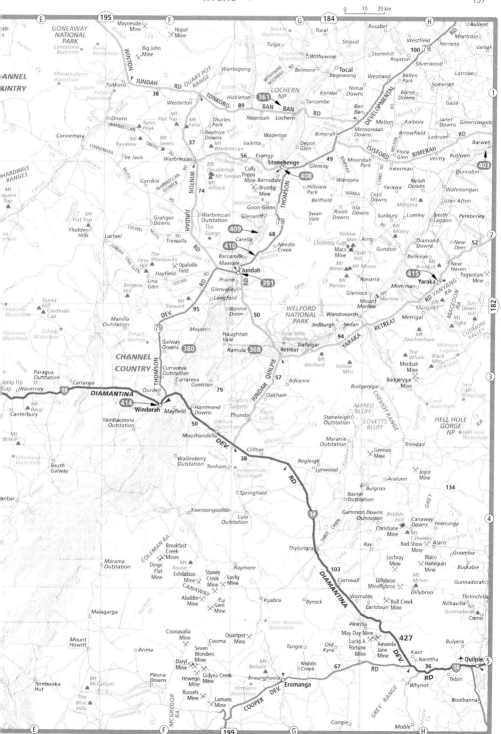

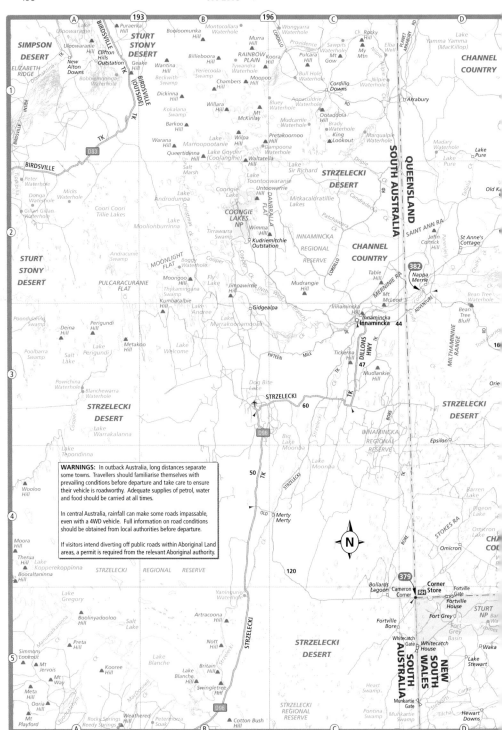

WARNINGS: In outback Australia, long distances separate some towns. Travellers should familiarise themselves with prevailing conditions before departure and take care to ensure their vehicle is roadworthy. Adequate supplies of petrol, water and food should be carried at all times.

In central Australia, rainfall can make some roads impassable, even with a 4WD vehicle. Full information on road conditions should be obtained from local authorities before departure.

If visitors intend diverting off public roads within Aboriginal Land areas, a permit is required from the relevant Aboriginal authority.

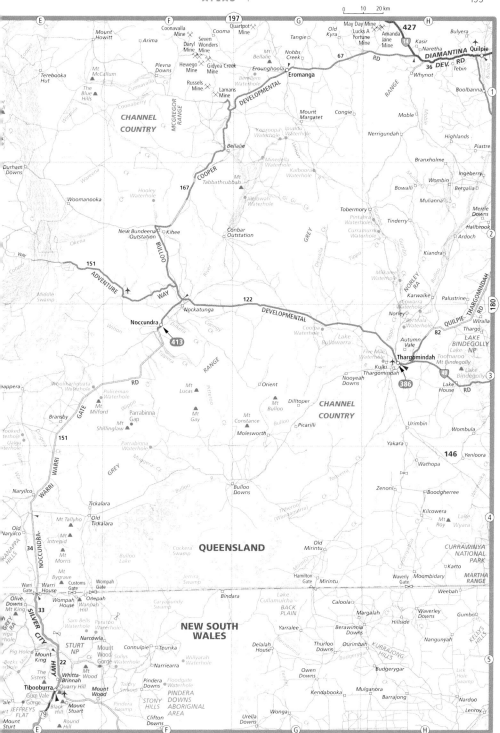

0   10   20 km

INDEX

This index includes all campsites, towns, localities, roadhouses and national parks shown on the maps and mentioned in the text.

For easy reference (where applicable), campsite names are followed by the national park, state forest or reserve in which they are located. This is followed by a map page number and grid reference, and the text page number on which that campsite is mentioned. A page number set in **bold** type indicates the text entry for that campsite. For example:

Crocodile camping area, Cape Melville NP 165 E1, 177 F3, **123**

Crocodile camping area	– campsite name
Cape Melville NP	– national park name
165 E1, 177 F3	– Crocodile camping area appears on these map pages
123	– the text entry for Crocodile camping area appears on this page

The alphabetical order followed in the index is that of 'word-by-word' – a space is considered to come before 'A' in the alphabet, and the index has been ordered accordingly. For example:

White Hills
White Mountains National Park
Whitefoord
Whiteheads Creek
Whitemark

Names beginning with Mc are indexed as Mac and those beginning with St as Saint.

The following abbreviations are used in the index:

CA – Conservation Area
CR – Conservation Reserve
NP – National Park
NR – Nature Reserve
SF – State Forest
SP – State Park
SR – State Reserve

Acknowledgements

Much of the material in this book originally appeared in *Camping around Australia (2nd ed)*, published by Explore Australia Publishing in 2013, where full acknowledgements for individual contributions appear.

The publisher would like to acknowledge the help of the following people in the production of this edition:

Project manager
Melissa Krafchek

Editing
Alison Proietto

Cover design
Leonie Stott

Layout
Megan Ellis

Cartography
Bruce McGurty, Emily Maffei, Claire Johnston

Indexer
Max McMaster

Photo selection
Alison Proietto

Pre-press
Megan Ellis, Splitting Image

Photography credits
Cover
Camping at Lake McKenzie, Fraser Island National Park (Richard Boll/ Photographer's Choice/ Getty Images)

Back cover
Kangaroo on Cylinder Beach, near Point Lookout on North Stradbroke Island (Jeff Drewitz)

Title page
Camping with the limestone pinnacles of Chillagoe–Mungana Caves National Park in the background (Sara-Jane Cleland/Lonely Planet Images/Getty Images)

Contents
Snappy Gums at sunset, Camooweal Caves National Park (Jeff Drewitz)

All other images are © Jeff Drewitz except for the images on the following pages:

Page 10 Tourism Queensland; 102 Andrew Bain/Lonely Planet Images/ Getty Images

Explore Australia Publishing Pty Ltd
Ground Floor, Building 1, 658 Church Street,
Richmond, Victoria, Australia 3121

Explore Australia Publishing Pty Ltd is a division of Hardie Grant Publishing Pty Ltd

hardie grant publishing

Published by Explore Australia Publishing Pty Ltd, 2013

Concept, text, maps, form and design © Explore Australia Publishing Pty Ltd, 2013

10 9 8 7 6 5 4 3 2 1

ISBN-13 9781741173796

This material first appeared in *Camping around Australia (2nd ed)* published in 2013.

Printed and bound in China by 1010 Printing International Ltd

Publisher's note: Every effort has been made to ensure that the information in this book is accurate at the time of going to press. The publisher welcomes information and suggestions for correction or improvement. Email: info@exploreaustralia.net.au

Publisher's disclaimers: The publisher cannot accept responsibility for any errors or omissions. The representation on the maps of any road or track is not necessarily evidence of public right of way.

The maps in this publication incorporate data copyright © Commonwealth of Australia (Geoscience Australia), 2006. Geoscience Australia has not evaluated the data as altered and incorporated within this publication, and therefore gives no warranty regarding accuracy, completeness, currency or suitability for any particular purpose.

Copyright imprint and currency – VAR Product and PSMA Data

"Copyright. Based on data provided under licence from PSMA Australia Limited (www.psma.com.au)".

Transport Data (November 2012)

Aboriginal lands, parks and reserves based on data provided under licence from the following jurisdictions:
Queensland Aboriginal Lands (2010) – Land and Indigenous Services, Department of Environment and Resource Management
South Australia Protected Areas – NPWS and Conservation Reserves (2010) – Department of Environment and Natural Resources
South Australia Aboriginal Freehold Land (2010) – Primary Industries and Resources, South Australia
New South Wales National Parks and Wildlife Reserves (2010) – NSW Department of Environment Climate Change and Water
Northern Territory Aboriginal Land Trusts (2010) – Northern Territory Department of Lands and Planning (2010)
Northern Territory Parks and Reserves (2010) – Parks and Wildlife Service – Department of Natural Resources, Environment, The Arts and Sport

Disclaimer
While every care is taken to ensure the accuracy of the data within this product, the owners of the data (including the state, territory and Commonwealth governments of Australia) do not make any representations or warranties about its accuracy, reliability, completeness or suitability for any particular purpose and, to the extent permitted by law, the owners of the data disclaim all responsibility and all liability (including without limitation, liability in negligence) for all expenses, losses, damages, (including indirect or consequential damages) and costs which might be incurred as a result of the data being inaccurate or incomplete in any way and for any reason.

www.exploreaustralia.net.au
Follow us on Twitter: @ExploreAus
Find us on Facebook: www.facebook.com/exploreaustralia

Queensland	Bowen	Brisbane	Bundaberg	Cairns	Charleville	Charters Towers	Cooktown	Cunnamulla	Emerald	Gladstone	Hervey Bay	Karumba
Bowen		15:00	10:10	7:25	13:55	3:35	11:20	16:10	6:25	7:55	11:25	13:10
Brisbane	1141		5:20	22:10	9:30	16:30	26:00	10:00	10:30	7:25	4:35	26:00
Bundaberg	813	363		17:20	10:15	12:40	21:20	11:30	6:40	2:35	2:00	22:20
Cairns	548	1703	1354		16:55	6:23	4:25	19:15	12:20	15:05	18:35	9:15
Charleville	1073	742	810	1370		10:50	19:35	2:20	7:30	9:50	10:25	17:10
Charters Towers	278	1309	1026	481	904		9:55	13:05	6:00	10:30	13:55	9:40
Cooktown	849	1982	1655	327	1593	814		21:55	15:50	19:00	22:30	10:50
Cunnamulla	1272	807	953	1569	200	1103	1793		9:45	11:40	11:30	19:25
Emerald	541	832	549	956	532	477	1291	731		4:30	8:00	15:40
Gladstone	633	515	187	1173	812	845	1474	971	369		3:55	20:05
Hervey Bay	919	219	124	1460	805	1132	1761	928	655	293		23:35
Karumba	1089	2158	1839	759	1494	814	730	1694	1290	1659	1946	
Longreach	800	1175	965	1109	515	524	1147	715	416	785	1072	979
Mackay	192	968	623	735	915	463	1033	1114	384	443	730	1235
Maroochydore	1056	105	279	1597	788	1263	1898	856	787	430	207	2077
Maryborough	909	264	114	1450	769	1122	1750	891	645	283	36	1936
Mount Isa	1045	1810	1612	1207	1162	769	1218	1362	1063	1432	1719	569
Noosa Heads	1043	138	266	1584	791	1250	1885	890	774	417	175	2064
Normanton	1019	2087	1769	689	1424	744	720	1624	1220	1589	1876	70
Port Douglas	615	1748	1420	67	1414	634	268	1613	1023	1240	1527	804
Quilpie	1198	956	1020	1387	210	922	1611	298	736	1022	1016	1512
Richmond	639	1549	1335	714	885	364	938	1085	786	1155	1441	656
Rockhampton	525	634	288	1069	795	747	1366	954	271	108	395	1561
Roma	944	478	542	1358	268	879	1693	466	402	544	538	1680
St George	1139	513	659	1553	372	1074	1888	294	597	677	634	1802
Toowoomba	1138	127	404	1662	620	1183	1997	681	706	542	358	2032
Townsville	201	1358	1007	345	1038	137	649	1238	611	827	1113	856
Warwick	1220	158	485	1744	701	1265	2079	694	788	624	440	2113
Weipa	1337	2471	2143	815	2082	1302	650	2281	1779	1963	2249	864

Distances between towns are shown below the white line (km). Travel times between towns
Distances/travel times on this chart have been calculated over main roads and do not necessa